Contents

TOM MURPHY — The Plays

On the Outside (with Noel O'Donoghue), Radio Eireann, 1962

A Whistle in the Dark, Theatre Royal, Stratford East, 1961

Famine, Peacock Theatre, 1968

The Orphans, Peacock Theatre, 1968

A Crucial Week in the Life of a Grocer's Assistant, Abbey Theatre, 1969

The Morning after Optimism, Abbey Theatre, 1971

The White House, Abbey Theatre, 1972

On the Inside, Project Arts Centre, 1974

The Vicar of Wakefield (adaptation), Abbey Theatre, 1974

The Sanctuary Lamp, Abbey Theatre, 1976

The J. Arthur Maginnis Story, Irish Theatre Company, 1976

Epitaph under Ether (compilation from Synge), Abbey Theatre, 1979

The Blue Macushla, Abbey Theatre, 1980

The Informer (adaptation), Olympia Theatre, 1981

She Stoops to Conquer (Irish setting), Abbey Theatre, 1982

The Gigli Concert, Abbey Theatre, 1983

Conversations on a Homecoming, Druid Theatre, 1985

Bailegangaire, Druid Theatre, 1985

A Thief of a Christmas, Abbey Theatre, 1985

Too Late for Logic, Abbey Theatre, 1989

The Patriot Game, Peacock Theatre, 1991

Tom Murphy:

THE POLITICS OF MAGIC

For
Mary and Sammy O'Toole,
with love.

TOM MURPHY:

THE *P*OLITICS OF *M*AGIC

FINTAN O'TOOLE

New Island Books / Dublin
Nick Hern Books / London

Tom Murphy:
The Politics of Magic
is published in 1994

In Ireland by
New Island Books,
2, Brookside,
Dundrum Road,
Dublin 14

& in Britain by
Nick Hern Books,
14 Larden Road,
London W3 7ST.

ISBN 1 874597 75 8

New Island Books receives financial assistance
from
The Arts Council (An Chomhairle Ealaíon),
Dublin, Ireland.

An earlier edition of this title was published in
1987 by The Raven Arts Press, Dublin, who have
originated this updated and expanded version.

Cover photograph by Richard Cummins.
Cover design by Jon Berkeley.
Typeset by Graphic Resources.
Printed in Ireland by Colour Books, Ltd.

Introduction

"I never saw such rubbish in my life." The words "confided" to friends in stage whispers loud enough to echo in the following day's papers, were those of Ernest Blythe, Managing Director of the Abbey Theatre. It was the night of 1st March 1962, and Blythe was leaving the Olympia Theatre in Dublin after the opening there of a production of Thomas Murphy's play *A Whistle in the Dark*, a play which Blythe had rejected as unsuitable for the Abbey and which had since then played at both the Theatre Royal, Stratford East, and The Apollo Theatre on London's West End. His reaction, with an added edge of outrage at Murphy's dragging down of the good name of Ireland, was shared by very many people in Ireland, and by a substantial number of English theatre critics.

Though Murphy was later to become himself a director of the Abbey Theatre (from 1972 to 1983), and to have many of his plays produced there, he has never found an easy acceptance of his work in Ireland. In England, meanwhile, the lines laid down in the reaction to *A Whistle in the Dark,* his first full-length play, continued for three decades to confine and determine a reputation which has been at best elusive, at worst non-existent. When *The Gigli Concert* was produced to great acclaim at the Almeida Theatre in London in 1991, it was the first British-originated professional production of a Murphy play since 1961. No other dramatist of his stature in the English-speaking world has been so marginalised for so much of his career.

In Murphy's case, the normal pattern for a playwright of a period of neglect followed by an established reputation and a more or less receptive audience was reversed. At the age of 26, when *A Whistle in the Dark* was first produced at Stratford East, Murphy was for a time the most controversial new playwright in London and the Irish papers were expressing concern that he was "in danger of becoming lionised by the 'arty' set." By the age of 30 he was already in something of an artistic wilderness, unable to have his plays produced and with a series of disappointments to look back on and forward to. Since then he has known periods of full-throated acclaim, followed by successive commercial disasters. Until the 1990s, the extraordinary consistency and coherence of his dramatic achievement over more than a quarter of a century had yielded only a delicate and unstable reputation.

Those reactions to *A Whistle in the Dark* to a large extent remained emblematic of the diverse responses which his work provoked, and help to explain why, for very different reasons he continued to be at an angle to both the British and the Irish theatres for so long. In London, where *A Whistle in the Dark* opened in September 1961 and transferred to the West End the following month, those who saw Murphy as vile and those who saw him as brilliant shared one central idea: that he was quintessentially an Irish playwright and that Irish playwrights had a particular role to play in relation to the British theatre.

The idea had long been established in English theatre criticism that it is the function of Irish theatre every so often to provide a playwright who would kick the London scene in the backside. Even while praising an Irish playwright, therefore, the tendency was to see his achievement entirely in terms of the English theatre. Murphy and *A Whistle in the Dark* fell directly into this category, the untutored, unknown West of Ireland schoolteacher come in from the wilds to lob grenades at London's staidness.

Even in their physical descriptions of Murphy, the English papers invented an image of him which fit the pre-ordained category. While Irish descriptions of the time portray Murphy as a quiet, reserved and slightly-built young man, the English papers managed to suggest that he might be a wild navvy who could handle himself in a brawl, that, as one paper put it, "he looks as though he could wield a powerful hurley." What is interesting is that this unconscious image-making seeped directly into the criticism of *A Whistle in the Dark*. Here is the opening paragraph of a review in The Observer by the most elegant, most perceptive and most intellectually accomplished of English critics, Kenneth Tynan:

"Thomas Murphy is the kind of playwright one would hate to meet in a dark theatre. I have always been obscurely frightened of loudly singing Irishmen, and of Irish debaters, who, corrugating their brows and stubbing my chest with an index finger, beg me to prove them wrong, and I am now convinced that I am scared of Irish dramatists as well. I have not met Mr. Murphy, but something whispers that he might unnerve me — me, who never flinched from meeting Brendan Behan, even when his shirt was unbuttoned."

The automatic image, based on no personal knowledge, of the dramatist-as-Irish-thug, the notion that Irish playwrights are primarily personalities and only secondarily dramatists, and the inevitable comparison with Behan, to whom Murphy bore no relation whatsoever, betoken an innate, and somewhat racist, set of expectations about what an Irish playwright should be. As another reviewer, Tom Milne of the Financial Times, bluntly expressed it, "I declare Thomas Murphy to be the Irishman to end all Irishmen."

This innate and latent racism became explicit and naked in many cases, making *A Whistle in the Dark* the occasion for straightforwardly anti-Irish outbursts. Felix Barker, reviewing the play, wrote that "If there's a single

Irishman who hasn't been deported from England by next weekend I shall write to the Home Secretary. I shall be enclosing tickets for the current play at the Theatre Royal, Stratford East. In *A Whistle in the Dark* by Thomas Murphy he will see just what bog vipers we are nursing in our bosom — savage kerns like the five Carney brothers."

Fergus Cashin called the play "a spew of stewed Irish that fouled the London stage . . . This kind of play relies on morons screaming in the vernacular for dramatic effect . . . Author Thomas Murphy has done the biggest disservice to Irish poetry and art since Mother O'Riley." Milton Shulman claimed that "Mr. Murphy has undoubtedly invented The Most Anthropoidal Family of the Year. The only thing that separates his characters from a bunch of wild gorillas is their ability to speak with an Irish accent . . . (The play) will probably set back Ireland's reputation for civilisation at least 100 years."

Even those to whom images of bogs, savages and gorillas did not come naturally when dealing with an Irish play persisted in seeing Murphy and *A Whistle* as some sort of genetic outgrowth of Irish racial deformities. Tynan concluded that "What blights this play is something endemic in the Irish temperament — a compulsion to turn drama into melodrama, and comedy into farce." Bernard Levin saw it as "The Irish Problem, again, with a vengeance" and was able to praise it only in terms of a view of the Irish that again borders on the racist: "For his rich, ripe, oath-laden language is much more than the usual flow of Guinness that poured forth when they struck the Blarney Stone."

The point about this response is that it created a critical context in which Murphy could only be judged as a broth of a boy, an ape-man. a savage come down from the hills to thrill a London theatre that was in perpetual danger of dying of ennui. To maintain this reputation he would have to say "fuck" on television, disrupt his own plays in performance, and drink himself into an early grave. He did appear on television, to be interviewed hy Cliff Mitchelmore on Tonight, but he did not manage to say "fuck."

And, more seriously, while *A Whistle in the Dark* had matched the expectations by being shocking (Tynan called it "arguably the most uninhibited display of brutality that the London theatre has ever witnessed. This is not American "Method" violence, slowly burning through understatement to eruption: it is naked, immediate and terrifying." and the *Guardian* called Harry, one of the Carney brothers, "one of the most vicious characters to have appeared on a London stage.") Murphy's two subsequent plays, *The Fooleen* and *The Morning After Optimism* could not be seen in the same sensational way. They were plays, not assaults from the hills on the London stage. Murphy was a playwright, not a performing Irishman. Although Michael Craig, the actor who brought *A Whistle in the Dark* to the Theatre Royal and who played Michael in the original production, took an option on *The Morning After Optimism*, he never managed to get it staged. Neither of the plays has ever been produced in London. and it was 1969 and 1971 respectively before they received Irish productions.

What might have kept his reputation alive was the film version of *A Whistle in the Dark*. Almost as soon as the play opened in London there were enquiries about the film rights and Murphy set about writing a film script. Rumours had Dirk Bogarde offering large sums of money and anxious to play in the film himself. The London Evening News ran a headline "His First Play Hits Jackpot" and the story that "A schoolmaster's first play, *A Whistle in the Dark* produced in the West End this week, is today on its way to Hollywood. I understand that the price suggested for it is 150,000 dollars (£50,000)."

The rights were in fact bought by Peter Rogers, a producer best known for the *Carry On* series of films, who paid £6,000 for them. Rogers was anxious to do something "classy," but still prided himself on his reputation for family entertainment. He sent Murphy's first script to the film censor's office and got back a reply which included the sentence "We'll be watching this one." Murphy did a second script for Rogers, but Rogers had gone off the idea of making the film and sold the rights again. The film was never made.

If Murphy's relationship with the English theatre dwindled into a very simple and straightforward indifference, never recovering from its spectacularly unreal beginning, his place in the Irish theatre has been more complex. For a start, the very racist outpourings provoked by *A Whistle in the Dark* induced a complementary sense of shame in some Irish commentators, who saw the play as portraying a side of Ireland best left unrevealed. While some of the critical reaction was positive and perceptive, much of it was informed by the notion that there were no such people in Ireland and that if there were, to show them was to demean the theatre. Des Rushe, writing in the *Irish Independent*, said of the Dublin production that "My ultimate reaction to Thomas Murphy's savage play at the Olympia Theatre, *A Whistle in the Dark*, was one of nausea, and I do not think the theatre is an institution which should nauseate . . . There are in short no real human beings (in the play)."

The *Evening Herald* saw it as "a play which will anger many Mayo people" and found it "distressing that this account of Irish savagery has been written by one of ourselves... It is a mournful thought that this was the picture of the Irish race that was paraded for three months last year to the wondering gaze of London theatregoers." The same reviewer also refused to believe that Dada in the play could have been a member of the Irish police force: "It is hard to credit his statement that he was once in the Civic Guards. The Force would surely have left some element of order in his personality."

This sort of reaction seems to have had some effect. *The Fooleen* (afterwards called *A Crucial Week in the Life of a Grocer's Assistant*) was offered to, and provisionally accepted for, the 1963 Dublin Theatre Festival. The Festival, however, then declined to produce the play and failed to find a Dublin management to take it on "because of the enormity of the set required and its big casting problem." The London producer Oscar Lewenstein flirted with the idea of staging the play, but also failed to do so.

To this broadly political antipathy to Murphy's work must be added the related fact that the predominant style of the Irish theatre, its production and acting values, were vastly out of keeping with the formal openness of his plays and their drive towards expressionistic, tragic, epic and melodramatic forms. Murphy's plays are large-scale in their concerns, dealing with the big questions and the grand forces of life; Irish theatre has been largely small-scale and domestic, in spite of its antecedents in the poetic drama of Yeats and Synge.

Murphy did begin to find some sort of place in the Abbey Theatre after the departure of Ernest Blythe and the onset of a more open policy in the sixties under Tomas MacAnna. It was *Famine* which, because of its recognisable historical setting, re-established him in Ireland when it was staged in the Peacock, the smaller of the Abbey's two houses, in March 1968 and later transferred upstairs to the Abbey itself. The epic scale of the play, however, has always provided problems for Irish theatres, and in spite of a number of good productions (including one by Murphy himself at the Project Arts Centre in 1978 and another by Druid Theatre Company in Galway in 1985) it tok Gerry Hynes's 1993 production at the Abbey to finally establish it in the repertoire. *The Orphans* which was staged at the Gate Theatre in the same year's Dublin Theatre Festival was met with general indifference.

Three years later the Abbey finally staged *The Morning After Optimism*, almost a decade after it had first been written, to a mixture of critical acclaim and bafflement. *The White House*, produced by the Abbey in March 1972, was more immediately recognisable and apparently naturalistic, and was, for the most part, well received, though there was controversy over the changing of the running-order of the two halves of the play and it aroused a furious reaction when it was televised by RTE in 1977.

Throughout the next ten years, however, Murphy's career, measured in terms of box-office and critical success, was something of a shambles. *The Sanctuary Lamp*, produced for the Dublin Theatre Festival by the Abbey in 1975, provoked a reaction which was compared at the time to that which greeted *The Plough and the Stars* in 1926: members of the audience walked out; some of them very noisily, and the controversy was such that a public discussion of the play was mounted in the theatre on the Friday after its opening. The hostility ranged from those outraged at the anti-clericalism of the play to those who argued that it was mere emotional bombast, devoid of intellectual substance.

Its defenders at the symposium, however, included the then President of Ireland, the late Cearbhall O Dalaigh, who said that "I would think that this play, which I do not require to see a second time, as some critics have said, ranks in the first three of the great plays at the Abbey Theatre — *The Playboy of the Western World, Juno and the Paycock, The Sanctuary Lamp.*" Such passionate opinions did little, however, to establish the play as a permanent part of the Irish repertoire: exactly ten years later, in October 1985, an admittedly mediocre production of *The Sanctuary Lamp* at the Abbey was a box-office disaster, and lasted for less than half of its allotted run.

The play which followed *The Sanctuary Lamp*, a light-hearted burlesque of Irish history called *The J. Arthur Maginnis Story*, which Murphy accurately characterised as a "romp," was firstly rejected by the Dublin Theatre Festival, and then, when it was produced by the Irish Theatre Company for a tour in 1976, was hammered by the critics and largely ignored by theatre audiences. After it, Murphy retired from playwrighting for over two years, spending his time as a "frontiersman" in the hills of Dublin, clearing and planting a vast garden in his Rathfarnham home.

When he returned in March 1980 with *The Blue Macushla*, again written in a "popular" style, though given a ludicrously elaborate production at the Abbey, it was an even worse disaster. After just two weeks and tiny houses *The Blue Macushla* was taken off, at Murphy's request. Although it resurfaced in a revised version in 1983 for a tour by the Red Rex company, it was only moderately successful. Some of its ideas found their way into Murphy's version of Liam O'Flaherty's novel *The Informer* presented by the Noel Pearson commercial management at the Olympia Theatre in Dublin. Reacting in part to the general lack of sympathy for his work in the Irish theatre, Murphy chose to direct the production himself, investing enormous energy and commitment in a script which was closer to an original Murphy play than to an adaptation. But again, the critical response was overwhelmingly hostile and the production was not a box-office or critical success.

This failure to find an audience even in Ireland was not counterbalanced by any great success in television or the cinema. Although he worked consistently for the BBC and Thames Television throughout the sixties, his television work was undertaken very much in default of stage productions. Indeed, most of his television work comprises versions of his stage plays, such as *A Crucial Week in the Life of a Grocer's Assistant* screened by the BBC in 1967, or *Famine* and *The White House* produced by RTE. *Snakes and Reptiles* was broadcast by the BBC in 1968, as the station's first ever colour broadcast of a drama, but it, too, is close to his stage work, being a version of the second part of *The White House, Conversations on a Homecoming*. Murphy's most interesting television play, *The Patriot*

Game, commissioned by the BBC to mark the fiftieth anniversary of the 1916 Rising, was never produced because of the projected cost.

His film scripts were no more successful. *A Whistle in the Dark* was not made. In 1969, he was commissioned to write a film treatment of Mary Webb's novel, *Precious Bane,* to be directed by John Huston, and to star Paul Newman. Again, in spite of plaudits from Newman and the enthusiasm of the would-be producers, the film has never been made.

Nor, in spite of a reasonable number of productions of his plays there, has America provided Murphy with a consistent audience. As in England, it was *A Whistle in the Dark* which introduced Murphy to American audiences. It was directed by Arvin Brown at the Long Wharf Theatre in New Haven in February 1968 and the production transferred off-Broadway to the Mercury Theatre in October 1969. The response was largely positive, with both *Time* magazine (where Ted Kalem called it "a play worthy of every tribute" and spoke of its "strength, wisdom and broody, disconcerting beauty") and the *Boston Globe* nominating it among their Plays of the Year. *The New York Times* called it both "strong and fiercely sustained" and "a strange, ugly, impressive play."

There was some of the hostility which had been evident on its first production in London, with George Oppenheimer in *Newsday* calling it an "evening with a group of anthropoid apes, indulging in such violence as has not been witnessed since television turned to talk." But even the best criticism of the play was ill-informed as to its context in Murphy's work as a whole. America's finest critic, John Lahr, writing in *Village Voice,* recognised that the play "transcends with its fury the limits of naturalism" and saw it as having "a tremendous visceral appeal." He also recognised that the play formed a model for Harold Pinter's 1965 play *The Homecoming* and put forward the comparison "to associate Murphy with the best in modern theatre." But his comparison was made in ignorance of Murphy's later work, and he claimed that "His literary instincts are sociological; Pinter's are metaphyscial," a judgement which could not have been made with any knowledge of *Famine* or *The Orphans*, which had been produced in Dublin before *A Whistle* opened off-Broadway. In this way even perceptive and appreciative criticism of Murphy in America failed to create any kind of coherent context within which his work could be understood.

Even more seriously, although *A Whistle* got better reviews than any other off-Broadway production for many years, and ran for a very respectable 102 performances at the Mercury, it did not make much money, and Murphy did not become a bankable playwright. Subsequent Murphy plays, including *The Orphans*, *The Morning After Optimism*, *On the Inside / On the Outside*, *The Informer* and *The Gigli Concert* have had American productions, but they have not collectively created a particularly responsive theatrical environment for Murphy in America.

The period since 1983, however, has been a strikingly successful one in Murphy's career. Firstly, *The Gigli Concert*, produced by the Abbey for the Dublin Theatre Festival, though by no means universally hailed, was given a production which came close to matching its stature, and emerged as a major European play. Secondly, Murphy began a highly fruitful period of collaboration with the innovative Druid Theatre Company in Galway. Between 1983 and 1985, *Famine* was revived, *On the Outside* produced, *Conversations on a Homecoming* was given its premiere, and most triumphantly, *Bailegangaire* given a superb first production, with Siobhan McKenna in the central role of Mommo. This concentrated association with Druid provided Murphy with a period in which his work, in something approaching its full range, was seen in a coherent series of sympathetic productions.

Druid also toured Murphy's work, bringing it to Dublin, New York (*Conversations on a Homecoming*), Australia (also *Conversations*) and London where their presentation of *Bailegangaire* at the Donmar Warehouse was the first time a Murphy play had been seen in London since *Famine* at the Royal Court in November 1969.

What is most extraordinary about *The Gigli Concert* and *Bailegangaire* is that, at first glance, they seemed to represent a retreat from the large-scale expressionistic or melodramatic plays of the previous decade — *The J. Arthur Maginnis Story*, *The Blue Macushla* and *The Informer*. Both look initially like naturalistic plays and follow, as many of Murphy's plays do, the so-called Aristotelian unities of time, space and action. Both are also, in practical terms, small-scale, requiring only three actors rather than the much larger casts of *The Informer* or *The Blue Macushla*. And yet both use an apparently small-scale set of theatrical resources to produce theatre that is concerned with the largest forces of life, that is both philosophically and theatrically expansive.

That the drive towards an extravagent theatre remains in Murphy's work is clear from the almost operatic form of his most recent plays *A Thief of a Christmas* and *Too Late for Logic*. The former had, at one point in its Abbey production, about forty actors on stage. Yet he has managed to achieve this extravagence without resorting to any such indulgences.

In spite of its public vagaries and reversals, Murphy's career as a playwright has been extraordinarily consistent and coherent. It has reached from tragedy and a sense of doom to the magical redemptions of *The Gigli Concert* and *Bailegangaire,* but in doing so has remained remarkably true to the same central concerns. This pilgrims's progress appeared to have reached a destination with the exorcism of sorrow, grief and guilt that is *Bailegangaire,* presenting a body of work which moved from a ferocious conflict to some kind of resolution. It is appropriate therefore to try to put some shape on what often seems to be a fractured and awkward achievement.

The argument of this book is that the achievement is in fact highly unified, and that what binds it together is the fact that it forms a kind of inner history of Ireland since the momentous changes which were set in motion in 1959, the fact that it reflects in a more sustained and accurate way the Irish society of those years than does the work of any other writer. Murphy's work has cleaved to the contours of a society's intellectual and emotional struggles, making the metaphysical and psychological elements of his work always firmly grounded in a specific reality.

This is not to argue that Murphy is primarily or exclusively an Irish playwright, ploughing a small and peripheral field, but to say the opposite. It is argued here that, because of its peculiarities and because of the truncated nature of the changes which took place in Irish society in the period in which Murphy was writing, it was possible for him to do things which are of enormous significance for the modern theatre as a whole: to write tragedy when many have argued that tragedy can no longer be written; to restore a religious sense to the theatre in a world which has lost a sense of the religious; to move beyond absurdity without denying its claims; and to produce theatrical images of transformation at a time when the world seems all too fixed and inescapable. To put it another way, Murphy has been able to dramatise an entire society at a time when the theatre has been forced to retreat into the dramatisation of individual lives or of the lives of confined strata of society. In confronting Ireland, Murphy has been able to confront an entire universe. It is this which makes him a great playwright.

Fintan O'Toole
Dublin, 1987 and 1993

I

A Haven of Rest and a Valley of Tears

In December 1992, the President of Ireland, Mrs Mary Robinson, herself a symbol of hope and change, paid an official visit to Tuam. For the occasion, the outside of the Town Hall was redecorated, so that, as she stood in the square, it would speak to her of civic pride and confidence, of an Ireland that was whole and undefeated. The spruced-up exterior, though, was an illusion, concealing the fact the building was in such a poor state inside that the Tuam Theatre Guild had been locked out of the little theatre inside that was its home because it had been declared dangerous. The illusion may have been unedifying, but, however unwittingly, it provided an apt image of one of the town's most distinguished sons. A ragged, awkward theatre abiding behind the walls of a spruced-up public illusion — a fitting monument to Tom Murphy's work.

The wall at the corner of the Town Hall is worn shiny where, for a hundred years, generations of young men have lounged and loitered watching the life of Tuam pass through the Market Square. The Hall itself, built "by the pennies of the poor," symbolised the Victorian aspiration to mercantile prosperity, its peculiar onion-domed spire rising to dwarf the ancient Celtic Cross, embodiment of Catholic steadfastness, that stands opposite. But for those generations who stood beneath it and watched the merchants on their way to any one of the town's four banks, the functionaries entering the hall behind them, the priests and nuns going to and from the town-within-a-town of convent, cathedral and college that forms the heart of Tuam, the diners and imbibers of the Imperial Hotel across the square, that prosperity was a taunting mirage.

As Irish Freedom came and went, the "shams" stood on the corner and watched. Some stayed, most drifted off to America or later to England where many saved their money only so that they could return for two weeks of the year in flash clothes and spend it in proving that they had, after all, joined the prosperous society. But one day, one Sunday morning in 1959, as Ireland stood on the brink of momentous social change, two of the loiterers stood there in the Market Square and one of them said "why don't we write a play?"

Tuam is in the West of Ireland, but to some observers it seemed more like the Wild West than the Irish West. The land around it has the pattern of stone walls typical of the West of Ireland, but it is better land than the scrub and rock of Connemara, good enough for its farmers to keep Tuam's merchants, joiners, cart-builders, blacksmiths and colleges going even when, in the nineteenth century, the town's incipient industrialisation was stunted by English colonial policy. The land is so flat that the few small hills seem like outstanding monuments and have attracted to themselves all the accretions of local legend, so that this one is the site of a great battle between the mythical peoples of ancient Ireland, the Tuatha de Danann and the Fir Bolgs, while that one is still echoing with the crash of swords where the last Irish kings slaughtered each other.

But the flatness gives to Tuam the feeling of being open to the world around it, unlike the enclosed air of hill-ringed towns, and this has been reflected in its culture. An American journalist visiting the town in 1897 found it "a sort of headquarters of every tramp going the road who, no doubt, looks upon it as a haven of rest and a valley of tears." Unlike most Irish small towns with their suspicion of "blow-ins," Tuam has a history of welcoming the outsider, even placing the outsider on a pedestal of awe. The two young men in the Market Square that Sunday morning in 1959 were already aware of the broader world around them. When Tom Murphy asked Noel O'Donoghue "What would we write about?", O'Donoghue replied "One thing is fucking sure — it's not going to be set in a kitchen."

Later, when Murphy became a playwright, his plays would be full of the nineteenth century and the effect of its deprivations on the life of the twentieth. Just forty years before he was born, and well within the lifetime of his father, a British visitor looked at Tuam and wrote: "Many of the streets are wretchedly built and the Galway Road shows how easily the Catholic poor are satisfied. Not only are the cabins in this district aboriginal in build but they are also indescribably filthy and the conditions of the inmates . . . is no whit higher than that obtaining in the wigwams of the native Americans. The hooded women, black-haired and bare footed, bronzed and tanned by constant exposure are wonderfully like the squaws brought from the Far West by Buffalo Bill."

For all its aspirations, Tuam had its own shanty town of squalor whose inhabitants ended up in America or in England. Another late nineteenth-century visitor described the town thus: "The mud lay thick everywhere. Many of the houses were simply shanties and squalid in appearance and the people whom one mostly met were painfully poor. Every little while I came upon a few words over a door that the party inside was licensed to sell beer or porter. Going into one of them, I found an earth floor, a wall immediately on the right, with a long bench in front of it, a small bar on the left covered with stains, and a roaring fire-place at the end of the bar. Hanging from a hook in the chimney was a large pot of boiling potatoes. I talked with the bar-tender (who was every time a woman) and found she had a cousin in America who was doing well."

The resonance of this hidden world continued to sound in Tuam when Tom Murphy began to write plays and the legacy of that poverty and emigration weighs down on those plays like the burden of history.

Tom Murphy was born in 1935 in a solid detached house which his father, a carpenter, had built on Church View. It is a square country house, with long windows each side of the door on both stories, bigger than a council house but by no means spacious for a man, his wife and their ten children. On either side of the house, straggling along the road were six thatched cottages, the dark, pokey dwellings of the shanty Irish. By the time Murphy was born the cottages were deserted and ruined, their roofs collapsed, their inhabitants either gone to England or moved to the new council houses of Tierboy.

As a child he played among the ruins, the low walls that were all that remained of the lives of the nineteenth century poor who had passed anonymously into unwritten history. The cottages are gone now, replaced in the 1960s by the bright new bungalows of the economic boom. The aborigines and squaws are gone too, the only reminder of Buffalo Bill's Far West being the crop of American-style fast food shops which has sprung up in the town. Murphy's plays and Murphy's times are circumscribed by that shift from the shanty shebeen to the hamburger joint, from the thatched cottage to the bliss of the bungalow.

From the front of the Murphys' house in Church View, the view is of the town's remaining symbol of the old Protestant ascendancy, St. Mary's Cathedral, seen across what was once a field and is now a cattle mart, built after Ireland's entry to the EEC in 1973 made cattle a big business. St. Mary's dates back to the twelfth century, but now that the power of the Protestant landowners and merchants has been replaced by the big farmers and the Catholic businessmen, it has declined to a museum piece, where a sign announces that restoration work has been carried out by AnCO as training for the unemployed.

From the back of the Murphys' house, you can see Tierboy. Tierboy is the town's working-class enclave, successor to the shanties and thatched cottages of the poor of the nineteenth century. A hundred years ago, there were evictions there, and a newspaper report of one remarked that "The houses there are not mansions but still, horrible as they are, the residents cling to them and there is no desire for a change." Those houses were, by Murphy's time, replaced with council housing, but Tierboy was still rough, the sort of place you wouldn't go at night. That sense of a social underbelly to the town runs through Murphy's work, with its concern for the outsiders, the dispossessed, the unrespectable.

In his 1994 novel *The Seduction of Morality*, for instance, the social division of the fictional town of Grange, clearly modelled on Tuam, is essential to the plot. The most scandalous aspect of the behaviour of Vera, the heroine, is not that she is a New York prostitute, but that she, a woman from the town's business class, holes up for a few days in a house in the New Estate, colloquially referred to as "the Punjab." Her sister Marcia's tearful outrage — "In this town, in-this-town, living with tinkers! Henry! With that old thing, with that old sponger, that old layabout, Reilly, Finbar Reilly! Up in the New Estate!" — identifies the estate with the shifting, mistrusted, pariah class of travellers, an unsettled encampment of outcasts on the edge of civilisation.

At one end of Church View is a crossroads. There, opposite what was Connolly's forge and is now a bicycle shop, the young unemployed men would gather to play pitch and toss. From the age of four or five Murphy would watch them as they pitched passionately for a few pence. Out of boredom, they would perform tricks, feats of strength to assert the manhood that unemployment seemed to threaten. One man could do a "flagpole," holding a post with only his arms and levering himself out straight until he was parallel to the ground. These performances came, as Murphy's plays would later, from the bitterness and frustration of being on the outside of the town's respectable life.

The official ideology of Irish politics at this time was that the ideal Ireland was rustic and Gaelic. Eamon de Valera's famous vision of a bucolic rural paradise was broadcast when Murphy was fifteen, and it held little for the urban working-class of which he was part. The men who played pitch and toss at the crossroads would wait for countrymen, farmers from the surrounding land, to pass on their way into town and would taunt them as "culchies." The hope was that the taunts would lead to a fight, that the resentment at being left outside of the official Ireland could be given vent in violence. Sometimes, the young men would go on raids into the countryside, hunting foxes with their terriers or raiding henhouses to drink the raw eggs. Though Murphy was too young to be part of the group, he would tag along with his older brothers. Once he was given a young vixen which they had caught, and raised it as a pet. As he grew up, he always thought of himself as an urbanite, though Tuam was then a town of less than 5,000 people. But this sense of not being a part of the rural Ireland that was the established ideal was crucial in his consciousness as it would be in his plays.

Towards the far end of Church View from the crossroads, there were other landmarks. There was the grocer's shop, now a derelict corner invaded by grass and weeds, whose owner formed the basis for the character of Uncle Alec in *A Crucial Week in the Life of A Grocer's Assistant*. There was Egan's Mineral Water bottling plant, which has now been replaced by a Coca-Cola bottling works, and whose transformation is influential on *The White House* and *Conversations on a Homecoming*.

But most importantly there was the railway station. The station is now closed, a piece of local history which has been taken over by a railway preservation society. But when Murphy was young, it was possible to go to the platform and buy a through ticket for Euston in London. The railway station was the most important place in Murphy's early life.

Murphy's first two full-length plays, *A Whistle in the Dark* and *A Crucial Week in the Life of A Grocer's Assistant* both focus, at the beginning, on the arrival or departure of a train. In *A Whistle in the Dark*, the opening scene is dominated by the impending arrival of a father on a train. In *A Crucial Week*, a young man in a dream is being called away to a train which we hear "whistling impatiently."

In Murphy's childhood, the heaven of anticipation was waiting for his father to arrive home from England on the train. The hell of misery was standing on the station platform, with the line stretching visibly away, to see off either his father, going back to Birmingham, or another of his brothers or sisters going to join him. By the time Murphy reached the end of childhood, nine of the twelve members of his immediate family had emigrated. During the Second World War, as the Irish building trade slumped into depression, Jack Murphy, his father, went to work in Birmingham and stayed there for the rest of his working life. As the youngest of the ten children, Tom was condemned to watch the others go one by one. "Birmyham," as it was called in Tuam, became the centre of a family-in-exile of which he was only occasionally a part.

Because there was a gap of up to twenty years in age between the elder members of the family and himself, Murphy's elder brothers, whom he saw only on rare visits home became, and remain, strange and mysterious creatures, connected to him but absent, tied to him by the closest bonds of blood and family but yet only vague figures in his memory. His work is full of brothers and parents who are absent and who yet haunt the imaginations of his protagonists.

In *A Whistle in the Dark*, Dada is an inescapable presence for Michael, even though they live in different countries. In *A Crucial Week*, John Joe's missing brother

Frank flits around the dark corners of his imagination and refuses to be forgotten. In *The Morning After Optimism,* Edmund is looking for his long-lost brother. In *The Orphans,* Kate and Roddy's parents are dead and they themselves are searching for some connection between them as brother and sister.

And even where there are not literally lost parents or siblings, there are metaphysical brothers who must find each other in order to be whole. Harry and Francisco in *The Sanctuary Lamp,* Tom and Michael in *Conversations on a Homecoming,* Eddie and Danny in *The Blue Macushla,* JPW and the Man in *The Gigli Concert,* Christopher and Michael in *Too Late for Logic,* are all two halves of the one mind, each of which is tormented by a sense of absence without the other. In *Bailegangaire,* the child Tom is both the young boy waiting at home for the adults in his family to return, and, after his death, himself the missing sibling whose absence is haunting the memory of his sisters and his grandmother and will not let them rest.

Murphy's theatre is a theatre of ghosts, of potent absences, and it is hard not to see the imagery of the broken family which gives flesh to his work as having its genesis in the mind of the boy on Tuam railway station in the 1940s. In this way economics, the bitter economic facts of poverty and emigration, and politics, the political ideology which excludes some of the children of the nation, find their way onto the stage in the intimate actions and thoughts of Murphy's characters. The dialectic of exile and homecoming which dominates Murphy's plays is rooted in the realities of Irish life and of his own life.

At the centre of Tuam which lies beyond Church View is a clerical corral of church buildings and lands. The same observer who described Tuam's poor women as squaws also saw the town as "a poor town of which the staple trade is religion" and it remains true that religion and religious educational establishments are among the town's main industries. Grouped together are the Catholic Cathedral, where Murphy served Mass and sang in the choir, the Archbishop's House, the Presentation Convent, the Mercy Convent, the two schools of the Christian Brothers and the boarding college with its Gaelic football grounds, St. Jarlath's.

In Murphy's childhood, this physical domination of the town by religious institutions was matched by the moral and emotional dominance of Catholicism and its clergy. Not only did the clergy control education, but they also took a hand in all aspects of social life, from sport to entertainment. Most societies had a priest on their committee, and the first thing a new society did was to seek the patronage of a member of the clergy.

As a child, Murphy was devout. Noel O'Donoghue who stood with him on that Sunday morning in 1959 and suggested that they write a play remembers Murphy reminding him to say a prayer each time the clock struck. Not only was it required that you blessed yourself passing a church, but also that you did so passing the statue of the Blessed Virgin in the grounds of the Mercy Convent. It is said in Tuam that some people blessed themselves passing the Post Office clock. By the 1940s and 1950s, the residual political passions of the Land War, the War of Independence and the Civil War had dwindled into something approaching apathy. With no rival centre of interest, the only challenge to religion as a source of passion was football, and in this, too, clerical influence was dominant.

For a child, contact with the religious was daily. Murphy went first to the convent school, then to the Christian Brothers when he was seven. He stayed with the Brothers until after his Intermediate Certificate, when he was fifteen. It was for him a time of almost unmitigated brutality and unhappiness, a time which would lead to the association in his plays between religion and violence. His later recollections of those who educated him were largely of their stupidity, of the fear of violence from frustrated men, of a "very evil minded man" who was the head of the primary school, of the black soutane and leather strap. Secondary school was worse, the mediocrity of the education more obvious, the violence of the teachers more pronounced. He himself was cunning and intelligent enough to avoid the worst of the punishment, but the atmosphere of terror pervaded. At times, of a class of forty or forty five, thirty five would by ten o'clock in the morning be standing at the walls around the room waiting to be beaten. The leather was the most common punishment, but children were also punched in the face or beaten with a board from a packing case or a stick from the garden.

The terror was not conducive to education, even to the narrow achievement of examination results. Murphy was one of only five out of a total of forty pupils at the Christian Brothers who passed the Inter Cert. He did so with the minimum possible qualification: five bare passes. His experience was by no means untypical of Irish education until the late 1960s. The Christian Brothers saw themselves preparing boys from less well off homes for accession to the pinnacles of civil service jobs and company clerkships, the only social mobility available to the working-class in a stagnant society. Murphy chose to opt out of the competition and to go instead to "Tech" where trades were taught, after his Inter Cert. The Christian Brothers greeted this decision with the words "You can go to Hell or you can go to the Tech." To go to the Tech was to be damned forever to the exterior darkness of menial working-class life, outside of the pretentions of petty social advancement. Murphy went and was happy there.

But it was not just inside school that the church and its attitudes dominated life. A virtual segregation of the sexes was in force. Men and women, even good Catholic husbands and wives, could not sit together at Mass, but were arranged in rows on opposite sides of the church. Groups of boys went round together and when they passed similar groups of girls, there was a round of embarrassed banter. Though Murphy himself is remembered as a rare case of a young man who could talk to women, his plays reflect the failure of communication between the sexes, often erupting into violence. Men hunt in packs and women hang on, often becoming the victims of the male's frustration.

In *On the Outside*, Frank and Anne are kept apart. In *A Whistle in the Dark*, Betty hovers on the sidelines and ends up being struck by Michael. In *Famine*, Mother is killed by John Connor. In *Conversations on a Homecoming*, Peggy is on the fringe of a male drinking group and is insulted and humiliated by Tom. In *The Gigli Concert*, the Man's wife is insulted and abused by him. In *Bailegangaire*, the relationship between Mommo and her husband is one of cold and silent resentment and Dolly is beaten up by her husband Stephen. In almost every case, the women are abused by the man who loves them: love paralyses and frustrates Murphy's men, placed as they are in a world in which there is an unbridgeable gulf between men and women.

In Tuam, too, the only source of outside women who might be freer of the social conventions were the four banks, whose female employees were often from outside of the town and generally unattached. This fact, too, is reflected in Murphy's plays, where Mona, who represents sex for John Joe in *A Crucial Week*, is a bank-clerk and thus, according to Mrs. Smith, a "pitfaleen," and in *Conservations on a Homecoming*, where Josephine "our new bank clerk" is rumoured to wear no knickers and to be "a right one." The mythical allure of such women serves only to underline the actual segregation of the sexes in small town Ireland.

There was, however, a counter-attraction to the church and its controls, one area of life which escaped its dominance: the cinema. Books were censored, and without television there was no medium in which Irish urban

society could find an image of itself, no reflection of the
lives which the people of towns and cities led. Murphy's
father moved his lips as he read, and the collection of books
in the house was a strange amalgam of popular education
and nostalgic Irish history. There was Scott of the Antarctic
and books on the Egyptian tombs, whose pictures of naked
women painted on vases held a particular attraction, side
by side with patriotic histories with titles like *True Men*,
magazines like *Ireland's Own*, with its folksy stories,
sentimental ballads and practical hints on rural living, and
there were the collected nationalist songs of Thomas Davis
from *The Nation*. But the state censorship of practically
every book about contemporary Ireland was re-inforced by
the religious embargo on reading books which were on the
Vatican Index. Noel O'Donoghue recalls reading Voltaire's
Candide at this time, a book which was on the Index. When
he got a toothache while reading it, he became convinced
that it was punishment for his sin. In this context, the only
imaginative relief was to be found in the fantasy of the
cinema.

Tuam had two cinemas, the Mall and the Odeon,
compared with three for the much larger city of Galway.
For Murphy, the Sunday matinee at the Mall was the
heavenly reward for the purgatory of the week. The diet
was of serials — *The Red Baron* and *Flash Gordon* — but
the audience was not confined to children. In the world of
prolonged childhood which he was to capture in *A Crucial
Week in the Life of A Grocer's Assistant*, it was possible for
a grown man and a young boy, one on the way to work, the
other to school, to walk down the street discussing what
would happen to the Red Baron who had fallen through a
trapdoor and into a pit of snakes and tigers the previous
Sunday. As Murphy remembers this incident, the man
predicted that the Red Baron would remove his braces and
use them as a lion tamer uses his whip to control the
animals.

When Murphy began to write as a young boy, he wrote wild adventure stories, and the imaginative leaps of the cinema continued to be an influence in his early move away from the naturalism which was the dominant mode of the Irish theatre. Most obviously in *The Blue Macushla*, but also in the form of his plays and their search for wonder and the spectacular, there is the mark of an imagination shaped by the flights of fantasy movies. His plays, unusually in the modern theatre, still contain heroes, men and women struggling to wrest some triumph from a hostile world as the cowboys and spacemen of the cinema screen strived to do.

There was also music, an enduring source of imagery and inspiration in Murphy's theatre. In every town in Ireland in the forties and fifties, there were obsessional devotees of classical music, particularly of opera, for whom the drabness and confinement of life were negated by the colour and expressiveness of this expansive sound. In Tuam there was a railway worker with an extensive collection of records who was happy to let Murphy and anyone else listen with him. Murphy's parents both sang at home and he himself has a fine tenor voice. At concerts in Tuam, he would not only sing himself but he would also parody the warblings of other bar tenors of the town, making his singing into an incipient theatrical performance of the sort which is so important in some of his plays.

Murphy has gone much further than almost any other playwright in his integration of music into his plays, making it not just a device or a relief from the action, but a central image of his characters' aspirations. This arises at least in part out of the fact that Murphy's own voice is both a blessing and a curse: a blessing because it is good. a curse because it not good enough to make him a great singer, to allow him to express himself through his voice, directly and without mediation. The imagery of singing in *The Gigli Concert,* the dramatic use of Peggy's singing of

All in the April Evening in *Conversations on a Homecoming,* the desperate tribal rendition of *The Boys from the County Mayo* in *A Whistle in the Dark*, the use of Gluck's opera *Orpheus and Eurydice* as a template for *Too Late for Logic*, the desire in all of his plays for "a sound to clothe our aspiration and emotion," the musical structuring of Murphy's dialogue, all of these arise from that desire, a desire that is at once personal to Murphy and typical of small town Ireland before television.

After two years at the Tech, Murphy went to work as an apprentice fitter/welder in the factory of the Irish Sugar Company. The sugar factory was one of the few successes of the years of Independence, a nationalised attempt to provide jobs in the town, a finger in the dyke against the flood tide of emigration, which, by 1953, when Murphy went to work, meant that 25,000 people a year were leaving Ireland. At this time he had stopped writing and read very little. But he was able to observe much in his two years at the factory, to watch the daily stratagems of camaraderie, cruelty and playfulness through which men coped with deadening realities and the petty tyrannies of factory life. And he had also begun to explore the new world of the theatre. At the Tuam Little Theatre Guild, a better than average local amateur group, he saw plays by Gerard Healy and Louis Dalton and was affected by the darkness, the magic, the comparative silence of the Market Square afterwards. He saw Anew McMaster, the last of the great repertory Shakespearians, play *Othello* to a nearly empty house.

In 1955, he saw an advertisement offering scholarships for young men to train as metalwork teachers. Metalwork had been his worst subject at the Tech (woodwork was his best, as it had been his father's) but the offer was a way out of the factory. He was sent to Ringsend Technical School for two years where he saw the "mysteries of the world" contained in books on biology, horticulture, surveying, physiology. He immersed himself in the workings of physical things: tools, valves, machinery, lathes, welding, car parts, tractors. His education was in putting things together, in shaping and honing, not in ideas or literature. The memory of working with metals seems to lie behind the detailed descriptions of Finbar Reilly's attempts to make his holy medals look more expensive than they should be in the novel *The Seduction of Morality*. Less directly, the images of alchemy, the metaphysician's metalwork, which crop up in *The Gigli Concert* and *The Seduction of Morality*, linking Murphy's erstwhile trade with the mythic Faust, may also arise from such humdrum beginnings.

He returned to work as a metalwork teacher in Mountbellew, a few miles outside of Tuam, where he began to see "the disasters of the night before" on the faces of his students. He also joined the Theatre Guild and acted in plays by Blessing, Synge, O'Casey. He began to read again, but this time to read plays, particularly Synge and Lorca, two urban playwrights who had written about and criticised the remnants of Catholic peasant civilisation which they found around them.

Not only had Synge written of the West of Ireland, he had done so in a language charged with poetry, a non-naturalistic language imbued with a sense of scale and power. He had been followed by M. J. Molloy, a playwright from Milltown, a few miles outside of Tuam, to whom Murphy pays a passing tribute in *A Crucial Week in the Life of a Grocer's Assistant* where John Joe refers to "Gardenfield Wood whispering to Molloy," a reference to Molloy's play *The Wood of the Whispering*. In Synge, Lorca and Molloy, Murphy found at least the possibility of a non-naturalistic theatre which could yet reflect the reality of the world around him.

Though he cannot have been aware of it at the time, the year in which Murphy (in collaboration with Noel O'Donoghue) chose to write his first play could not have been a more symbolic one. 1959 was not just the end of a disastrous decade for the Irish economy, a decade in which the slide into ever-deepening recession was made psychologically much more damaging by the contrast with Britain's booming economy, it was also Year One of the Irish Industrial Revolution, the first year of the First Programme for Economic Expansion. The Programme had been published in 1958, the year in which *On the Outside*, its later companion piece *On the Inside*, and *A Crucial Week in the Life of a Grocer's Assistant* are all set. In this sense, Murphy's most important contemporary writer is Dr. T. K. Whitaker, the Secretary of the Department of Finance and author of the Programme, an economic policy which was to have dramatic cultural effects.

The effect of the plan was to recognise that Independent Ireland had failed as an economic entity and that the nationalist policy of enclosing the Irish economy behind high tariff barriers in the hope that a native industrialist class would emerge to provide jobs for the people was simply untenable. In the face of massive and steady emigration, which had led to serious discussion of the possibility that the Irish as a race would vanish altogether, Whitaker proposed the abandonment of economic nationalism and the provision of tax advantages and grants to attract foreign investment. It was a plan for urbanisation and inevitably for opening up the country, which had tried so hard to shield its Catholic purity and homogeneity from alien influences, to foreign money, foreign ideas, foreign culture.

These influences had long been present, through the cinema, through the music of the dance halls which had replaced traditional music as the accompaniment to popular dancing, and through contact with English and American-based relatives, but now they were no longer to be controlled by an official culture which could claim to be Gaelic and pure. American multinational industries began to establish themselves in Ireland: Hallmark Cards in 1958, Burlington Textiles in 1960, General Electric in

1962, until, by 1983, foreign firms had invested nearly six billion pounds in the Republic of Ireland, four and a half billion pounds of which came from America. Ireland was gradually ceasing to think of herself as the Island of Saints and Scholars whose greatest export was missionaries to the Black Babies, and to try on the image of what the Industrial Development Authority's advertisements in *Time* and *Newsweek* would soon be calling "The Most Profitable Industrial Location in Europe."

Murphy's play, *On the Outside*, though a short one-act piece, gives a remarkably precise and compressed sense of the tensions which led to this change and a remarkably accurate foretaste of some of its consequences.

T. K. Whitaker himself, as a cultured man, was not unaware of the cultural consequences of such massive socio-economic change. But he believed that Irish civilisation could absorb the changes and remain true to its own essential nature. His own cultural ideology, based on a long view of Irish history, stressed Ireland's ability to assimilate and make her own the cultures of invading peoples. His combination of reverence for Ireland's Catholic past and confidence in its ability to cope with alien influence was a useful frame of mind for a man who was about to open the floodgates. When Whitaker made a pilgrimage to the shrines of the saints and scholars from Ireland who had evangelised the barbaric Germanic tribes in the seventh and eighth centuries, he found that their altars had been invaded, in Saint Gallen and Salzburg, by the statues of local German saints. He was able, however, to console himself with the thought "I suppose Irish initiative and devotion needed eventually to be underpinned by German organisation and method!"

But Whitaker was sowing the seeds for the abandoment of nationalism as an economic, and gradually as a cultural force, and this fact had enormous consequences for a writer like Murphy setting out to address an Irish audience. For nationalism in Ireland was the great binding force which united culture and politics, literature and economics, writers with their audiences. The strength of the nationalist movement was its inclusiveness, the way in which it managed to find a place within its political programme for everything from social justice to religious righteousness, from the words the Irish were to speak to the games they were to play, taking theatre and literature effortlessly into its warm embrace.

The advantage, albeit a highly problematic one, from the point of view of the Irish literary and theatrical movement, was that writers could see themselves and their concerns as allied to those of the public, external world, bound up in the higher unity called "Ireland." The writers embraced, and were embraced by, a single broad movement which, by and large, also included their audience. Irish theatre before Murphy, with the exception of O'Casey, assumes a single unified society, in line with nationalist ideology. But the economic revolution that is contemporaneous with the writing of *On the Outside* broke that ideology's binding force.

After 1959, it became impossible to think of an Irish literary movement, because it became impossible to think of "Ireland." Movements need common points of reference, but in the Ireland of the years after 1959 it was precisely the reference points of cultural and political homogeneity which were being removed. Whitaker's revolution called into being new class forces, new divisions of urban and rural, new consumer choices, new modes of behaviour, so that "Ireland" itself as a fixed and coherent notion which could underlie the work of a writer ceased to exist. It was replaced by a series of divisions, a series of variations on Ireland, a range of individual responses to the problems, not of unity and homogeneity, but of discontinuity, disruption and disunity.

Where so much of Irish theatre had been a theatre of social unity, *On the Outside* is most definitely a play of division. Where nationalism proclaimed the unity of the classes in the common name of Irishman and the unity of city and country in the common land of Ireland, *On the Outside* creates its extraordinary impact by showing the division of the classes and the antagonism between city and country. That this could be done in one short play, far from a full-scale drama, is a mark of how strategic was the moment at which Murphy was impelled into playwrighting, a moment at which the social tensions of the country were so compressed and stark that they could be encompassed in a one-act play.

The setting for *On the Outside* is very specific and very important to the workings of the play. It is "a quiet country road outside a dancehall." That the setting is in the country, and that Joe and Frank, the play's two central characters, are from the town, places them immediately on foreign territory. That the Irish countryside should be an alien place for two young Irishmen is itself a startling breach with the conventions of Irish literature since the Revival, in which the countryside is the essential Ireland, the natural habitat of the Irishman.

Since Yeats, Synge and Lady Gregory promulgated the ideology of the peasant as the true representative of the Irish people, the countryside in Irish literature had been the realm of nature, innocence and truth, set against the artifice, corruption and deceit of the city. Even in the fifties, when rural Ireland was being bled dry by emigration, and its people were finding their own way to urban life in Britain and America, the myth of the impoverished but wise Irish peasantry persisted to the degree that it was possible for a playwright like Paul Vincent Carroll, regarded as a realistic depicter of Irish life, to write that Ireland "may well be destined to be the saviour in a world jungle of rank material weeds, and perhaps distracted foreigners, driven to despair by the ever-multiplying complexities of a machine — and gadget — ridden age, will visit her to try to relearn, from that tattered woman trudging her way to the slum hospital to have her baby, or from that peasant lost in wonder at the yellowing barley, the unutterable simplicities of living . . . If *that*, instead of prosperity, population and efficiency, is the destiny of Ireland, then surely she is the divine instrument of a pitying God, and I, as one Irishman, will be well content."

This vision of an Ireland which existed for others, as a spiritual haven for tourists rather than as a place for its own people to live in, was written in 1954, just five years before *On The Outside*. Nor was it an eccentric vision, for it was matched by the vision of Ireland's messianic mission to save the world through its "spiritual empire" put forward in his public speeches by the Taoiseach Eamon de Valera.

Similarly, emigration was seen not so much as a problem in itself, but as carrying with it the attendant problem that it removed pure, Gaelic peasants from their contemplation of the yellowing barley and placed them in the urban mire of corruption and sordidity. While the unwanted young of rural Ireland were getting the necessities of life denied to them at home in the industrial cities of London, Birmingham, or Coventry, even an intelligent "realist" novelist like Bryan MacMahon could come to bemoan the fact that "The pattern of Irish life in the shoddy towns of industrial England has yet to reveal itself; it seems rather a pity that the rural Irish did not emigrate to rural England."

The cast of mind which associates "town" with "shoddy," explains much of the alienation which Joe and Frank in *On the Outside*, themselves "townies," feel. MacMahon's refusal to countenance the fact that Irish people might actually choose to live in towns is evidence of the persistent refusal to recognise urban life which remains in the official Irish culture at the time *On the Outside* is written.

On the Outside confronts this official culture not only by showing Joe and Frank's resentment against the countryside, but also by its very setting outside a dancehall. For the same conventions which allow for a vision of the countryside as a place of innocence also allow for only two possible rural settings: the inside of a thatched cottage, or an outside which is pure natural landscape. By presenting us with a setting which contains both a quiet country road and a dancehall with a poster advertising The Marveltones and a garish revolving crystal ball sending its glints through the window, Murphy presents us with an immediate image of a countryside that is not just thatched cottages and lovely landscapes.

For the dancehall is a very specific symbol of contrast between the idealisation of the countryside and its actuality. Nowhere was the official reverence for traditional Gaelic culture more ironically at variance with the real political practice than in relation to dance music. The social basis of Irish traditional dance music was in the informal dances held at crossroads in the summer and in houses during the winter. But at the same time as he was espousing the revival by the new state of the traditional culture of the countryside, de Valera was introducing, as one of his first pieces of legislation in power, the Public Dance Halls Act of 1935. The Act required the licensing of dances, which meant that they had to be held in halls and could no longer continue in houses or at crossroads. This suited both the clergy, who could now more easily supervise the dances to ensure that they did not become occasions of sexual sin, and the petty rural businessmen who built the halls and made money from the dances. In the process, traditional music was replaced by American-style dance bands, such as The Marveltones of *On the Outside*.

The setting of the play outside of a dancehall, therefore, takes us immediately into a rural world that is far from the innocent centre of Gaelic civilisation that it is supposed to be.

The central and simple metaphor of *On the Outside* is that of exclusion. Frank and Joe are waiting outside the dancehall because they have not enough money to get inside, where Frank has a girl waiting for him. The immediate reason for the exclusion is economic, but there is also a sense that Joe and Frank are on hostile territory out here in the countryside. They are apprentices in a factory in the town, members of the working class rather than of the agricultural economy of the country. When they try to get into the dancehall using "pass-outs" they have cadged from a couple who are leaving, the Bouncer throws them out, using what for him is obviously the ultimate insult — "Townies." Frank remarks bitterly that "These buffers will soon object to us walking on the roads. He wouldn't be so tough in town."

In this exchange there is the sense of a deep division between town and country: the Bouncer, on his own rural territory, defeats Frank and Joe; if they were to get him on their territory, the town, the positions would be reversed. This is an antagonism between two neighbouring countries, a state of undeclared war within the nation that goes against every assumption of nationalism.

But to this image of division and exclusion is added another, deeper divide, that of class. Where the official ideology of nationalism had always placed country above class, founding itself on the belief that what united Irishmen was infinitely more important than the petty economic antagonisms which might divide them, *On the Outside* is immersed in the minutiae of class division and of social mobility. The opening section of dialogue between Anne, the girl whom Frank is supposed to have met for a date which he cannot afford, and Kathleen, her friend, is entirely to do with social status. Kathleen, wiser in the ways of the world than Anne, reminds her of the importance of a man's economic status and the danger of being misled:

"I was going with a fella last year in Dublin . . . Richard Egan. And then one night we met — yeh know Mary O'Brien nursing in the Mater? And later she took me aside. 'Do you know who he is?' she said. 'No'. 'He's the porter at the hospital'. The shagging porter. And his name wasn't Richard."

While it might be acceptable in the end for a man with a vast private income not to be Earnest, a hospital porter cannot afford not to be Richard. The opening scene of *On the Outside* establishes with economy and immediacy the fact that love is bound up with economics. Appearances, the stuff of sexual attraction, are subordinated to social status in a deadly serious game where it is the business of men to conceal who they are and the business of women to find out. Already Murphy is making the connection between the intimate sphere of love and sexuality. the world of the mind and the personality, and the public sphere of economics and history.

Kathleen's hopes for Anne are not that she might encounter a compatible lover, but that she might "meet someone with a car." The only appearances which matter are those that betoken social and economic status.

From Joe and Frank's first entrance there is a clear indication of the degree to which they are on the other side of the class divide from "them with the cars and money." Not only have they been hiding behind the wall in order to avoid having to pay for the girls to get into the dance, but they quickly discover that they themselves have not enough money to get them inside. They are at the mercy of those who are in a position to exploit them, in this case, the organisers of the dance who have raised the admission price "Just because there's no other dance on around here tonight." They are on the receiving end of the law of supply and demand.

This economic exclusion is reflected in the language which Joe and Frank speak. Being cut off from respectable society, they express their sense of being separate by their use of small town argot. In his first line of dialogue, Joe refers to Frank as "sham," a word which in the Tuam idiom is used to indicate another Tuam person. It is used so much that even outside of the town, Tuam people are called

"shams." This in-talk is scattered through Joe and Frank's
dialogue in the play, identifying them with each other in
the face of a hostile world around them. Words like "whid"
(look at), "buffer" (country dweller), "choicer" (nothing), "a
bull and cow" (a row) strengthen the impression of Joe and
Frank as being in league against everyone else around
them.

Joe and Frank also recognise that the language of heroic
Ireland, the tales of peasant life and of gallantry in defence
of Irish nationhood against the Saxon foe, is not theirs.
They mock the school rhymes of *The Old Woman of the
Roads* and of Custume's stand at the bridge of Athlone:
"Oh, to have a lickle house, to own the hearth and stool
and all; in the dear little, sweet little emerald isle, in the
county of Mayo. Break down the bridge six warriors
rushed, and the storm was shot and they shat in the storm.
And Sarsfield strung up by the nockers behind them!" All
the romantic history of Ireland, all the hymns of Saint
Patrick and the songs of patriotic love of place and the
sorrows of the nation, are reduced in Joe and Frank's
minds to a meaningless gabble of overwrought posturing
which is immediately followed and undercut by Frank's
despairing reminder of economic realities: " Look, let me
go in and borrow the money for you."

The meaning of this alienation from the conception of
Ireland which they have been taught at school is made
clear in the play — their exclusion is a matter of class. Joe
remembers a man at work whom they soft-soap for
cigarettes, and thinks of the way he "nearly tore the head
off himself pulling off his cap" when called into the boss's
office. Frank takes up this reminder of servitude and
extends it to the whole town, making it clear that not only
is there a division between town and country, but there is
also a division within the town:

" No, but the job. You know, it's like a big tank. At home
is like a tank. A huge tank with walls running up, straight
up. And we're at the bottom, splashing around all week in

their Friday night vomit, clawing at the sides all around. And the bosses — and the big-shots — are up around the top, looking in, looking down. You know the look? Spitting. On top of us. And for fear we might climb out some way — Do you know what they're doing? They smear grease around the walls".

Frank's imagery is related to an incident of which Mickey Ford later reminds him: "Think back what happened with you and your auld drunken auld layabout auld fella last year: Oh, didn't quiet, cunning Frank stand beside him kicking in the shop window, and stand beside him wanting to take on the town. The priest saved you from being arrested, but he mightn't bother a second time." Frank's outburst of violence, his wanting to take on the town, has only served to grease the walls of the tank, putting him more in debt to the clergy, giving the likes of Mickey Ford something to hold over him to keep him in line.

The image of being trapped in the tank, of not being able to get out, combines with the play's central image of not being able to get in, to redouble the sense of being caught in a purgatorial world. For Frank and Joe this is made all the more intolerable by the presence in the play of a figure who represents an embodied image of their own future, Daly the drunk. From his first entrance, Daly is treated with contempt by everyone, and indeed, before he appears at all he has been dismissed as "some old drunk" by Kathleen. Joe and Frank treat him as they would a smelly old dog, toying with him, telling him to "scram," calling him names, patting him on the head when they think he might have money, then ordering him to "go home." Joe, in fact, refers to him as "like a stray dog." Daly is manhandled out of the hall by the bouncer who refers to him by name, giving the impression that he is thrown out on a regular basis.

By the end of the play, however, when Daly reappears, Frank attacks him with a peculiar intensity tinged with fear, clearly recognising in Daly the ghost of his own future: "You! Keep away from me!" Daly is left on stage as Frank and Joe exit, kicking impotently at the poster advertising the dance, a spectre of what they may become. In this use of an image of the future, Murphy is already breaking out of the apparent naturalism of the play, prefiguring the use of not one, but two, registers of time in his later plays from *A Whistle in the Dark* onwards.

Daly may be the harbinger of the future for Frank and Joe if they do not escape, but *On the Outside* also has an embodiment of the country's future, one which clearly does not include them. The world of the new American consumerism into which Ireland at the time of the play is about to launch itself is hinted at in the language borowed from the movies and rock 'n' roll, like "Okay Elvis," "Annie get your gun," "Makum joke for squaw," and the conversion of Irish coinage into American values in the phrase "half-a-dollar" used for half-a-crown.

But this world is chiefly present in the character of Mickey Ford, whose very name associates him with the great success story of American industry and who drives "round the town always with one arm sticking out the window," who sports an "American-style tie" which Frank later calls his "Florida Beach tie," and who "affects a slight American accent whenever he thinks of it." Mickey says "Gee, fellas" or "Gee, guys" when he is being suave. When his guard slips or he is trying to be sincere in explaining to Frank and Joe that he cannot afford to lend them money, he reverts to "Aw jay, lads." Mickey's Americanisms are not just a vulgar affectation: they reflect the fact that he has money, that he is a young man on the up and up. As the country's economic future is being entrusted to American hands, Mickey is merely going with the national tide.

At first, Frank and Joe are confident enough in their townie swagger to treat Mickey as a joke. They laugh at his affected accent, Frank explaining it by the fact that "He has an uncle in America and they get letters home from him." They laugh at his flash vulgarity, suggesting that Henry Ford should "invent a car — great idea — with an artificial arm fixed on and sticking out the window. The hard man car they'll call it. Then fellas like Mickey can still be dog tough without exposing themselves." They are prepared to put up with the mindless boasting about the speed he travels in his car while they think there is a chance that they might be able to cadge some money from him.

But the joking turns sour when they learn that Mickey has been dancing with Frank's date Anne. In the end, as Mickey emerges with Anne, they are reduced to impotent name-calling. Frank's resort to "Shout, shout, shout at them!" as Mickey and Anne exit is a recognition of futility and powerlessness. Mickey has won. The future lies with him, for all that they might taunt him as a yank. Frank's final joke about Mickey and the car is sour and despairing — scorn cannot stop Mickey from being the coming man.

What is extraordinary about *On the Outside* is not just its economy and accuracy as a sounding of its times, but also the fact that it is already beginning the process in Murphy's theatre whereby immediately social observation is transmuted into the metaphysical and the metaphorical. The closing line of the play is Joe's "Come on out of here to hell." This is at once a normal piece of naturalistic dialogue and a lifting of the play onto a level of quasi-religious metaphor.

On the one hand, it suggests that Joe and Frank's only future is in emigration, a prospect that has been constantly before our eyes in the play with Bridie and Mickey's brothers being home on holidays from England. On the other hand, if Joe and Frank are now going to hell, then they have been, throughout the play, souls in purgatory seeking admission to heaven. This last line subtly imbues the play with the emotional strength of Catholic language without diluting the passion of the attack on established values. In fact, it prefigures, in the turning away from

heaven towards hell, JPW King's plea for assistance from
the devil at the end of *The Gigli Concert*, after he has
realised that no help will be forthcoming from God. It
makes Joe and Frank the first in the long line of
metaphysical outsiders in Murphy's plays, the damned
who are the only ones who can ultimately expect salvation.
To remember that Murphy's spiritual outsiders in plays
like *The Gigli Concert* and *The Sanctuary Lamp* are the
lineal descendants of a pair of apprentice fitters roaring
abuse at their bosses is to keep in mind the ultimate
political derivation of that spiritual malaise.

On the Outside prefigures, too, one of the central devices
of Murphy's theatre, the use of two men who are in a sense
two halves of the one whole. In *Conversations on a
Homecoming* it is said of Michael and Tom that "the two of
ye might make up one decent man" and this idea is present
in embryo in *On the Outside*. Joe and Frank are not
literally brothers, but they are alike enough in age,
language, social standing and attitude to be two aspects of
the same personality. And they have within themselves the
possibility of making up one whole: Frank suggests that
Joe should give him his money, so that he can get in to the
dancehall and try to borrow enough to get Joe in after him.
"It's the only chance we have." Joe responds that he should
go in and try to borrow the money for Frank. Neither is
prepared to fully trust the other, so they are both doomed
to remain outside. As in Murphy's later plays, the two
halves of a whole personality must be joined before
salvation becomes possible.

On the Outside was submitted by Murphy and
O'Donoghue to the manuscript competitions at various
amateur drama festivals, winning for its authors the
fifteen guinea prize at the All-Ireland Festival in Athlone.
It was given an amateur production in Cork, and then
broadcast by Radio Eireann. When the play was given its
first professional production in 1974, however, Murphy
wrote a companion piece, *On the Inside*, showing the

situation inside the same dancehall. *On the Inside* re-inforces the sense that Frank and Joe have little option but to choose hell, for the putative heaven of the dancehall is little better than the purgatory outside. In fact it shares the same feeling of people in a state of suspended animation, of immobile yearning. The plays are linked only in a casual way through character or incident (Bridie of *On the Inside* is mentioned by Mickey Ford outside the hall; Anne and Katherine's discussion about fellows who lie about their social status is mirrored by Malachy pretending to Bridie that he is a teacher, when in fact he is unemployed; and there is a passing, ironic reference by Mr. Collins, the organiser of the dance, to the fact that "Six bob was too pricey").

The relationship between the plays lies more in the way in which their similarity of atmosphere reflects on the pointlessness of illusions about the possibility that physical location can make any difference to the prospects for happiness. Having seen *On the Outside*, and knowing as we now do that Frank and Joe's belief that things would be better inside the dancehall is mistaken, we are in a position to judge the futility of Kieran's belief in *On the Inside* that he and Margaret would be happy in Canada because "It's different there." The ironic juxtaposition of the two plays suggests that it is not different anywhere, that flight is impossible.

At one level, *On the Inside* is a reflection of Murphy's educational experience, both as a pupil and as a teacher. Most of the characters are teachers; the dance is organised by the Irish National Teachers' Organisation. They talk shop, quoting their pupils. Mr. Collins the headmaster warns Kieran not to be late for his classes. The arrogance of the teacher's assumption of complete knowledge of anyone who has ever been his pupil is caught in Collins' dismissal of Malachy: "That layabout is still as thick as ever." And Malachy, for his part, has all the old pupil's resentment of the violence and ignorance of his teachers.

Deliberately misquoting Goldsmith, he jibes about how "The village master beat his little school." His greeting to the group of teachers at the soft drinks bar is "Still beating the children up there?" Malachy's head is full of snatches of school learning and his attempt to pass himself off as a teacher in order to impress Bridie produces a conscious parody of learned conversation: "The square on the hypotenuse is equal to the sum of the squares on the other two sides! Are you enjoying yourselves?"

A picture of stultified education tied to the stultification of lack of money is painted in. "What kind of job is teaching anyway?" asks Kieran. "When you're slave-driven. Four hundred and two pounds a year! And it's so dead, so dead around here."

Along with this sense of the oppressiveness of education, the world of *On the Inside* is also groaning under the weight of clerical control. Church and school come together to create a climate in which sexuality is without meaning or content. Malachy "endeavouring to ascertain the essence of love" with the help of large quantities of drink, diagnoses the "celibate personality" of the Irish male:

"From birth to the grave, Baptism to Extreme Unction there's always a celibate there somewhere, i.e., that is, a priest, a coonic. Teaching us in the schools, showing us how to play football, taking money at the ballroom doors, not to speak of preaching and officiating at the seven deadly sacraments ... And without any malice aforethought as the fella said, the priest is imparting his attitude which is all very fine for him, but of no use to a fella like you with different aspirations. Do you follow me? Only a few of us escape ... And the nuns — And the nuns nursing us in hospitals in between. And doing our laundry for us. Think of that for a complication!"

The blind craving for sexual pleasure free from greater meaning is seen in the play as the obverse side of this coin. The story is told of Jimmy Wilson in Galway who makes seven women pregnant in three months of "the holiday season." Malachy considers this "poetic justice" because Wilson's adventures took place "In the furnace room at the back of that church near Seapoint" and the priest from that church "was the guy who used to be out letting the air out of the tyres of the cars parked around there at night," presumably as punishment for courting couples. *On the Inside* creates a mechanical world where the action of the "coonics" has an equal and opposite reaction, and where freedom is not accounted in the equation.

And it is precisely that freedom which Kieran is seeking. "I'd love to be free ... I mean — FREE! Free, free!" Set, like *On the Outside*, in 1958, at a point where economic change is about to bring about new freedoms of behaviour, particularly sexual freedom, *On the Inside* is a reflection, albeit with the benefit of hindsight, on the worth of that freedom. The play projects back to 1958 some of the changes in sexual mores which followed the opening up of the country in the years after that date, in order to catch a point of transition, when Malachy's question "What would you say love is?" is not just an academic speculation but an attempt to understand how people should respond to changing times.

Kieran reflects on the "progress" in sexual relations. Things have changed in a few years from the time when "you'd get maybe half a dozen kisses of an evening and you're in love." Since then the "rummagin'" has started. "That's all we progress to. Fronts of cars, backs of cars, doorways, steering wheels, gear-levers, and love starts to fade, and we've all had our chips." Just as Frank and Joe were caught between the "tank" of the town and the hostility of the country, Kieran is caught between the new, fumbling sexuality and the old celibate repressiveness.

Besides his vision of sex in cars, he has before his eyes in the dancehall "the unhappy picture of Mr and Mrs Collins," the headmaster and his wife whose relationship is so dessicated that, we are told in the stage directions, Mrs Collins is "at her best" when her husband is not with her. Collins and his wife have the same dramatic function here as the drunk has in *On the Outside*, as the ghost of a possible, and awful future. Between false freedom and repression Kieran seeks something that makes sense. "Holy medals and genitalia in mortal combat with each other," as Malachy says, "is not sex at all."

The crux for Kieran in his attempt to make sense of love and freedom is his relationship with Margaret, whom he may have made pregnant. He is no longer fascinated by her; he wishes to be free of her. At the same time, he is afraid of losing her, feeling that his initial rapture has forced responsibilities on him. If nothing else, he cannot be true to himself without being true to the feelings of wonder which he once felt in Margaret's presence. To be unfaithful to that would be to plunge into self-contempt, and, as Malachy puts it, "How can you, I ask myself, love someone, if, if, first, you do not love yourself?"

On the Inside is, therefore, a play not so much about the relationship between a man and a woman, as about the relationship between a man and himself in changing times. Margaret is an entirely passive character, a sounding board for Kieran's emotions, humble and anxious to cause him the least possible grief. The real dialogue is typically between Kieran and Malachy, who are again those two halves of the one whole — Malachy knowing and speaking the truth, Kieran feeling and attempting to act it. It is Malachy who expresses the logic of Kieran's dilemma, though his own actions are as sterile as any which he describes, but Kieran who must feel it and act his way through it.

That they are in fact two halves of the one whole is made clear in the play: Malachy, in pretending to be a teacher, addressing Kieran as a "colleague," takes on some of Kieran's attributes; Kieran, for his part, adopts Malachy's hard-bitten man-of-the-world act, trying to be more like his experienced and cynical friend. In the end of the play, their roles are merged: Kieran takes the keys of Malachy's house and brings Margaret back there, while Malachy, in rejecting Bridie's advances, kills some of his own former self. They each absorb a part of the other, making for some kind of tentative resolution. It is tentative because Kieran has merely talked himself into loving Margaret, but in Murphy's plays, as they develop, the speaking of words can have an enormous power to alter reality.

The words which Kieran refuses to speak are those which would tell Margaret that he loves her. The action of the play is a long postponement of these words. When Margaret first says "Love you," Kieran says "Look, will you excuse me for a minute?" Later, when she tries to get him to utter the words "I love you," his evasion is played out like a game of tennis.

"The only thing that I'm afraid of," she says, "is that you won't love me." "Oh don't . . . I mean, I wouldn't worry about that." "What?" "Don't worry about that." "What?" "Yeh know." "Always?" "Yeh . . . Yeh." "What?" "Always. Forever and ever."

It is only when he has been released from the grip of compulsion by the news that she is not in fact pregnant, that he utters the words "I love you too." It is a kind of exorcism, casting out the demons of the coonics and the car seats. It is also an escape from the necessity of emigration, for we know that Kieran, in saying this to Margaret, is also dropping his plans for emigration to Canada. He has, for the moment at least, beaten the seemingly invincible crush of time and circumstance. He has got out from under the burden of history.

The relatively upbeat ending of *On the Inside*, compared with that of *On the Outside*, is a mark of the fact that it was written in 1974, when Murphy's theatre had developed to a point where redemption was a possibility for his characters. In 1960, however, no such possibility seemed to be available, and Murphy's first full-scale play *A Whistle in the Dark* is a tragedy. While still teaching metalwork at Mountbellew, Murphy drafted a play to be called *The Iron Men*, about an Irish family in Coventry and their involvement in tribal faction fighting with other Irish emigrant clans.

In the housing estate behind him in Tuam, he had sensed at times "the atmosphere of a frontier town in the old West, with feuds in which entire families faced one another in phalanxes on either side of the street." On these days of pre-arranged warfare, members of the families scattered to England would return to take their place in the ranks. There was some hint of this tribal family warfare in *On the Outside*, where Frank and Joe are afraid to attack Mickey Ford because his brothers are home from England, and they would fight in a pack to protect one of their own who was under threat.

Murphy asked Noel O'Donoghue to collaborate on *The Iron Men*, but O'Donoghue felt that the idea was dwelling too much on the past, too locked up in an Ireland that would be best forgotten. In fact, when the play reached its final form, it was not so much a reflection of the past, as a dramatisation of the tensions arising from the transition between the past and the future, a tragedy of the change that was taking place in Ireland at the time in which it was written.

The Iron Men was submitted for the Charleville Amateur Script Competition, which it won. In his adjucation, the actor and producer Godfrey Quigley spoke for twenty minutes about the play, and told Murphy that he would produce it for that year's 1961 Dublin Theatre Festival. In the meantime, the script was submitted for the All-Ireland competition at Athlone, and won the first prize of thirty guineas. The money was witheld, however, on the basis that the play would never be produced by anyone. In fact, Quigley's plans for a Dublin Theatre Festival production fell through, and Quigley himself left to work in London. While there he showed the script to a number of producers and it was accepted by Joan Littlewood's Theatre Royal at Stratford East. Before that acceptance, however, and after the Dublin Theatre Festival plans had fallen through, Murphy sent *The Iron Men* to Ernest Blythe, Managing Director of the Abbey, Ireland's national theatre.

Ernest Blythe replied to Murphy on behalf of the Abbey not merely with a rejection slip, but with an abusive denunciation. The characters of the play, he said, were unreal, and its atmosphere was incredible. He did not believe that such people as were to appear in *A Whistle* existed in Ireland.

In a sense, Blythe was right. Such people did not exist in the Ireland of nationalist ideology to which Blythe most fervently belonged. He was himself the living symbol of the relationship between theatre and politics in Ireland. Blythe was one of the founders of the state. As Minister for Finance in the first governments of that state, he had done everything possible to defend and preserve it, supporting the execution without trial of his opponents in the Civil War, and taking a shilling off the Old Age Pension. He was deeply committed to Gaelic Ireland and to the integration of the cultural nationalist movement with state policy, obtaining for the Abbey Theatre the first state subsidy of any theatre in the western world. When, on his retirement from party politics, he was made Managing Director of the Abbey, it was a startling symbol of the theatre's retrenchment in line with the gathering gloom of social conservatism and intolerance of the new state. Tom Murphy, in sending his play to the Abbey in 1961, was seeking access to the theatre, not of Yeats, Synge and O'Casey, but of Ernest Blythe.

The theatre was not only a theatre of petty domestic dramas, it was also a theatre of stilted naturalism. The critic and director Eric Bentley who visited Dublin to direct *The House of Bernarda Alba* at the Abbey in the fifties, summed up the prevailing style of Irish theatre which was the context in which Murphy's plays emerged:

"In Germany the actor takes pride in being a master of the metier. He expects to rehearse four or five hours daily as well as give a performance. At the Abbey, I had the greatest difficulty getting the actors to rehearse more than two and a half hours. In Germany the regisseur has authority; his staff is a well-oiled machine; leadership and an interpretation of the play is expected of him. In Ireland, the director is often only the chap who tells the actors how to avoid colliding with each other and where to stand. Or, more often still, where to sit: for the method of the Abbey director, consonant with that of Abbey playwrights, is to have a table centre stage and the cast sitting round in a semicircle. Scenery is a matter of repainting the standard box-set representing a kitchen. Lighting is something added at dress rehearsal pretty much at the discretion of a lighting man who has not read the play."

"Habits are sanctified by traditions. Departures from tradition are permitted, if at all, with the sulks and much mumbling of 'What the hell does he think he's doing?' A director ... will ask an actress to wear her shawl like this and be refused with the declaration that Sara Allgood (who has never appeared in the play in question) wore it like that . . . At the Abbey there is no habit of 1920 or even 1910 that does not have its guardian. The one that the visiting director falls over most often is that of deferring to the actor who is speaking at the moment to the extent of keeping everyone else on stage quite still and looking at him. In this manner the Abbey blithely forgoes one of the great opportunities of theatrical art — the opportunity of showing several things happening at once."

With these standards and practices, it was not merely a matter of not wanting to put on Murphy's plays, though certainly their vision of Ireland was totally counter to the theatre's ideology, but also of the Abbey being simply unable to do so. If Murphy's theatre is anything, it is a theatre of "several things happening at once," with the stage full of oppositions and collisions, presenting both a world of actuality and a world of metaphor, in a way which moves vastly beyond the crude naturalism that was the Abbey's staple fare. It was effectively impossible for him to stay in Ireland.

The Iron Men had become *A Whistle in the Dark*, undergoing several changes before and during its highly successful run in London, where it transferred from Stratford East to the West End. The play had opened with Michael and Betty talking, but this was changed to make it more "arresting." The other changes, made over a period of time, stressed the tragic structure. Originally in *The Iron Men*, the play had ended with a policeman leading the brothers off stage, as some kind of crude symbol of justice. Dada, in the original production, was more triumphant, the play ending with him on his own on stage, adjusting his hat in a mirror, still preening himself. After the London production, the order of two crucial speeches in the last act, Harry's "thick lads" attack on Michael and Dada, and Michael's attack on Dada, was changed so that the latter should come second, placing the emphasis of the play more decisively on Michael, focussing on him as the tragic protagonist.

With the play being hailed as, amongst other things, the most uninhibited display of violence ever seen on the London stage, Murphy made the decision to leave Tuam for London. Before he left he sent a new play, *The Fooleen,* which he had written towards the end of 1961 and into early 1962, to Blythe at the Abbey. It was rejected.

When Murphy had taken up the scholarship to train as a metalwork teacher, he had signed an undertaking that he would teach for five years. Four years and seven months later, he was a fêted playwright, but still a scholarship boy. He applied for two years leave of absence and was refused. He resigned from his teaching job, and, being in breach of contract, was ordered to pay £97 / 4 / 7 before leaving. When he attended the West End opening of *A Whistle In the Dark*, and *God Save the Queen* was struck up, he stood.

II

The Wild Irish

Good manners, in an industrial society, are more than just a pleasant adornment. They are an expression of the order of things. Discipline, self-control, deferring to others, keeping one's impulses in check — these are things which the lower orders had to be taught if they were to be useful in industry. As the centre of power moved from the open spaces of the countryside to the confined order of towns and cities, the struggle for that power came to have more to do with being civil than with being physically strong and dominant.

Good manners were essential to the regulation of commerce, since commerce involved trust and trust depended on a series of practices and conventions which convinced those you were dealing with that you were a civilised, trustworthy person. To fit into this society, you had to be able to subdue irrational drives and impulsive behaviour. You had to act in a manner altogether different from the Carneys, a family struggling with an industrial civilisation in *A Whistle in the Dark*.

In Ireland the lower orders learned these things late. Being a rural, peasant people, the Irish had little use for good manners. They were immodest and given to violence. They were "savage" rather than "civilised," and, as the Bishop of Ossory described them in 1835 "The people has some of the characteristics, and, unfortunately, some of the defects of savage people... they basically lack the civil virtues. They have no foresight or prudence. Their courage is instinctive: they throw themselves at an obstacle with

57

extraordinary violence and if they do not succeed at the first attempt, give it up." As sociologist Tom Inglis has pointed out, it fell to the church to civilise the people, bringing them into richly adorned chapels and enforcing rules of etiquette and mannerly behaviour there and through the schools. This discipline became the mark of accommodation to the modern world, a world increasingly organised according to the values and standards of the commercial bourgeoisie. But since much of Ireland remained unindustrialised until the 1960s, the work of the church and the school had not yet been completed by the routine of the factory and the office. *A Whistle in the Dark* dramatises the tensions of a society on the brink of industrialisation, about to become belatedly "civilised."

The opening moments of the play present the audience with an immediate and stark image of the contrast between "civilisation" and "savagery." The civilisation of the Irish involved changes in the way they regarded living space: getting them from one-roomed cabins to multi-roomed houses, from sleeping with animals to sleeping only with humans — first with the whole family, then with one's brothers and sisters, and, finally, on one's own. But the opening of *A Whistle in the Dark* is a scene of this arrangement of domestic space being frantically disrupted. Betty is rushing in and out of the room with bedclothes and pillows. We are told that Iggy is going to sleep on a camp bed. Harry is invading the privacy of Michael's domestic effects by rummaging in his drawer to borrow his socks. We are taken immediately into a world where the normal physical arrangements of space which signify domestic order and civilisation in modern urban society are being overturned.

And this visual chaos is quickly re-inforced by the complete lack of manners which the Carneys display. The opening of the play up to the arrival of Michael is full of questions, but not one of them is answered. Harry is more interested in talking to the sock which he is hunting than to any of the others. Hugo is singing an idiotic song to no one in particular. Iggy completely ignores Betty's question about the camp bed, and is himself ignored as he repeatedly asks "Are we r-r-ready?" The art of polite conversation has not yet been born; the brothers content themselves with making vague noises to establish their presence.

Iggy, the only one who is anxious to communicate something — the fact that they will be late for the train bringing their father and younger brother from Ireland — is impeded by a stammer, while the others use language often without conventional syntax, language as pure, harsh sound. These are men who have not internalised the rules and regulations of life in an industrial society, the system of discipline known as good manners. Their impulsive, careless behaviour is embodied in the contempt for domestic order as Hugo throws at Mush a cup which smashes against the wall.

The chaos of this opening scene invites an immediate sense of anachronism, of people from a previous time living in a contemporary world. *A Whistle in the Dark* is not a play about emigration, even though it is set in England. It is set in Coventry because Coventry is a completely industrial city. With Ireland embarking on a rapid programme of industrialisation, Coventry is the Ireland of the future. And the Carneys are the Ireland of the past located in that Ireland of the future.

Tom Inglis has argued that the "transformation of Irish society was essentially based on the transformation of space and time. In pre-Famine Ireland there was an impressive programme of building churches and schools. Within these large ordered spaces, priests and teachers began to define and regulate time. In the decade after the Famine this civilising and moralising process reached down to the smaller ordered spaces of houses, and within these to the even smaller spaces of rooms. It was in these new houses and rooms that behaviour became regulated and supervised by mothers."

But the Carneys have yet to undergo this transformation of space and time. The domestic space of the set is insufficient to contain them and they do not recognise the distinctions between rooms, eating and sleeping in spaces other than the kitchen and the bedrooms where these activities are meant to be performed. Nor do they allow themselves to be fully regulated by time. Iggy's constant concern with time — the arrival of the train — is ineffectual in motivating his brothers, and eventually he himself is distracted from it by the opportunity for a childish prank to be played on Michael. Divorced from basic concepts of space and time which regulate industrial society, the Carneys are immediately recognisable as creatures of the past, the remnants of the Wild Irish.

This means that, in a relatively conventional three-act, apparently naturalistic play, history is present on the stage. We have the past — the Carneys; we have the future — Coventry; and we have an individual, Michael, who is caught betweeen the past and the future. Already, in his first full-length play, we have the roots of a notion which is essential to Murphy's theatre as it develops over a quarter of a century, the notion of time as being, not linear, but simultaneous. In Murphy's plays time does not pass in a straight line, with one event following another as cause follows effect. Instead, there is more than one time frame in operation on stage, with things being connected by the fact that they occur simultaneously in different time frames, rather than by the fact that they follow one another logically. As we shall see, this notion is essential to the great leaps into magic of Murphy's later plays, and to the politics of transformation which informs them. It is this same notion which makes it possible for *A Whistle in the Dark*, in spite of its naturalistic surface, to go beyond naturalism and into tragedy.

Naturalism and tragedy are incompatible, because naturalism requires the presence on stage of one world — and one world only — while tragedy requires two. Naturalism assumes that there is a rational universe in which things happen because something else has happened before. The ripples reach the edge of the pond because someone has thrown a stone in the water; Hedda Gabler kills herself because every action of the plot has been leading towards that point and there is nothing else for her to do. Tragedy, however, is irrational. It happens because there are two worlds on stage and these two worlds collide.

Agamemnon suffers because he gets caught up in two different systems of logic — the logic of the gods and the logic of humanity — and no rational action on his part will allow him to escape being ground between these two forces. Antigone suffers because she falls between the logic of the state and the logic of her duty to honour her dead brother. Macbeth suffers because he is at the confluence of two worlds, a world of hierarchy which values order above all things, and a world of rising ambition which encourages the breakup of that hierarchy. The same is true of Othello, who is stuck on the border between a system of pre-ordained rank and a system which rewards ability. In tragedy, the past and the future diverge, leaving an abyss into which the hero must inevitably sink. Tragedy sees history as a process of great leaps in which there are yawning gaps; naturalism, as a quintessentially bourgeois form, sees history as a seamless garment, in which change happens by a process of minute accumulation. *A Whistle in the Dark* is much more a tragedy than it is a naturalistic play.

In Ireland, in 1960, it was possible to write a tragedy. The possibility existed because of the rate of change. With an economic and social revolution in progress, the past was receding rapidly and the future approaching at a pace which often seemed alarming. If tragedy is about a man falling into the gap between the past and the future, then that gap was clearly opening up as a highly traditional, rural society transformed itself into a modern industrial one. Michael Carney is in many ways a typical Irishman of his day: trying to settle down in an industrial society, with a factory job, a neat well-kept estate house, the rules of self-betterment in a developing capitalist economy. His aspirations are those of T. K. Whitaker's Ireland — material security, social acceptability, a respectable life. But he is also corralled into another world, the world of Ireland's past with its dark patriarchy, its lack of civilisation, its twisted pride and its burning tribal resentments. Michael is caught between the future and the past, not merely his own, but Ireland's, and it is this which makes *A Whistle in the Dark* the tragedy of an entire society.

The tragedy of the play arises from the unresolved tensions of two massive changes taking place in Ireland at the time in which it was written. These changes are, firstly, industrialisation, and secondly, the shift from the extended family to the nuclear family as the basic unit of society which accompanied that shift.

It is clear from early in the play that the Carneys have left a depressed economy at home. Mush remarks that "The economy (is) destroyed since the demand for St. Patrick's Day badges fell," summing up the underdeveloped, gombeen nature of an economy dependent on religiosity and sentimental patriotism for its survival. He also draws a picture of a land in which opportunity is dependent on crawthumping and nepotism: "The ones that say 'Fawther'— like that: 'Fawther'— to the priest. And their sons is always thick. But they get the good job-stakes all the same. County Council and that." Mush's vision of the Irish economy contains everything that is opposite to the values which the sixties were to foster — opportunism, meritocracy, cosmopolitanism.

But the play also emphasises the rate of change. For while Mush's memory of Ireland is an exactly accurate picture of the gombeen republic he would have left a few years before, Michael's vision of an upwardly mobile society in which material progress is coming on stream is also accurate. The fact that the play contains two contradictory but equally true versions of Irish economic life, expounded by Mush and Michael, does more than emphasise the difference in world-view between Michael and the rest of the Carney clan. It also tells us directly that we are being presented with a contradictory world on stage, a world in which things are changing so fast that opposites can be equally true. And a world where opposites can be equally true is a world where tragedy can happen.

What Michael sees in Ireland is a place that is changing, a place that now offers the prospect of a living for his younger brother Des who has come to visit along with their father, Dada. Michael's interest is in preserving the innocence he sees in Des and he believes that it is now possible to do this because of what is happening at home. There is a new factory, one of the many being built, even in small towns, as the foreign investment boom gets under way. Michael wants Des to work there, to buckle down to the new ways of industrial life. He holds up as an example the Carneys' old neighbours, the Flanagans, who have moved to a new and better house. The Flanagans were the children of a roadsweeper; now they are making their way into the middle-class.

"That's right. He was a road sweeper. And one of his sons became an engineer, and there was a girl that became a nun, and another of them was at the university when I left. All from the dirt of the roads."

In Michael's vision of Ireland, the last can become the first, there is hope and opportunity even for the most derided. The road sweeper Flanagan, kept in his place with the nickname "Pookey," has risen out of the hard times to become a proud paterfamilias.

Michael's confidence in this vision is such that he allows himself an ironic joke about the manners of the Wild Irish. When Betty complains about the destruction of the house and its contents by his brothers, Michael laughs:

"We can drink out of the saucers; it's an old Irish custom . . . And we'll get a little pig, a bonham, to run around the kitchen as a house pet . . . And we'll be progressive and grow shamrocks instead of geraniums. And turn that little shed at the end of the garden into a hotel of the fairies and leprechauns."

He can laugh at the uncivilised, superstitious Paddies, not yet used to living in houses without the animals, because he feels sufficiently far away from them. The bitter irony is that he, and his brothers, are not as far away from that world as he thinks. Just before he says this we have seen, as he has not, Iggy, Harry, Hugo and Mush violate the civilised order of his house with their carry-on. And later Michael's innocent mockery of a tourist vision of Ireland full of leprechauns and fairies is turned to a cold and sinister image when Harry taps him on the shoulder with a knuckle duster and calls it a "souvenir from Ireland." The knuckle duster is a donkey's shoe, the sort of rustic, folksy object which a tourist might hang on a suburban wall as a souvenir from the romantic West of Ireland. By using it to smash people's faces in, Harry takes a sentimental image of Ireland's past and makes it the stuff of viciousness. For Harry himself is an embodiment of a past that refuses to lie down and be smothered in folksy nostalgia, a past that is alive and kicking its way through the walls of Michael's suburban aspirations.

What Michael does not understand is that the Carneys cannot and will not adapt themselves to industrialisation. Their refusal to accommodate themselves to the regulations of time and space make it impossible to imagine them as industrial workers, and Des reacts to Michael's hopes that he will get a job in the new factory at home with "There's too many bosses in that factory job.

Slavedrivers. You don't have to lick no one's shoes over here." Dada re-inforces this refusal, appealing to a notion of pride that is a tribal anachronism: "The trouble with you, Michael is you've no pride. I don't want people, twopence-half-penny guys, ordering a son of mine, a Carney, to clean up after them." Instead, the Carneys cling to a notion of economic advancement that is entirely individual rather than social, leading them onto the fringes of criminality. Harry is a pimp. Iggy is a foreman on a building site who hires Harry's clients and then takes "a pound or two" from their wages in return. The reaction of Dada, a former policeman, when he hears this is one of hope rather than shock, seeing their scheme as "a good thing, opportunity."

The roots of this tribal pride are historical and Dada's appeal to it brings the play back again to Ireland's dark past. Murphy, in *A Whistle in the Dark* as in all of his subsequent plays, is no moralist. In his theatre, virtue and vice are relative and historical, reactions to time and circumstance. *A Whistle* brings two worlds into conflict and each of those worlds has its own proper set of values. The problem for Dada is that his belong to a residual tribal Ireland, a place which no longer exists. He imagines himself as a warrior chieftain, believing that the fact that Des is a Carney should exempt him from the realities of the modern world. In this fantasy, he carries with him the burden of the dispossessed: the notion that they are still kings in hiding, lost princes waiting only to be recognised so that they may claim the honour that is rightfully theirs. Dada's appeal to Michael's family pride taps into a sentimental notion of Irish history which allowed the grubbiest peasant to imagine that he would really be a king if only the English had not dispossessed his forefathers. It is the same notion which allows John Mulryan, leader of the rival family which the Carneys are to engage in pitched battle, to call himself "The King." The disdain for industrialism with which Dada has imbued his sons is not genuine pride but a plebeian version of aristocratic hauteur.

Michael and Dada share one thing: the belief that they can be, or are, as good as their betters. But in sharing this view, they expose the complete incompatibility of their respective ideologies. Michael holds the belief that he and his brothers — or at least Des, who has yet to fall into the corrupting grip of the big bad world — can advance themselves on the basis of the economic optimism of his times, the doctrine of opportunity for all who are prepared to work hard. He believes in Pookey Flanagan's alchemical miracle of turning the dust of the roads into gold dust. Dada, however, believes that the Carneys have no betters to become as good as, that they are already, by right of their family name and pride, entitled to a place of honour at the top of the heap as the "World Champ Carneys." He thinks that this superiority can be established in the fight with the Mulryans, a tribal conflict whose rules and methods are more primitive than the polite struggle for power in the industrial war.

Dada's disaster, however, is that this fantasy of being as good as the best of them is relentlessly and ruthlessly exposed by events. The more he clings to his family pride, the lower in the social order his family has slipped. He has declined from the position of policeman, a respected place in the community, to selling clothes around the countryside and, finally, to parasitic unemployment. Dada's economic progress has proceeded in the opposite direction to that of everyone else. While they have prospered, he has become more and more marginal to that prosperity, to the point where the Carneys have become open to the jibe that they belong to the ultimate category of the dispossessed in Ireland, the hated travelling community.

The travellers are hated most by those who are economically closest to them, because they are a reminder of a past that needs to be forgotten in the new world of material progress. The Carneys, by their lack of civilised behaviour, become vulnerable to the taunt that they are "tinkers." Just after he has told of the rise of Pookey Flanagan, Michael bitterly recalls that, when he was younger, he was blamed for a violent incident in which he had no part and jeered at "Go home, you tinker! Go back to your tent, Carney!" This ultimate insult is repeated by Mush after he has been banished from the Carney tribe for daring to challenge Dada's superior intelligence: "Tinkers! Carneys! Tinkers! Tinkers!" The jibe hurts because in reality there is so little to separate the Carneys from the tinkers.

Dada's fantasy of being at one with the respectable middle-class of the town is played out by his drinking at the golf club with the architects and the doctors. He embodies the dream of nationalist Ireland, the dream of a country in which the common name of Irishman would serve to diminish differences of class and status. The political ideology of the Irish state was founded on the faith that all lesser divisions were subsumed in the greater unity of being Irish. In this ideology, the peasant and the businessman, the poor and the rich, the worker and his boss all belonged to the mystical body of nationality. Its rhetoric was full of exhortations to be "oblivious to the differences carefully fostered by an alien government," to "abolish the memory of all past dissensions," to "cherish all the children of the nation equally." Nationalism sought, not to abolish the actual differences between the rich and the poor, but to treat them as ultimately less important than what the poor and the rich had in common with each other — Irishness.

Dada's drinking with the doctor and the architect is an attempt to live out this supposed unity. He uses one of the great badges of nationalism — the Irish language — as part of this pretence, telling Hugo that "often, for the sport of it, we talk nothing but Irish all night. At the club." The image of architect, doctor and dosser discoursing through the night in fluent Gaelic and drinking heartily at the golf club is a risible and pathetic fantasy which is the product not just of Dada's delusions of grandeur, but also of a whole nation's political delusions. And it is cruelly undercut when we learn first that Dada has been barred from the club for stealing the architect's coat and throwing it over a wall, and then of the reason for that pitifully ineffectual act of revenge:

"They drank with me. I made good conversation. Then, at their whim, a little pip-squeak of an architect can come along and offer me the job of a caretaker. To clean up after him!"

The fact that the offer of a job is clearly made in good faith and without any intention to insult Dada is a mark of the gulf between Dada's world of tribal pride and nostalgia and the architect's world of economic exchange in which Dada's delusions could not even begin to be understood. For the time when *A Whistle in the Dark* was written was a time when, for the new middle-class, the old egalitarian pretence was already being dropped in favour of conspicuous consumption.

In the play, it is Harry who most clearly dissects the emerging divisions. While others are rising through the power of a good education, Harry recalls the teacher at school searching his head for lice with the blade of a pen-knife and mocking his fantasies of being a priest. Against Michael's dream that Des might improve himself by going to night school, Harry sets a vicious parody of self-improvement:

"But we just want you to know we just turned over a new leaf. And we come to the conclusion that Des is going back to Mary Horan's country. And Hugo is going to university, and I'm going paying for his fees. And Iggy is going joining the Foreign Legion of Mary. And Dada is going off, with his old one-two, killing communists. And I'm going joining the nuns."

Against the ideology that says that all Irishmen are the same and only the English are different, Harry sets "The bloody Englishmen, the lousy Englishmen. And there's a lot of lousy Irishmen too. Isn't there?" Against Michael's belief that respectability is the route to equality, Harry sets the insight that "Your big mistake is thinking they don't do it to you . . . wrinkle up their noses." This constant sense of irreconcilable division between different kinds of Irishman makes *A Whistle in the Dark* a specifically post-nationalist play and this in turn has a profound effect in shaping the story it has to tell, in making it a tragedy.

The great Irish works of literature of the nationalist revival, Synge's *The Playboy of the Western World* and Joyce's *Ulysses* are both about the relationships of sons to their fathers, and are both comic. This fact is, as Declan Kiberd has pointed out, connected with the symbolism of the revival itself. At the time of the revival there was the notion of a new Ireland about to emerge in the nationalist revolution. Synge's Christy Mahon has to kill his father in order to win the freedom to become himself, a story which takes its configuration from the attempt of political nationalism to "kill" its colonial overlord and so win the freedom to emerge in its own colours. Joyce's Stephen Dedalus has to reject the "boozy bravado and heroic posturing" of his father Simon in order to be free to invent himself. The point about both of these stories is that they are comic: the father is slain, the freedom is won. They were written at a time when it still seemed possible for a new, young Ireland to emerge. "The revolt against provincialism that underlay the Irish revival was a revolt," according to Kiberd, "by young men against their fathers, against men like Joyce's Simon Dedalus who had inured themselves to repeated defeat by declining into 'praisers of their own past'."

After four decades of the new Ireland that Joyce and Synge looked forward to, *A Whistle in the Dark* shows a similar struggle between a young man and his father, a similar revolt against a man who is a praiser of his own past, who is, like Synge's peasants dependent on a false notion of heroism in order to stem the pain of failure. But this time the father is not so easy to kill and the outcome is tragic rather than comic. This is what makes it a post-nationalist play.

A Whistle in the Dark could, indeed, be seen as a direct inversion of *The Playboy of the Western World*. There are enough similarities to justify the comparison. Both plays are set among the poor of Mayo. Both are concerned with what Pegeen Mike calls the "great gap between a gallous story and a dirty deed," the gulf that separates heroic talk from vicious action. Both are animated by a notion of heroism which includes sordid violence: Christy's listeners are enthralled by his killing of his Da; Dada sees the vindication of the Carneys' manhood in their ability to smash the heads of all comers.

In its examination of this gap between words and actions, *The Playboy* gives us language as a self-conscious accomplishment, something used for its own sake, with Christy constantly congratulating himself on his fine talk. *A Whistle* examines the same gap and its characters are equally conscious of language as an end in itself, from Dada's pathetic triumph in the fact that "Irish people talk better than English people," to his constant speech-making and his claim to respect for the fact that he is able to make "good conversation," and to Harry's "You like the ways I talk? . . . I like the ways I talk too . . . I like the ways our Michael talks too." Dada's obsession with speech is partly based on the belief that by "talking proper" ("If the Mulryans is bragging about what they'd do to sons of mine, then they have to be learned different. Differently.") he can dissolve the differences between himself and the town's middle-class. Like Christy Mahon, he sees speech as itself a social accomplishment worthy of honour.

But this thematic similarity merely underlines the starkness of the reversal that has occurred between the writing of the two plays. In *The Playboy*, Christy metaphorically kills his Da and goes forth to face his own, brighter, more expansive future. In *A Whistle*, Dada is in a sense already dead — a defeated, emasculated man, dependent on the generosity of his sons — but he cannot be got rid of with the belt of a loy. He still holds sway over the destinies of his sons. It is not Dada who is killed at the end of the play, but Des: the symbolic killing of father by son is replaced by the all too real killing of brother by brother. And when Michael kills Des, he is also killing his own future, for it is in Des that he has invested all his hopes for what he himself might have been. Michael and the Carneys have seen Christy Mahon's future and it didn't work. For them and their likes, the years of Irish nationhood have been a matter of pretending to speak Irish at the golf club while watching the "fly shams" inch their way upwards.

Michael could never kill Dada because, beneath the skin of defiance and suspicion, they are too alike. Besides sharing the belief, which none of the other Carneys profess, that they can be, or are, as good as their betters, Michael and Dada are infected with the same confusion of words with action. The identification between them is made starkly clear in the third act and underlines Michael's doom. For just as we see that Dada's bragging and his promises to be with his sons in the battle against the Mulryans have come to nothing, so we also see that Michael's dramatic exit at the end of the second act, ostensibly to join the fight, has been a trick. Dada's earlier taunting of Michael with the difference between saying and doing ("You can talk a bit, but you can't act. Actions speak louder than words. The man of words fails the man of action.") is the poisoned chalice now proferred to his own lips, making Michael a living reproach to Dada for his own failure, and causing him to push the others to torment and

71

goad him. And the language of the play is constructed to underline the identity between them. Of the Carneys, only Michael and Dada try to speak conventional fluent English. Iggy can't speak much without stammering; Hugo says virtually nothing; and Des is initially so shy of speaking that he refers to the toilet as "the, yeh know" and only finds his tongue when drunk on violence and alcohol.

Harry, on the other hand, uses language less as a tool of communication than as a weapon. His speech deliberately uses idiom and slang: he is not interested in talking proper. His sentences generally lack a subject and Murphy's revisions of the text for the 1984 edition strengthen this feature of Harry's language — making them seem like objects divorced from their speaker. What is more, when Harry sets speech against action, as when he says "A souvenir from Ireland" while tapping Michael on the shoulder with a knuckle-duster or when he utters the seemingly mild and courteous "The beds and things are fixed up" while violently tearing the lining out of the sleeve of his jacket, it is in order to undercut the speech. When Dada and Michael set speech against action, it is the action that suffers.

The whole grain of the play's language and action, therefore, is towards the identification of Michael with Dada. Betty, listening to Dada's drunken outpouring of self-contempt and hatred for the world recognises her husband in his father: "Michael talks like that sometimes ..." Instead of symbolically allowing sons to kill their fathers as the literature of the nationalist renaissance had done, *A Whistle in the Dark* has father and son locked in an embrace of impotent self-loathing from which neither has the energy to break free. There is no bright national future beckoning at the door, only the spectre of tragedy. In comedy, the future is ready to be entered; in tragedy, the future and the past are in conflict and the protagonist, in this case Michael, is not free to embark from one onto the other.

If the tensions of industrialisation are one source of that tragedy, the other is the unresolved contradictions thrown up in the shift from the extended family to the nuclear one. The play is more a conflict between two competing ideals of the family than it is a conflict between individuals. It dramatises tensions which were coming to the surface in Irish theatre at the end of the fifties, most directly in John B. Keane's play *Sive*, which, in this respect at least, it resembles. Keane showed the tragedy of a woman trying, in keeping with social change, to turn a tribal, extended family into a nuclear family of husband, wife and children and in the process getting caught in the gap between the past and the future.

Murphy, in *A Whistle in the Dark*, shows the same clash with similar tragic consequences. Michael's dilemma is that he is pulled between his loyalty to an extended, tribal family, and his aspirations to belong in a modern nuclear family, the powerhouse of industrial society. Unable to decide between them, he ends up by being cut off from both, and is lost.

At the end of the 1950s, the Irish family was in crisis. On the one hand, it was, in the political ideology of the state, much more than a mere social arrangement. It was the guarantor of social stability, the focus of continuity in a changing and threatening world, or, as the Constitution of the Irish Republic has it, "The natural, primary and fundamental unit group of Society . . . a moral institution possessing inalienable and imprescriptible rights, antecedent and superior to all positive law." But this absolute reverence for the family as an institution went hand in hand with an official disgust for sexuality, a mistrust for relationships between men and women, which gave Ireland the lowest marriage rate in Europe. In the years before *A Whistle in the Dark* was written, 64% of the Irish population was single; 6% widowed; and only 30% married. This combination of an overwhelming emphasis by church and state on the value of the family with a very half-hearted commitment to the nuclear family based on marriage, made for the strength of a different kind of family unit: the extended family of unmarried brothers, sisters and cousins, held together by the family name on which Dada places so much emphasis.

Like many of Murphy's later plays, *A Whistle in the Dark* is haunted by a potent absence, and in this case it is appropriate that the haunting should be done by the figure of an Irish Mother. In the first minutes of the play, Harry searches in Michael's drawer, finds a pair of socks and then spots a hole in one of them. He is exasperated, even shocked. He roars at Betty, who is in the kitchen, "Oi! No use English birds." His anger at this failure in the domestic order is testimony to the ideal of the Irish Mother who would never allow her son's socks to go undarned. Harry's expectations of the role of the woman fall immediately into the stock categories of the domestic and the sexual: a woman must either be, like an Irish Mother, a good domestic servant, or else be good flesh. Anything else is a waste of good money. Harry's contempt for Betty's home-making skills draws immediate attention to the fact that he and his brothers are, in Coventry, motherless. And, because the Irish Mother was the mainstay of the civilising process in the country, to be motherless is to be outside of the confines of the Irish family as the fundamental unit group of society.

Much of the early action of the play is concerned with establishing this tension between two competing notions of the family. Betty complains to Michael of the attempt by Harry and the other brothers to sleep with her, a direct assault by them on the sanctity of the nuclear family which Betty and Michael are trying to establish. Harry, in fact, refuses to recognise Betty as a wife, regarding her as either a servant or a whore. Harry's ideal of the family is tribal, embodied by the Muslims with whom he identifies: "But I still like them. Respect them. Blacks, Muslims. They stick together, their families and all." What he respects in the

Muslims is a male bond of loyalty and mutual support in the face of a hostile world, not a bond of love between men and women. Betty recognises the threat of this competing bond, which is destroying the sexual relationship at the core of her and Michael's family. "I married you, not your brothers. Since you asked them here we've hardly gone near each other."

This threatened sexuality is set against the sexlessness of the other Carneys. Harry's sexuality is entirely a matter of commerce, of what he can, as a pimp, buy and sell. Iggy, Hugo and Harry hold up as an ideal male figure the cowboy eunuch Hopalong Cassidy, whose reputation as a "tough-un" is, in Hugo's eyes, enhanced by the fact that "I never seen him kiss a jane once." Harry does recall seeing Hopalong kiss a woman once, and his description of the scene on the prairie, with her dying and him close to tears is a comic travesty of unrequited love. The sexlessness of this ideal is underlined by the fact that Iggy refers to Hopalong throughout as "her" and "she."

Against this ideal of asexual camaraderie, Betty's desperate attempt to dragoon Des into the pleasures of marriage with "That pretty girl in the paper shop on the corner" is clearly doomed, and Des almost immediately undercuts it by jibing about the evils of "wives." At that point we know that Des has been drawn into the exclusively male tribe of his brothers, and also that Michael, who encourages Des's put-down of Betty, is hovering between his commitment to Betty and his loyalty to the extended family of the Carneys. As he has said in reply to Betty's insistence that he choose between her and his brothers "They're my brothers, I have a responsibility. It's our family." By using words like "responsibility" and "family" in relation to his brothers, words more appropriate to his relationship with Betty, Michael reveals the extent of his confusion about what precisely is the fundamental unit group of his society.

Haunting this dilemma of Michael's is the image which gradually emerges of his mother at home in Ireland. Though she never appears in the play and is only referred to in the sparsest of words, it is Mama who fills the play's silences, whose pain flickers in its darknesses. Michael, we sense, is stricken with guilt in relation to his mother, and what he is seeking throughout the play is forgiveness and absolution from that guilt. He wants Des to go back to Mayo because "there's no one left at home now with Mama." He uses Des throughout as a surrogate for his own ambitions, and his hope that Des will comfort and console Mama is a hope that he himself will be forgiven by her for abandoning her to the mercies of Dada.

That she has been abandoned and neglected, we sense from Dada's suspicious and defensive reaction when Michael asks simply "How's Mama?.." Dada, according to the stage directions, "feels there is an accusation in such questions." Dada is so touchy about his home life that he even takes Michael's polite banter about how difficult it must be to keep Des fed as an accusation. It is only at the end of the play that we learn that Mama has been scrubbing the floors of the doctors and architects with whom Dada drinks, a viciously ironic counterpoint to Dada's earlier insistence that he will not have his sons cleaning up after anyone. Dada's reaction to the revelation is to retreat into outrage at this irreverent way of referring to Mama. For in his tribalistic family based on false authority, Mama must draw her respect from an idealised notion of motherhood, while he himself depends on a heroic ideal of fatherhood. "Don't you know," asks Michael, "fathers don't have to gam on to their children the great men they are?" But in Dada's version of the family, the relationship of fathers to their children is deeply problematic.

With the failed, bitter marriage of Dada and Mama haunting him, Michael is unable to cut himself off from it and build his own marriage freely. Dada and Mama's marriage is the embodiment of his past, the past which impels him towards tragedy. Because he is unable to free himself from that past, Michael thinks himself into the role of husband in that marriage rather than in his own. He tries to usurp Dada, both in being the comforter and protector of Mama, which Dada ought to have been, and in being the father figure, guiding and advising, which his younger brothers never had. He cannot be a husband and father in his own right because he is already, in the role he has imagined for himself, a husband to Mama and a father to his brothers, particularly Des.

There could be no more direct and dramatic image of the seeping of one type of family into another, and therefore of one idea of society into another, than this confusion of roles which Michael plays out. It is the physical realisation of the abyss between two worlds into which he has fallen, the heart of his tragedy. Because he is caught between two shifting periods of history, Michael does not know the most basic things about himself in relation to his own family history: he does not know whether he is father or son, husband or child. For every individual, the family is the living embodiment of history, the structure in which we place ourselves in relation to the past and the future. Michael, caught at a time when the nature of the family is changing, is unable to place himself. His universe is irrational, absurd, and therefore tragic.

This underlying confusion in Michael's mind between himself and Dada, his imaginative attempt to usurp his father, is the reason why the action and language of the play work to identify Michael and Dada with each other. If they are locked in an embrace from which neither can break free, it is because that embrace is the confrontation of a man with a past which he cannot escape. Dada's struggle with Michael's attempt to usurp him takes the form of an insistence that Michael is still a child — "Up, muck and trash, we'll put him to bed like in the old days!" — since fathers are fathers and children are children and there can be no confusion between them. But in the act of running away from the fight, he makes himself all the more like Michael, until in the end, they are virtually indistinguishable. Michael, in killing Des, becomes more like Dada. Dada, in his physical isolation from the rest of the family at the end of the play, is in exactly the position which Michael occupied at the end of the first act.

In spite of its surface naturalism, therefore, *A Whistle in the Dark* manages to dramatise the tensions of an entire society and to achieve a sense of tragedy. The aura of a Greek tragedy is suggested by the story of a house accursed and by the triumphal return from bloody battles which the Carneys make after their defeat of the Mulryans. A father who kills a child returns in triumph from war, a bargain-basement Agamemnon. These mythic dimensions are added to by the Oedipal tinge to Michael's make-up. There are also the formal premonitions to which Michael is subject, an essential feature of Greek tragedy. Michael twice speaks of "this awful feeling that something is going to happen me" and "this awful feeling that something terrible is going to happen." The hanger-on Mush acts to some degree as a chorus, immortalising the deeds of the Carneys in his bathetic ballad of Iggy the Iron Man, and then cursing them as tinkers, showing all the fickleness and opportunism of a chorus from Sophocles or Aeschylus. And the naturalism of the action is also disrupted by its formal framing by anarchic bustle at the start of the play, moving to a frozen tableau around Des's dead body at the end.

But this formal sense of tragedy should not be taken as an attempt at timelessness or abstraction from the real world of Irish society. Tragedy is always based on an identity of interest between the hero and his society, so that Agamemnon's disaster is inseparable from that of his polis, and Macbeth's sickness plunges his Scotland into chaos. By dramatising the tensions of both the great world of industrialisation and social change and the small world of the family, Murphy makes a connection between what happens in history, politics and society, and what happens in the intimate mental and spiritual life of individuals, a connection which remains at the heart of his theatre over the next quarter of a century. He creates a theatrical context in which a man (Dada) who is stung by petty humiliation, can say not merely that he hates his persecutors or that he hates his own life but that "I hate the world!" In that hatred for the entire world, that desire to sweep everything away, is the root of an apocalyptic theatre.

The connection between the social and the psychological, between disorders of the body politic and of the individual mind is made in Murphy's plays through the idea of a sickness which is shared by both realms of existence: the holding back of unspoken griefs, the refusal to utter dark secrets which then fester and become dangerous. The psychologist Ivor Browne has written of this psychological phenomenon in relation to Murphy: "when a person, particularly in early life, is faced with an experience which is so painful, so threatens to engulf him or her, rather than go through the pain and the suffering which would be too much at that time, the person brings into play a capacity which we all appear to have: to inhibit, to deny, to quite simply put the experience on ice so that it remains unlived, held out from us, waiting to be experienced with all its pain and immediacy at some later time." And what is true of individuals, is true of societies also, that at times of change and crisis the past and the future come into collision and the unspoken traumas of the past demand to be uttered. This is the process of the play which followed *A Whistle in the Dark*, and which, with it and *On the Outside*, forms a thematic trilogy that comprises Murphy's early work.

A Crucial Week in the Life of A Grocer's Assistant, originally called *The Fooleen*, and published under that title in the United States, was written immediately after

A Whistle in the Dark, but not performed until 1969, by which time much of its impact had been lost because of its outward similarity of theme to Brian Friel's very popular play *Philadelphia, Here I Come!*, which had been premiered five years earlier. Even when the play was first published in 1970, it suffered from the fact that it was then set in 1968, rather than, as in the original and definitive versions, in 1958. This confusion disrupted its relationship to its context: it is very much a play set just as the Irish industrial revolution is about to begin rather than a decade into its advance, and it is also very much a companion piece to *A Whistle in the Dark* from which, by virtue of the delay in its production, it seemed to be separated in time.

Like *A Whistle in the Dark* it is concerned with the legacy of the nineteenth century past in an Ireland facing an industrial future, with the ties of the family on an individual facing the industrial world, and with the schizophrenia of the Irish male. Unlike *A Whistle in the Dark,* it seeks a comic resolution rather than a tragic one. And it looks for that resolution in the power of speech to affect things, the magical notion that the uttering of certain words can change the world. It is the beginning of Murphy's politics of magic.

The idea that words can transform the world is one which is deeply rooted in the Irish psyche, through the power of Catholicism. Irish Catholicism in particular mixes magical beliefs with the strict adherence to the rules and regulations of the church. It draws much of its strength from the idea that by speaking out one's deepest sufferings and desires in prayer, the material world can be changed to one's benefit. A survey in 1974 found that 97 per cent of Irish people prayed at least once a day, and 45 per cent said that they prayed for material reasons, for protection from illness, for comfort and prosperity. Even fifteen years after Ireland started to become a modern industrial society, the magical notion that one's lot in the world can be transformed by the speaking of certain words remained deeply embedded. Beginning with A *Crucial Week in the Life of A Grocer's Assistant*, Murphy began to make use of that connection in his theatrical language and imagery. While developing into an increasingly anti-Christian writer, he has been careful to retain much of Catholicism's language as a way of dealing with transformation and the power of speech to change things.

This idea that words can change the world is linked to the idea of hidden things coming to the surface and being spoken out at last. A *Crucial Week* is full of this sense of things that have been hidden being spoken out, of the past being dealt with. But, as in a much later play *Bailegangaire*, the festered secrets have the power either to maim or to heal, to kill or to cure. Partial, selective revelations are used as weapons to hurt others, and only a full, cathartic exorcism of past secrets can have the effect of changing things and making a new wholeness possible.

A *Crucial Week* is set in "a small town in rural Ireland," in fact, as we learn, fourteen miles from Galway — probably Murphy's native Tuam. As a small town, its setting is neither fully rural nor fully urban, but a place in transition between the two, with a toe in the waters of the coming change. It is a gombeen world of small time huckstering, in which everyone knows everyone else's business. But it is threatened by fearful change, as the small-time businessman Mr. Brown tells the mother of the play's hero, John Joe Moran:

"You see, Mrs. Moran, take up the newspaper any day of the week, and what does it say? What will you see there as plain as the nose on your face, in capital letters of black and white? You will find it says what? You will find it says 'Times Are Changing'. The world is upset, sir ... the universe is trembling."

This trembling universe is a schizophrenic place, clinging to the past but being impelled into the future. *A Crucial Week* is an examination of that schizophrenia, and like *A Whistle in the Dark* it finds both social and psychological sources for it.

All throughout his work, Murphy tends to use the kind of small town in which *A Crucial Week* is set as a metaphor for schizophrenia, as the locus of a neurotic in-betweenness of mind and soul, a social version of Purgatory. There is a mechanism in his mentality by which the half-and-half status of Tuam, neither city not country, comes to represent the purgatorial state, neither despair nor salvation, which he cannot abide. The city of *The Gigli Concert*, or the forgotten countryside of *Bailegangaire* are places in which transformation are possible, because they are definite, clear territories. The half-and-half territory of the town, neither one thing nor the other, is, in *A Crucial Week*, in *The White House*, in *Conversations on a Homecoming*, a no man's land dominated by gombeenism, a place of eternal transience in which time and human development seem arrested. The feeling is summed up in the pun on the word "mean," with its meanings of both middle-of-the-road and money-grubbing, used to describe Vera in his novel *The Seduction of Morality*:

"Extremes seemed to suit her. The unapologetic directness of New York, the elemental simplicity of life in the countryside with Mom. But how to deal with the mean of the town?"

John Joe Moran in *A Crucial Week* is nailed to this far from golden mean of the town by two related forces: his schizophrenogenic dependence on his mother, and his confusion about whether to stay at home or to emigrate. He is at the mercy of a history which has left him with an impossible choice and that history is embodied in his mother.

!n *A Crucial Week,* the Irish Mother who haunted the silences of *A Whistle in the Dark* is incarnated on stage. The stage directions make it clear that Mother is an anachronism, as the Carney brothers were, a survival from the past which refuses to fade in the white light of a technological age: she is "a product of Irish history — poverty and ignorance; but something great about her — one would say 'heroic' if it were the nineteenth century we were dealing with." She is, indeed, a tragic figure stuck with the values forged in one age while facing the challenges of another, caught in the gap between two worlds.

The references to the nineteenth century are appropriate, because it was then that the Irish Mother as a species emerged, a creature moulded by the church as the centre of power in the home and the guarantor of social continuity. In *A Crucial Week*, Mother is a powerful, inventive and complex character; Father a defeated and emasculated being, wandering sadly and ineffectually in and out of the action. Mother is, in fact, more than an individual character: she is a dramatisation of an entire category of Irish humanity, conforming closely to the generalised picture of the Irish mother presented by Tom Inglis:

"The mother maintained her power within the home in the same way as the church did in wider society. She did the dirty menial tasks involved in the care of members of the household. She looked after the young, the sick, the elderly, the weak and the distraught ... She slaved, especially for her husband and sons. She encouraged her daughters, as part of their training to be good mothers, to do likewise. By doing everything for her sons, the mother made them dependent on her. But by limiting and controlling the physical expression of her affection, she inculcated an emotional awkwardness in her children. The denial of the physical expression of affection was a major child-rearing practice in preparation for emigration, postponed marriage and celibacy."

Nancy Scheper-Hughes has argued for a direct connection between this relationship between mothers and their sons and schizophrenia; maintaining that Irish mothers tend to be schizophrenogenic because, while they are too protective and extremely possessive of their sons, they are at the same time unconscious of — and ignore — their expressed needs and demands.

This is why, in *A Crucial Week*, there is no difference for John Joe Moran between his dilemma over whether to emigrate and his confused relationship with his mother. If the way mothers brought up their sons was determined by economic circumstances, then the economic choice which John Joe faces is the same as the emotional one: a choice between dependence and independence, between wanting and having. John Joe's mother taunts him with her combination of protectiveness and a failure to meet his needs. She tries to run his life, getting him to work in the morning, attempting to control and discourage his relationship with his girlfriend Mona, getting him a new job when he loses the previous one she has got for him. We see her brushing the dust off his collar, fussing over him, using her charms to defuse the anger of his employer.

But in John Joe's dreams, this avalanche of affection threatens to suffocate him. He sees her using her affection as a prod to keep him in line "That's the son I reared. The favourite child I lavished with praise, the plans I had for his economy; the spotless boy, in days of old, who was so nice and knew his place ..." And, in a sense, she represents not merely an internal authority within the family, but external authority as well. For she is in alliance with Father Daly, the town's main figure of authority, and this makes her the enemy within. When John Joe loses his job, Mother's immediate concern is that Father Daly "will say we're a nice crowd." She goes to tell him immediately "before someone else brings him the news." Mother is not just the heart of John Joe's family, she is also the embodiment of the social order for him. He cannot reject his society without also rejecting her.

John Joe's dream of economic advancement is much more than a search for material prosperity, therefore. It is also a hope of psychological health. Again, for Murphy, the connection between economics and psychology is made. What John Joe wants money for is to enable him to resolve the intolerable tension between his dependence on his mother and his need to separate himself from her. "If I was rich," he tells Mona, "the first thing I'd do is give a million pounds to my mother. Pay her off." Later, in his second dream sequence, he imagines the riches that he will find at the end of the rainbow of emigration: "See that box over there? Treasure, gold. Big box — the big box — bigger box — the biggest one! To be sent home to Mammy, cause now I'm of use."

Money will either buy off his mother or prove him to be an adult in her sight. In this he is not unlike Pakie Garvey, home from England for his father's funeral, who dreams of having enough money to buy out the town and "burn it to the ground." John Joe and Pakey don't talk about money as giving them access to houses, cars, record players, foreign travel, the usual consumer desires. For them money is merely a way of destroying the past — Mother, the town, the world of childishness and humiliation — and coming to psychological terms with themselves.

In this, John Joe, too, represents the coming Ireland of his times. Like the nation of which he is part, he is trying to emerge from childishness into adulthood, to shake off the shameful past of prolonged dependence and step forward into a new self-confidence. The town as we see it is full of grown-up children. John Joe is 29 but, at the start of the play, in the dream sequence where his fears and desires contend, he is "childlike." Mona talks to him in a childish language, dreamy and stylised: "My suitcase is

85

outside on wheels for away, on wheels for away on the puff-puff." And in that dream, Mona turns into John Joe's mother, her attempt to seduce him away being spliced into his mother's attempt to rouse him for work: "Quick, before you're thirty! Quick, get up, it's Monday morning!"

This image of John Joe's lover turning into his mother establishes immediately the depth of his failure to rid himself of Mother's all-embracing dominance. It is counterpointed by the other half-adults of the town. Agnes Smith who is almost as old as John Joe, still wears ringlets and carries a prayer-book. Her defiance of her ever-present mother is confined to the fact that she chews sweets without her knowledge or permission. Miko, whom we meet at the end of the play, has a similarly childish relationship with his mother, who asks him "What does the clock say, Miko, son?" "The cow says moo-moo, Mother; the duck says quack-quack, and the clock says tickety-tock!"

In the language of the play, this sense of a childish world is re-inforced by the constant use of the diminutive "-een" added to the ends of words, in particular by Mrs. Smith who even manages "The pitfaleens, darlin'." That this is a way of robbing men and women of their threatening adulthood is clear from the way in which Peteen Mullins, emasculated by his conformity as "a top member of his Sodality and a non-drinker," is denied his proper name.

John Joe's first act of truth-telling, of faith in the power of words to transform things, is to call Peteen "Peter." He has learned from Pakey Garvey of the way in which nicknames and diminutives are used to keep people in their place. Pakey's father, who couldn't afford a decent suit, was called "Rags"; Pakey himself "Bags." John Joe realises that "they call us nicknames too" and the realisation brings home the extent to which the use of childish language makes people childish, the way in which langauge can be abused in order to keep people from coming into the dignity of adulthood.

This image of grown people as children is the int rnalisation of the coloniser's image of the colonised. In *The White Man's Burden*, Kipling pictured the coloniser as represented by "manhood" which has "done with childish days," the colonised peoples as "your new-caught, sullen peoples, half devil and half child." In colonial ideology, the subject peoples came to be seen as innocent and incapable children, crying out for discipline and betterment to be imposed by the selfless motherland. The Victorian image of the Empire as a family, with the Queen as the loving mother bringing her children under strict but beneficent tutelage, is the apotheosis of this ideological vision. The Irish were the first and most direct objects of this imperial motherhood and the theatre, with its stock character of the Stage Irishman, half-devil and half-child, was an important vehicle for its promulgation.

The image became internalised, so that Irish writers, even those of the revival, came to see the ideal Irishman as a child-like peasant. It is no accident that in *A Crucial Week* John Joe expresses his ironic mock-vision of ideal Ireland in terms of the childish simplicity and rural utopianism of the colonial stereotype and that he uses the language of the Stage Irishman and of Mrs. Smith's diminutives to do it. He tells Mona that they will go and live in "The huteen! Up in the mountings!", at a time when what he is really thinking about is, as Mona knows, "England". His real dream address is not a rustic paradise but "Two-two-two A, Tottenham Court Road, Madison Square Gardens, Lower Edgebaston, Upper Fifth Avenue, Camden Town, U.S.A., S.W. 6." But the language of his ironic vision links it firmly with the stunted growth of himself and Peteen and Miko and Agnes. By connecting together the personal immaturity of these characters and the self-image of a post-colonial people, Murphy makes *A Crucial Week* into the story, not just of John Joe, but of a whole people struggling to emerge into adulthood. As in *A Whistle in the Dark*, the drama becomes that of an entire society.

This imagery of childishness in the play weaves its way into the imagery of schizophrenia. The child is a half-person, and John Joe's image of the schizophrenia of emigration is that "we're half-men here or half-men away, and how can we hope ever to do anything." The play builds a sense of a world in which everything is incomplete. The world of dreams is divided from the world of reality. Men are divided from women. The soul is divided from the body, as Fr. Daly warns John Joe in a dream:

"But woe, says he, to the fooleen that goes to Holyhead way-woe, and leaves himself behind . . . I have a bag here for his soul. Cause he'll have to leave it behind him. We insist on that . . . The soul is not a thing to be bandied about in any old way in any old place. Manchester for instance."

In this world of incomplete, stunted things, opposites offer themselves as alternatives only because the wholeness in which they should be bound together is missing.

As in *A Whistle in the Dark*, the embodiment of this lack of wholeness is the dissolution of the family. We see this in the opening of Scene 3 which is a ritual of the failure of family communication. Mother talks away to John Joe, giving out gossip and scandal. John Joe neither answers her questions nor appears to listen. Father sits on his own, intent on scraping the dirt off a penny he has found in the back garden, ignoring the stream of talk from Mother and singing softly to himself.

And like *A Whistle in the Dark*, this play is haunted by the absent member of the family, the personification of its lack of wholeness. If the mother flitted about in the silences of A Whistle, here the mother is all too present, but the absence is that of a brother, Frank. Frank is referred to only fleetingly but we know from the accusation which mother makes in John Joe's dream at the start of the play that he has ended badly — John Joe, she says, is "as bad, if not worse, than his brother before him." We learn that he has emigrated to America and that he has ended up in jail. He is the family's hidden secret, a limb that has been lopped off and has turned rotten.

In this sense, *A Crucial Week* takes up from where *A Whistle in the Dark* ends, with the death of a brother. For Frank is not merely physically absent, he is also linguistically absent, in that he is never spoken about. His physical absence cannot be overcome by John Joe, but his linguistic absence can. By speaking about him, John Joe can at least diminish his absence, and it is towards this that the play builds. Frank is a spirit who can be conjured by speaking his name. He is John Joe's other half, imprisoned abroad just as John Joe is imprisoned at home. By invoking his name, John Joe can metaphorically join these insufficient halves together and create one whole. In this sense at least, words can resurrect the dead.

And this resurrection would also transform the Morans' image of themselves and their role in the town. In the interwoven imagery of the play, the Morans are buriers of the dead. Father is a gravedigger, John Joe a gravedigger's son. The taunt in the town is "Dig a cold bed; Morans are going to bury the dead." They are associated with death and with the covering up of unpleasant realities. But the play is full of images of those realities being unearthed, coming to the surface. There is John Joe's father trying to scrape clean the penny he has found buried in the back garden. There is Peteen Mullins delving into his neighbours' privacies and unearthing their secrets. There is Alec's revenge on Peteen in his incantation of the secrets of the Mullins family, stretching back over the decades:

"None of them ever informed to the soldiers one time for twenty three shillings and got the legs shot off Danny Kelly! And none of them in later times did the quare thing to the hunchyback girl in Clonshee, before they had to marry the horse-faced one from Ballinasloe side!"

There is Mother's act of verbal violence in telling on Alec, her own beloved brother, when she informs the pensions inspector that Alec has a small shop, in the hope that Alec will have to give up the shop and pass it to John Joe. This latter act is the final proof for John Joe of the way in which secrets fester and become dangerous to those who hide them. Alec's petty dishonesty is an undead corpse which returns as a monster to destroy the bond of love between himself and Mother. As the supposed beneficiary of this breach of faith, John Joe is impelled to lift once and for all the spell of silence and deny to the secrets of the town their power to maim and oppress by speaking them out.

But this need to reveal the truth is also seen in economic terms in the play. Mother, in John Joe's dream, makes a declamatory defence of the economic state of things, a proud and resigned acceptance of poverty:

"Aren't we all right the way we are? And what have them with the gold to do with us? Now or ever? Let them afford their toothpaste and cosmetics. Let them afford their love, with their clean long legs. We will stick with our own and the soot, as we did through the centuries." The image of soot here is one which brings together economics and metaphysics. It is on the one hand a contrast with toothpaste, as soot was used to clean teeth in the pre-consumer economy, making it an embodiment of the world before materialistic consumerism which is, at the time of the play, about to be officially sanctioned as the new economic order. On the other hand it is also an image of a state of being, of the poverty of the body and the mind, the grime of the dark ages. In this double image, Murphy captures the sense that the new consumer economy is also breaking away from the ignorance and poverty of the past, and to that extent gives it a tentative endorsement. Mother's speech specifically links love with economics, seeing love as a luxury of the rich, making it inevitable that John Joe's search for love must also involve the acceptance of a new economy.

This is indeed what John Joe's great speech of revelation does. Having told out the family's secret of Frank's misfortune, John Joe insists on the recognition of the poverty that is in the town's anaemic blood, and aligns himself with the forces of economic change:

"We are badly off. And there are people trying to do something about it, and not getting much help. And some other people like it this way because we are a proof of their fortune. And there's some of ourselves like the pigs, happy and glorying in it, maggots feeding on this corpse of a street. Wives and husbands up and down the road, pots calling kettles black; the poor eating the poor. Anybody's business but our own. Not content with the hardships of today, the poor mouth whining about yesterday as well. Begrudging, backbiting, hypocrisy; smothering and slobbering in some cunning nineteenth century way."

That movement from physical poverty — "We are badly off" — to emotional poverty — "wives and husbands up and down the road" — is quintessentially Murphy. The possibility of some kind of wholeness for John Joe, the resurrection of Frank, goes hand in hand with a call for economic change.

John Joe's rhetoric of recognition, the bald statement of the fact of poverty, must be set against the political rhetoric of the Irish state before 1958, in which that poverty was obscured beneath an ideological mantle which was woven of Ireland's spiritual richness and the joys of frugality. In 1962, when *A Crucial Week* was written, John Joe's call for support for "those who are trying to do something about it" could only be regarded as an endorsement of the new mood of economic optimism and of, in effect, the Programme for Economic Expansion. That endorsement may be tempered by the distaste for the huckster class which is so much a part of the play, but it is nevertheless the fact that economic change is taking place as the play is written which makes a comic resolution of John Joe's dilemma possible. John Joe can choose to stay, not just because he has lifted a psychological burden, but because, when the play is written, emigration is no longer the only real option for most young men of his class.

Taken together, *On the Outside*, *A Whistle in the Dark* and *A Crucial Week in the Life of a Grocer's Assistant* follow a circular path leading from the inevitability of exile at the end of *On the Outside*, to the futility of exile in *A Whistle in the Dark,* and to the possibility of staying at home in *A Crucial Week*. In this they collectively constitute the search for a space in which human needs and desires can be pursued. And the conclusion to that search is the belief that escape is impossible, that there is no sanctuary or haven in which the reality of the world may be avoided. John Joe's relative optimism at the end of *A Crucial Week* is not the optimism of escape, since he has been able to lift the veil on the town's secrets only by confronting reality and speaking it out, not by leaving it behind. The play's endorsement of the Irish future is therefore tentative and tempered by the bitterness of social division and domination which John Joe has revealed. The play ends hopefully rather than triumphantly, and its theme of the breaking of the bonds of illusion is one to which Murphy would quickly return.

The irony of *A Crucial Week's* endorsement of the Irish future is that it was made precisely at a time when Murphy himself was preparing to leave for exile in London. Once there, he found himself with a hit play in *A Whistle in the Dark*, but virtually no theatrical context in which to work. He attended writing classes at the Royal Court Theatre for a period (among his fellow pupils was Tom Stoppard) but formed no permanent association with any group or theatre. He wrote television plays for the BBC, to whom he sold *The Fooleen*, as it was then called, when no stage producer showed a tangible interest in it, but he was far from being a member of that generation of playwrights which was content to work primarily for television.

He remained effectively as much of an outsider in the British theatre as he had been in the Irish. If he doubted this latter fact, it was amply confirmed for him when he submitted, over a period of a few years, two plays, *The Morning After Optimism* and *Famine*, for the Irish Life Prize, an annual award of £500 for new playwrighting put up by the state insurance company in Dublin. *The Morning After Optimism* did not get the award when it was entered; when *Famine* was submitted in 1966, it not only failed to win the prize, but the judges announced that the standard of entries had been so low that the money would not be awarded that year. *A Whistle in the Dark* had created a sensation in London in 1961. It would be all of seven years before Murphy would see another of his plays on the stage,

III

After the Golden Age

The years between 1922 and 1958 were the childhood of the Irish state. Central to the nationalist ideology on which it had been founded was the notion that, before the coming of the Saxon invader, Ireland had enjoyed a Golden Age, an age of innocence and bliss. This Golden Age could again be restored by the winning of freedom and the return of Gaelic civilisation. Ireland, not merely free but Gaelic as well, not merely Gaelic but free as well, would return to the childhood innocence of its once and future Arcadia. The public rhetoric of the state was filled with this notion of an ideal innocence, an innocence which would make Ireland a beacon to the world, the centre of a spiritual empire, which, at the most messianic heights of the rhetoric, might save Christian civilisation.

This rhetoric of innocence was continued in the literature of these years, which is essentially a literature of childhood. The short story was the dominant form, and short stories of childhood were its main achievements. And the Irish people, like innocent children liable to corruption from every side, were in need of protection from adult books, which they got from the rigorous censorship.

In a bitter irony, the facts of Irish economic life proved conducive to preserving the childishness of its people. For those who did not emigrate from rural Ireland, the prolonged dependence on parents and the interminable delay in marriage produced an extended childhood that dwindled into old age. Already, in *A Crucial Week in the Life of a Grocer's Assistant,* Murphy had shown this prolonged childhood and the attempt to leap beyond it. His next play, *The Morning After Optimism*, Is about the initiation from childhood into adulthood and the dispelling of the oppressive myths of the Golden Age which helped to keep people from growing up to face the world. "Yes" says James in the play, "you're coming of age at last, Jimmy kid."

The Morning After Optimism was not produced on stage until March 1971, at which time Murphy's exile in England was over and his association with the Abbey Theatre had begun. It is therefore generally thought of as belonging to the later period of his work, associated with *The Gigli Concert* and *The Sanctuary Lamp*. In fact it was written immediately after *A Crucial Week*, and belongs with it and *A Whistle in the Dark*, as plays of Ireland's painful transition from a rural to an urban, an agricultural to an industrial, society. The point is of some importance, for the play's absurdist and surrealist form, its self-conscious theatricality and its clearly pyschological connotations, can make it appear to be removed from anything other than the inside of Murphy's mind.

As with all of Murphy's plays *The Morning After Optimism* does reflect Murphy's own psychology, but as with his theatre in general that psychological concern also reflects the inner history of his country. As Eric Bentley has put it, writing about John Millington Synge, "Nor should one, like the crasser historical critics, take history as only that which is 'objective' and outside the artist. He himself is a part of history and his reflection of himself is a part of his version of history." In *The Morning After Optimism*, Murphy reflects himself, and in doing so reflects the history of what was happening in the greater world of Ireland.

In reflecting himself in the play, Murphy was reflecting his own departure from home and from Tuam. *The Morning After Optimism* is his first play to be written outside of Ireland, from the perspective of exile. He started the play in September 1962, shortly after he had settled in London and wrote two drafts of it in two weeks, beginning in his mind with the line "Once upon a time there was a boy." He was 27 and he had fled the nest, leaving behind his mother and family, Tuam, and Ireland. *The Morning After Optimism* is a play of emergence into adulthood, of the slaying of the dragons and witches that beset the childish world. It is also a play of the loss of faith in the Golden Age with which the Irish public world had been imbued, and as such it coincides with the new realism of the early sixties in Ireland, the abandonment of the dream of a Gaelic rustic paradise in favour of the more tangible dreams of the consumer world.

The setting of *The Morning After Optimism* is reminiscent of the setting of *On the Outside*. The play begins with the arrival into the forest of James and Rosie, a pimp and a whore. James and Rosie, like Joe and Frank in *On the Outside*, are modern urban creatures. Though their language is clearly a literary creation, it is equally clearly based on the rough talk of the city. They say "I done" for "I did." They talk in the insistent rhythms of street language, a language that must make itself heard above the confusion of competing sounds: "Let me be frank, I'm not complaining — I am complaining — I'd like to know, one way or the other that there is or is not, something more than the momentary pleasure..."

The forest itself into which they arrive is on stage; there are trees towering over them, verdant nature threatening to overwhelm them. This forest is, on the one hand, a theatrical convention, Shakespeare's Forest of Arden in which dreams are played out, in which reality melts into the surreal, and the iron rule of logic is overturned. It is a theatrical space in which things that have no place in the cause-and-effect world of naturalism can happen. It is the stage as a laboratory of human dreams and fears, nightmares and aspirations. But is also something more literal and with a more specific social meaning — it is the country as opposed to the city, an image of the Arcadia which was the ideal Ireland.

And what is more, it is, like the setting of *On the Outside*, a fallen arcadia, a countryside that is not, in fact, free from the realities of history and the commercial system. Just as the juxtaposition of the ballroom with the quiet country road in the setting of *On the Outside* provided a contrast between the idealised countryside of political fantasy and the reality of a place in which business is conducted, where social processes are enacted, so too is the forest of *The Morning After Optimism* a place of commercial transaction. For it becomes clear that this is no primeval landscape, innocent of the ways of modern men. Rosie suggests that "Perhaps we could rent a little cabin for the interim" and it becomes clear that there are plenty of such cabins to choose from. This untouched paradise is in fact a tourist resort, a place exploited for commercial gain. Like John Joe's mockery of "The huteen! Up in the mountings!" in *A Crucial Week*, this is an ironic joke on the notions of a rural paradise outside of commerce and history which lay at the back of the Irish political ideology of the restoration of the Golden Age. Already in the setting of *The Morning After Optimism*, there is an implied irony, contrasting illusions with realities, an irony which is social and political rather than simply psychological in its import.

James, in fact, has internalised the dream of a Golden Age. He is a ponce, malicious, vicious and vulgar. As the play opens he is on the run, probably from the aftermath of some vile crime. We learn later from Edmund that, in his search for James, he has heard of one of that name "accused of rifling boxes of the poor and convicted of the same offence 'gainst Convent postulants." James, in fact is a comically exaggerated version of vileness personified, a silent movie villain, lurking and sidling like a Grand Guignol assassin. He hates everyone and treats everyone, particularly Rosie, abominably. He is an exaggerated, stylised version of Harry in *A Whistle*, a misogynistic pimp. He wishes nothing but ugliness on the world: "It would suit me to see them all ugly as porridge . . . Mouths like torn pockets."

But in spite of all this he believes that inside him there exists an innocent child. He talks of "my hidden beautiful self" — "I'm very beautiful, yeh know, but it's in hiding or something. And I'd like to feel its twinge once more." That this hidden self is an aspect of the Golden Age is made clear later when James, Rosie and Edmund discuss the past. "What is the past?" asks James. "A fairytale" answers Rosie, and Edmund replies "Was not the past golden, nevertheless?" The fairytale which is the play is the search for, and abandonment of, the golden past which never existed.

For all their grizzled, world-weary air of bitter experience, Rosie and James are as much grown-up children trying to emerge into adulthood as were John Joe, Agnes and Miko in *A Crucial Week*. In taunting each other, they lapse into baby language and portray each other as children, even though he is middle-aged and she is 37. Rosie calls James "Jame-Jame, sniveller, cry-in-bed dreamer," painting him as a foolish infant. He calls Rosie "the middle-aged girl." And they both behave like children, showing all the petulance, the wilfulness, the demand for immediate gratification of their needs, of the child. They want what they want and if they can't get it, the next best thing is to spoil it for anyone else. Their relationship swings from the malicious desire to wound of children fighting over who is to get the blame, to the delight of children repeating each other's words with glee. When they like each other they repeat each others' phrases like this:

James: Do you remember, Rose — Wait a minute. Were we?.. Yes! When we were in love, do you?

Rosie: We wouldn't —

James: We wouldn't go to bed at night!

Rosie: We wouldn't go to bed at night!

James: Trying to stay awake!

The world of the fairy tale is the world of emergence from childhood into adulthood. Fairy tales do not take place in a pre-Raphaelite land of enchanting sprites, but in the Land of the Faerie, a perilous realm inhabited by dangerous fears which must be overcome before the passage into adulthood is possible. In psychoanalytic interpretations, the witch of fairytale is one's mother, the dragon one's father, and Murphy makes use of both of these identifications in *The Morning After Optimism*. When the play is seen in the context of its two immediate predecessors, *A Whistle in the Dark* and *A Crucial Week in the Life of a Grocer's Assistant*, all three plays being written in a three-year period, then the pointedness of this fairytale emerges. *A Whistle in the Dark* is about the attempt to "slay" a father, who is also the whole weight of Irish history and the past. *A Crucial Week* is a story of the "slaying" of a mother who is a personification of the Irish Mother, again the product of history. *In The Morning After Optimism*, James is pitched against both the dragon and the witch, the father and the mother. His initiation into adulthood involves the "slaying" of both.

If the failure to kill a father in *A Whistle in the Dark* was a mark of the failure to break with the past, and the success in defeating a mother in *A Crucial Week* the beginning of freedom to act, then James' attempt to do both is a final breach with the past and an end to domination and repression. At the end of *A Whistle in the Dark,* the killing of a brother is tragic because it is an emblem of Michael's failure to break free into the future. But *The Morning After Optimism* ends with the killing of a brother also, only this time, the act is comic. The change is possible because, when *A Whistle in the Dark* was written, Ireland was still struggling to break free from its past. By the time *The Morning After Optimism* is written, a decisive break with the past is already apparent in the country.

The man-child James and the woman-child Rosie
encounter in the forest the fantastic fairy-tale figures of
Edmund and Anastasia. Edmund and Anastasia belong to
James and Rosie's fantasies, embodying their own more
beautiful selves, but they also belong to the forest. Edmund
is identified with the forest by his Robin Hood hat, which
reminds us of the romantic outlaws of Sherwood;
Anastasia by the fact that she is an archetypal fairytale
figure, the orphan girl who lives in the woods. And since
the forest in the play is not the idyllic locus of innocence
merely but also an ironic landscape of oppressive myths,
we know that Edmund and Anastasia are not to be taken
on face value as inhabitants of a perfect world. They are
the embodiments of the Golden Age which James and Rosie
are tormented by and immediately want to capture.

James has dreamt of a woman for whom he could
maintain a pure love: "Once I saw a girl, her back in
headscarf and coat, once. I just passed by, I didn't see her
face, in my blue motorcar, and turned left for Eros and the
Statue of Liberty, and became a ponce in the graveyard.
She may have been Miss Right, she certainly was Miss
Possible, cause my hidden, real, beautiful self manifested
itself in a twinge... Just to hold her hand, yeh know." Rosie,
for her part has "dreamed, you see, that someone
someday'd come along and turn my working blanket into
a magic carpet." They both immediately identify Edmund
and Anastasia as the fulfilment of their dreams.

But while Rosie seeks Edmund, James is in flight from
him. For Edmund is his long-lost brother, representing the
whole world of family and the past from which he must
escape. James identifies Edmund with the dragon, the
fairytale image of the father he must slay: "Well, come on,
come on, come on, Dragon-Feathers, try me!" At the same
time, he identifies his mother with the witch: "And that
night-rambling corpse of a mammy! I'll lay that dead witch
sleeping!" Throughout the play, this image of the mother
as a witch recurs: "Nickerdehpazee, nickerdehpazee —

Dead hand so mottled, brow so worn with care! I'll nail you witch! I'll nail you! ...But how? Some bury them with a smile and a tear, some with a prayer and a nail ... I'll try. God gave me a wonderful mammy, her memory will never grow old, her smile was — (angrily) Aw yes — yes, her memory, heart, smile, head, hands, promises!"

James is not haunted by his father in this way, but Edmund, who pursues him, represents father as well as brother, the whole apparatus of authority within and without the family. Edmund, unlike James, is a prince, sired on their mother by a passing king. As Prince, he has authority in the outside world, making him a father-figure as well as a brother.

This identification of brother with father is not unparalleled in Murphy's plays. *In A Whistle in the Dark*, Michael's brothers are an outgrowth of the father he must face. In *The Gigli Concert*, the Man's brother Mick is the father-figure of his childhood: "Mick frightened us all. Shouting, kicking his bike. Like our house wasn't a house for luxuries, but there always had to be mustard — for Mick. And if there wasn't, like once, there was hell to pay. Kicking the doors, shouting. My mother thought the world of Mick." Given Murphy's own background, where his father was missing for much of his childhood, and some of his brothers were old enough to be his father, this slipping of brother into father in his plays is logical enough.

The idea that, through Edmund, James is half-brother to a prince also links Edmund into the oppressive fantasies which fed the violence of *A Whistle in the Dark*. There, the inability of men like Dada and "King" Mulryan to cope with the modern world was linked to their innate fantasy that they were kings in hiding, the dispossessed waiting for the day when the scales of history would fall from the eyes of the world and they would be revealed for the nobility that they truly were. This is one of the fantasies from which James is running. Edmund's quest to find his lost brother who may be living in the mire but is really noble, is from the fairytale world of the prince lost at birth, waiting to be discovered so that his true identity can be revealed to him, and this is clearly Edmund's plan for James. James is therefore pursued by something of the same fantasy which created the monster of Dada, and in this sense his fantasies are the product of history as much as they are of psychology.

James himself is clear that the fantasies which pursue him are the products of church and state rather than of his own mind. Both are present in the play. Edmund speaks of meeting a bishop on his travels, his description, in its association of the church with political power and oppressiveness prefiguring the attack on the clergy in *The Sanctuary Lamp*. The bishop, he says, was in "most imposing cleric's drag," guarded by "military P.P.s." Rosie's parents were members of the upper-class, her father a judge, her uncle a cleric, and James remembers that he had to "blow the lot" of his money "liquidating them," tying church and state into the dragons he must slay. "Clerics and judics!" he jeers. "Coonics and earwigs!"

The fairytales which James must escape are induced, not by his own mind, but by social indoctrination, the forces of school, family, church and state which Murphy's earlier plays attack. In a story which begins "Once upon a time" and ends with "and he lived happily ever after," James tells of how his mother promised that if he were good "there would be a lovely girl for him one day, and she would have blue eyes and golden hair" (a promise of which Anastasia is the apparent fulfilment); of how teachers were "saintly men and could answer all his questions" and "the books he read were filled with heroes; people lived happily, ugliness was sure to turn to beauty, and poor boys were better than rich boys because they were noble really ... And the Church told him of God, kind God and guardian angels. And how everyone was made just like God — even the little boy himself was. There was a devil but he himself was not alive ... And there were things called politicians for doing favours and seeing to things ... And there was a king there for — that was not quite clear. But he was there, like in all the other stories. Not that anything would go wrong, but he was keeping an eye on things all the same ... He was there, probably, to make the boy's life his dream... everyone gave the little boy balloons ... already inflated ... and they floated above him, nodding and bobbing, and lifting his feet clear of the ground so that he never had to walk a step anywhere. Until, one day, one of them burst, and it was the beautiful blue one. And he was not prepared for this .. And one by one the other balloons burst." God, the church, the politicians, teachers, heroes are so many burst balloons. James's disillusion begins with the public world of power.

As so often in Murphy's plays, the failure of James and Rosie's lives is a failure of the family and of the relationship between men and women. The family is the shape which disaster takes in Murphy's plays, the broken family the image of the breach of order in the world. James left home, Edmund says, because "twixt my ma and he, all was not well." Edmund tells James that "granddaddy, grandmammy, father and mother" have all died and that, before mother died "She said to tell James she forgave him." James has therefore become an orphan, without anchor in the world, and pursued by guilt at his mother's death.

And part of James's state of prolonged childhood is his inability to have children of his own. He expresses his disgust for children in language which itself identifies him as a child: he says he "wouldn't give any woman a baby," then "Hate smelly babies! — Hate them." But the desire persists. Later, in a litany of the trials of life which might be visited on Edmund and Anastasia, which he and Rosie are compiling as a game to console themselves for their failure to seduce them, they inadvertently arrive at the curse of having no children, and James asks plaintively "If we did have a little girl, what would we tell her?" Rosie remembers a moment in her life when the sound of a child momentarily lifted the ignominy of her situation and the despair of passing time: "Once in the dark, with a client in that boxy room, in the silence, for a moment, a child cried from the heights of the floor above ... And from the depths of the floor below, from the basement, for a moment, the shuffling of that blind old man stopped." Rosie has been "in and out of the club" and her catch-cry, introduced first as a joke to please James but gathering bitteress as it is repeated is "My brains are danced on like grapes to make abortions." The crushing of her personality, the dancing on her brains, has its outcome in her abortions. The fruitlessness of her union with James is the dead symbol of the barrenness of her world.

With such a universal failure of the family and of the relationshlp between men and women, the union of James and Rosie cannot be an easy one. Each is willing to desert the other if they can find a better alternative. James tells Anastasia, hilariously, that he was "practising monogamy for when the real thing came along ... See, I've thought of you a lot." He is searching for "Something more than momentary pleasure," but he is not prepared to find it with Rosie. Rosie in turn, is happy to cheer Edmund on in an arm-wrestling contest with James, and to try to seduce him.

It is only when each realises that their options for escape from the other are unfounded and illusory that they become, again, a supportive couple. Then Rosie uses the bitterness of her own fruitless union with James to give force to her curse upon Edmund and Anastasia: "Give them pains of the lack of pains of motherhood. The forty year pain of the frigid wife in bed with randy Andy. The pain of the secret birthmark, unwanted hair, wanted hair . . .Nothing achieved but memories — that pain." In this curse is all the sexual anguish of the childless or frigid or unattractive woman, an anguish which comes from Rosie's relationship with James, her rejection by Edmund, her life as a woman in a world where men and women are not happy together. But in saying this Rosie has emerged from out of James' shadow and after it she is in charge, taking the initiative and guiding James in his fight against Edmund.

But if the play is full of such understandable, historical griefs, it also contains images of horror, fear and disgust which are as deep and enigmatic as the nameless shadows that threaten to leap out of the forest at every turn as the children of fairytale pass through it. The play opens to the cawing of a crow, and the image of the crow as a harbinger of the dark forces of the psyche remains throughout. James later draws attention to it as an omen: "Didn't you hear a solitary bird sing over there just now? ... An omen." The crow, he says, "is my friend." To Edmund later, however, the crow is "the only bird I loathe!"

It can be taken as the nightmare at the heart of the fantasy. Just as the primeval forest is really a tourist camp, so Edmund's fantasy figure is haunted by a horror and disgust which belie his romantic jauntiness. For most of the play Edmund speaks a naive language of openness and optimism. But suddenly he too is plunged into a vision of death and desolation in which Anastasia and the forest, symbols of his romantic fantasy, become chillingly sinister. His purity and union with nature turn to terror and darkness, his lovely forest gives up its rotten secrets:

"Down in the forest ... I saw her. And my being fed to regeneration. And the meaning of everything became clear and unimportant. And once I closed my eyes to trap the angel self within me, but all of me had fused to become one sensitive eye, drinking in God, or was I radiating Him or was I Him ... Then (shivers) down in the forest ... I lay upon the fallen leaves, the only noise was dying hushed derision. And then the quietness of a smile, so strange and still, no sound to cheer the accomplishment of journey's end, for my mission was quite done. And then I looked up to see a crow alighting from a tree, to perch upon my breast. I wondered at his fearless apathetic eye more beadier than fish's fixed on mine; and I wondered at his mystery purpose: 'Twas not

105

good. The caked offal on his beak was grey, and then he opened it up to show the stiffened corpse of a maggot for a tongue. I knew that birds are sometimes known in vagary to offer their own store to human kind, and so I thought I would accept, for he was dark, his succulence, his relish, my disgust. And then I checked my mouth to find that it was shut as in paralysis. And then — O God! — my eyes I found were open with such tautness: They were gaping bulges wide. And though I would I could not race my fear towards liberating climax to release me in a roar. And on and on the insult of my tightened lips I stared back, in the innocence of silent nightmare. And then he pecked; I was so young, and that was that."

That passage of horror, with its juxtaposition of "innocence" and "nightmare," of nature and disgust is a surrealistic episode which breaks with the conventional imagery of nature in Irish literature, and in doing so also breaks with the ideological surround in which that imagery works. The literature of surrealism arises as a rejection of the world-view in which nature is separated from humanity and set over against it as an ideal world. In this, surrealism is a phenomenon of the dominance of the city, for when it shows man in contact with nature, it shows him not as a contemplative observer of its beauties, but as merging with it into a nightmarish image. In surrealism, most obviously in Kafka's story Metamorphosis, nature is threatening and invasive of man's identity, as when, in that story, a man turns into a giant insect. In Irish culture, where the glorification of nature and man's contact with it has had enormous significance in the maintenance of the myth of the superiority of the countryside over the city, and therefore of the political dominance of the rural over the urban, this kind of surrealism is subversive. The descent of the good, pure innocent Edmund into a nightmarish contact with nature in which he is assaulted and threatened by a bird and in which trees, fish and maggots also make sinister appearances, serves within the play to further undermine the ideals of the public world which James has found to be illusory. In this personal reflection of the processes of history, images of psychic horror are also images of the corruption of public ideals.

Other images of fear and trauma in the play are also drawn from nature. Early in the play Rosie launches into an enigmatic description of the holding back of grief, a repression which, as we have seen in relation to *A Crucial Week in the Life of a Grocer's Assistant*, is an important mechanism in Murphy's plays:

"I know of a person who, when she found out that things are really what they seem and not what they are supposed to be, instead of manifesting her reaction in a little tear, held back and clung to her pain. Until one day, as she was silently hanging out the washing on the line, a gander came hissing from the end of the garden, chasing her indoors. Then she cried. She nearly died. But too late. To this day that woman believes she is a goose."

This association of the gander with both childhood fears and with the repression of grief is something which recurs in Murphy's work much later. In a televison play written in 1983, *Brigit*, Tom, a child of four, will not go into the garden because, he says, "I'm afraid of the gander." And in *Bailegangaire*, Mommo, repressing her grief at the death of Tom, mentions him only to say "And Tom is in Galway. He's afeard of the gander." The image of the gander appears to be one of repressed childhood fear, the fear which must be banished in James's belated accession into adulthood.

James is the first appearance in a Murphy play of a figure who is to become typical: a man who is seeking to annihilate the world through utter despair. Because the virtues of the world have turned out to be so bitterly illusory, he can believe in nothing except utter debasement, a state which has cruelly eluded him. His goal, he says, is "rock bottom for my basis": "It's a simple case of honest terra firma or caput for me." The only firm ground is a complete denial of all ideals . Like Francisco in *The Sanctuary Lamp* he is trying to escape the dominance of a Catholic education which induces guilt by imposing impossible standards. Against the "guilt-ridden little-Jesus education" he sets ignorance: "And let's have done with the innocent shit. See, I'm a believer in honest, open ignorance, kid, not innocence. Don't you confuse the two like the hypocrites like to do. They manured our honest open ignorance on moral crap and fairy snow, then sent us out as innnocents to chew the ears off any man, wife, stranger, friend and kick their hearts to death in the name of Santa Claus or Jesus Christ to boot." To get away from "them" he is searching for some way to lose himself, to get "irretrievably lost," but he is unable to find it because of the fantasies of purity and love which continue to pursue him. His problem is that in a world where God is a burst balloon, there is no sin, and without sin he cannot get himself properly damned. His attempts to sin through sex are infected with innocence: "The amateurs came in to desecrate with innocence; everybody in, doing it with flowers; the pros were in despair, the cons were in confusion... Jesus, Mary and Joseph, where is the sin anymore, I said."

With salvation not an option, and damnation unachievable, James' only eventual course of action is to live in the world and face it. In this sense *The Morning After Optimism* is an anti-religious play, but religion is only one part of the entire package of social and political conditioning which is under assault. And if James is scornful of God, neither has he had much success with evil, a state of mind which he is unable to sustain.

James' enemy is the system which refuses to recognise reality and humanity and imposes instead a set of impossible, and at times nightmarish, ideals. His discovery is that dreams go sour, a discovery the play overall relates more to the general superstructure of public idealism which ignores real life than it does to the church alone. James wants ideals that are on a human scale and he suggests in relation to Edmund and Anastasia that " If we can't get to their ridiculous level, they must be brought to ours. What?" He offers to kill Edmund and Anastasia "with all that evil and the devil behind us," but Rosie has understood that what they need is what she calls "simple alive" — "No devil, no evil, no God, no crap ... We've tried all that. Kill them in our own name." God and the devil are replaced with simple humanity.

James fights Edmund, gains the upper hand, and appears to be about to kill him with a sword. He relents, drops the sword and is embraced by Edmund, who recognises him as a true brother. While they are embracing, James stabs Edmund in the back with his flick knife. He had to kill Edmund, not with the weapons of fantasy, but with his own weapon and in his own way. James and Rosie, who in turn kills Anastasia, are free to face a future which is entirely open, even to the extent that they cannot be sure as to the meaning of what they have done: "We done it, James." "We did." "What have we done?" "We'll see."

They can trust nothing, not even their own tears: "Don't be fooled by it, Rosie" says James as they leave, crying. "You can't trust it James." "We might," says James, "be laughing in a minute." They must re-learn the world from scratch, starting with their own emotions. But their relationship has changed in the play, as Rosie has gone from desperately trying to humour James at the start, to taking the decisive role in their escape from illusion. Having rid themselves of the past and of the mirage of the Golden Age inside themselves, there is at least the possibility that their dependence on each other will come to resemble a kind of love.

The Morning After Optimism is a playing out through a personal psychic history of the recent history of a nation. It is a negative play which clears space for an attempt at transcending history rather than actually invoking any images of such a transcendence. It is the beginning of a quest rather than the end of a voyage. But besides that clearing of the ground, it also represents a substantial development of Murphy's theatrical methods and use of language. The change in the setting of plays from *A Whistle in the Dark* to *The Morning After Optimism* indicates something of the distance that has been travelled. *A Whistle in the Dark* is set in the indoor, domestic territory of naturalism, and retains all of the outward trappings of naturalism in spite of its elements of an expressionistic representation of historical forces. *A Crucial Week in the Life of a Grocer's Assistant* is half-indoors and half-out-doors, spilling from the house onto the street, using the stage more as a theatrical space in which the conventions of naturalism can be either used or discarded. It is a play poised between the freedom of a non-naturalistic theatre and the restrictions of naturalism, as its hero John Joe is poised between staying and going. *The Morning After Optimism* moves into the purely theatrical use of space, with an expressionistic set and characters who are completely non-naturalistic. Edmund and Anastasia as fantasy figures are obviously so, but James and Rosie are also not "characters" in the conventional sense. Their language makes no attempt at internal consistency which is necessary in naturalistic portrayal: both of them shift from a spiky colloquial speeech, to babytalk, and on to a declamatory involuted rhetoric.

The language of the play is indeed its great achievement for it takes the dream language of some sections of *A Crucial Week,* and turns it into a sustained performance in which language itself becomes one of the "characters" of the play. Edmund in particular is made up of nothing else but his words, a showy array of archaisms, poeticisms, cliches, syntactical tricks, and romantic gobbledygook. James's victory, as much as anything else, consists in silencing this flow of talk. *A Whistle in the Dark* identified the affinity between fine talk and dirty deeds, and in *The Morning After Optimism*, Murphy uses language in such a way as to force the necessity of action. At the end of the play, after they had been spurred into action, James and Rosie are practically deprived of the power of speech. They are unable to describe what they have done or what it means. They are unable to put words to their own emotions. It is as if all of the contaminated words of the past have been excised from their vocabulary and a new language must be invented. This is true for Murphy also, for *The Morning After Optimism* represents a sharp break with the inherited language of the Irish theatre. After this play, there could be no going back to the kitchen.

IV

The Great Hunger

"The anatomy of man" says Karl Marx "is the key to the anatomy of the ape. The indications of something higher in the subordinate animal species can only be understood when what is higher is itself known." Similarly, the anatomy of the present is the key to the anatomy of the past. Far from understanding the present by reference to the past, we understand the past by reference to where it is going — to the present. A writer's relationship to history is not something which exists in isolation; it arises, rather, from his relationship to his own society and his own time. Historical drama, in particular, is a way of tilting the present at an angle in order to see it more clearly. This is especially true of Tom Murphy's play *Famine*, which dramatises the central event of nineteenth century history in Ireland, the great famine of 1845-1847, while being all the time a play about the twentieth century, about the spiritual and emotional famine of Murphy's own times.

Famine is in many ways the key play in the Murphy canon, for it is the work which most directly and most thoroughly explores the relationship between material and economic conditions on the one hand and the intimate life of the mind, the realm of one individual reaching out to or withdrawing from another individual, on the other. Murphy's early plays, as we have seen, try to embody past, present and future on the stage at the same time. *Famine* is concerned with achieving the same effect, but it does so in a new way, a way which has much in common with the Brechtian theatre.

For in *Famine* the conjunction of past and present takes place not so much on stage as in the mind of the audience. Just as Brecht was concerned that the real drama of a play should happen within the collective mind of the audience, *Famine* presents us with a story which does not so much engage our emotions, in spite of its deeply emotive nature, as force us to see the correspondence between what is happening in this nineteenth century setting and what the present is like. In this, it is an utterly theatrical work: its dramatic tension does not exist without the audience in the theatre, for that tension lies in the realisation by the audience that this horrible, extreme world of the past, full of starvation, murder and cruelty, is our world, the world of our present time.

Famine is a history play, and history plays are not written in times of stability and continuity. The great era of historical drama is the era of the shift from one order of society, the feudal, to another, the capitalist. Shakespeare, Corneille, Racine, Lope de Vega, all turned to the writing of history plays at a time when a society which valued hierarchy, order, tradition, communal values, was being replaced by one which valued freedom, material progress, social mobility, individualism. At such times, history provided a way of disentangling the contradictions of the present by placing them at a distance. Historical drama is, for these writers, a way of dealing with discontinuity. With *Famine*, Murphy uses Irish history in an analagous way.

For *Famine* is written at a time when Ireland is undergoing, in a truncated and much less dramatic way, the final breakup of one social order and its replacement by another. There is a decisive shift taking place, a shift towards industrialisation and urbanisation. And what is more, the play itself dramatises just such a shift. In *Famine*, the central characters, the people of the village of Glanconor, are faced with the collapse of one economic order, the feudal relationship between landlord and tenant, and the rise of another, the economic order of the

countries of the New World to which they are being
impelled to emigrate. In this way *Famine* dramatises
conditions which are analagous to those of the great era of
historical drama. If John Connor, the central figure of
Famine, sometimes has the air of a modern, downbeat
King Lear, it is because his world of shifting values and
crumbling authority is not unlike Lear's. Lear loses a
kingdom and a daughter; so does Connor. Both are
patriarchs caught in the breakdown of the feudal family.

That Murphy uses history as a way of dealing directly
with contemporary discontinuity is another example of his
going against the grain of modern Irish culture. For one of
the central uses of history in contemporary Irish culture
has been as a way of avoiding the radical discontinuity
which arose in Ireland as a result of the Sixties period of
modernisation. Take, for example, a poet like Thomas
Kinsella and a playwright like Brian Friel. Both were
acutely aware of the discontinuity of Irish life in the
Sixties. Kinsella, as a civil servant in the Department of
Finance under T. K. Whitaker, reflected in poems such as
Nightwalker on foreign investment and its impact. Friel,
in *The Loves of Cass Maguire* and other plays, uses
American idiom, giving us images of social mobility, and
even of the new bungalows which were beginning to
replace the thatched cottages in rural Ireland. But both
came to make that sense of discontinuity abstract by
locating it in the notion of what Kinsella christened "The
Divided Mind".

A rift which was social and economic in origin came to
be seen as cultural and linguistic, stemming from the
divide between the old Gaelic language and the new
English language. Kinsella pursued this lost sense of
continuity through his translations of Gaelic poetry in *The
Tain* and *An Duanaire*. Friel, too, in his play *Translations*,
located the crucial point of rupture, the beginning of
discontinuity, in the change-over from Gaelic to English as
the vernacular language of the people. The point is that in

doing this both used an idea of history to evade the actual social and economic rupture that had taken place in contemporary Ireland. In *Translations*, Friel shifts the point of rupture backwards from 1959 to 1833, using historical drama as a way of evading the present. This shift depends on a notion of history as a fall from a Golden Age, a time when people spoke Irish and were happier.

Famine however uses a quite different notion of history, one which stresses the ironic continuity behind the discontinuity, the continuing presence of those who are outside of official society in spite of what seem like great changes for the better. This is a way of dealing with the upheavals after 1959 which calls attention to their failure without evading them. The notion of history which animates *Famine* is articulated at the end of the play by an old man, Dan, lying delirious beside the body of his starved wife. Dan's view of history is sceptical of great historical changes in which the poor do not share:

"What year was I born in? 1782 they tell me, boys. There's change since, Brian? There is, a mhac. And Henry Grattan and Henry The Other and prosperity for every damned one. Hah? yis — Whatever that is." History and its great changes are the promise of prosperity to a man who is just about to die of hunger. Dan remembers "the comical small piaties in '17," the death of a starved man in 1822, the great wind of 1839, the coming of Catholic Emancipation. The latter event is remembered from the point-of-view of a man showing more signs of emaciation than of emancipation:

"'Tis, sure I seen O'Connell once. Yis, yis, yis. The Liberator — didn't we Brian? We did. And we waved. And he waved. And he smiled. On top of his horse. The lovely curly head on him. He did, did, waved with his hat. Aaaa, but the day we got our freedom! Emancy-mancy- what's that Nancy? — Freedom, boys! Twenty-nine was the year, and it didn't take us long putting up the new church. The bonefires lit, and cheering with his reverence. Father Daly, yis. And I gave Delia Hogan the beck behind his back. I had the drop in and the urge on me. Oh!-Oh!-Oh!-Oh! that is alright, said Delia, winking, but the grass is wet ..."

In Famine, underneath the great official events of history, the wretched on the sidelines continue to be wretched. The continuity which underlies historical events is that of the outsiders who must watch and suffer.

John Connor, the central figure of *Famine*, is not just one of the wretched, he is their king. Connor is a king for the same reason that Oedipus and Agamemnon and Macbeth and Lear are kings: as kings, they unite within themselves the public and the private domains. They are individuals, marked with all the distinctiveness of any private man, but they are also pivotal to their societies: their actions have consequences not only in the public sphere, but in the order of nature and of the universe. In a play which is concerned, as *Famine* is, with the conjunction between the private and the public, the shared economic world and the private emotional world, these connotations of kingship are essential.

But Murphy gives us a beggar king, a residual tribal elder whose authority exists only in tradition and only so long as he can prove his worth as a leader. The tribal notions of loyalty and a usurped kingship which are so pathetic in *A Whistle in the Dark* when they are evoked by Dada, here still retain some vestige of genuine respect, and one strand of the story of *Famine* is the charting of the disappearance of that respect. The village in the play, Glanconor, is named after John Connor's ancestors. Throughout the play there are references to the fact that the Connors were "kings here once." In the first scene, at the wake of Connor's daughter who has died in the famine, Mickeleen O'Leary intones his tribute:

"She was regal. And why wouldn't she? A descendant of the Connors, kings and chieftains here in days of yore. A true Connor she was. Of this village, Glanconor, called after the Connors ... You're a king, Sean Connor."

116

This is a tribal society in which family histories are the real history. One young villager, Liam Dougan, gets a job from the landlord's agent because "he said he never had anything against my father." Another, Mark Dineen, is cursed because of his family:

"The Dineen breed! And all his breed before him! His grandfather one time that stole the spade that was the only livelihood to Peadar Bane. His sister that used to give belly to the soldiers at the fairs in Turlough."

By right of inheritance John Connor, though he is clearly as poor as everyone else in the village, is "King Johnny," the man to whom the community looks in time of trouble to "think of something brave for us yet." This status makes Connor much more than a mere naturalistic character, investing him with something of the aura of a Greek or Shakesperian tragic hero.

Famine belongs to that category of theatre which includes both the tragic and the epic, forms which present the outer world, giving us the inner life of characters only insofar as it is manifested in deeds and actions, in a visible interaction with objective, outer reality. Tragic and epic plays, as Georg Lukacs has put it, are "compelled by their form and content to appear as living images of the totality of life ... No naturalist authenticity of individual manifestations of life, no formalist 'mastery' of structure or individual effects can replace this feeling of the totality of life." *Famine* belongs to this category of play which seeks to encompass a sense of the totality of life, but its uniqueness and to some extent its difficulty in production comes from the fact that it is straightforwardly neither tragic nor epic, but lies somewhere between the two.

In tragedy everything is concentrated around a central clash and every element of the play takes its meaning from that clash. In epic, on the other hand, all the elements of the play have a life of their own, preserving much more closely the "normal" proportions of the way things look in real life. *Famine* shares something of both of these forms.

The play is organised around the central clash of John Connor with a hostile world and with history. But on the other hand, because he is a king who is at the same time on the same level as the other villagers, they and the other individual elements of the play also work autonomously. *Famine* is a tragedy alright, but a social tragedy, whose real tragic hero is an entire community.

The epic elements in the play's construction are crucial to its dramatic effect. If, as is the case, the real dramatic tension of the play is in the mind of the audience, it is essential that the audience does not sympathise with the characters and become absorbed into their emotions and dilemmas. The audience has to retain a sufficient distance from the characters in order for it to be able to make the leap between the nineteenth century and the twentieth. This distance from the characters is carefully maintained by not allowing us to forget that we are watching a play.

The opening scene of *The Wake,* for instance, is stark and almost entirely formal, to the point where it takes on a ritual air. The play opens with a prayer "The Lord have mercy on the soul of the dead!" Conversation is interspersed with a liturgical poetry of mourning :

"I loved her better nor the sun itself!

And when I see the sun go down

I think of my girl and my black night of sorrow.

But a dark storm came on

And my sunshine was lost to me forever;

My girl cannot return."

This elegy not only re-inforces the sense of John Connor's kingship, with nature and the elements being disturbed in sympathy with the sorrow of a royal household, as they would be in Shakespeare or in the Greeks, it also lends to the scene a formal sense of distance. And what is more, these very words are repeated in elegy for his dead wife by Dan at the end of the play, making for a virtual framing of the action within this mournful ritual.

The action itself refuses to light for any extensive period on any one character, depriving us of any search for psychological insight and of any opportunity for sympathy with the characters. There is one long and very important scene, The Relief Committee, which has none of the villagers in it at all, but has characters who do not appear elsewhere in the play. All of these structural devices are, in a Brechtian sense, "alienating," in that they act to prevent our identification with the characters and to remind us that we are all the time watching a play which we ourselves must work to understand.

We are also made to think about the behaviour of the villagers by being given a view of them which we must either accept or reject. In the Relief Committee scene, Murphy has the landlord Captain Shine express a colonial view of the natives. It is one which, as Murphy's earlier plays had done, shows the dark side of the image of the Irish peasant as a childlike innocent. Plays like *A Whistle in the Dark* and *A Crucial Week in the Life of a Grocer's Assistant* showed the reality of this childishness, making it, not a state of untainted bliss, but a real imprisonment in an underdeveloped world. In *Famine*, Captain Shine takes the notion of the natives as wild children and lays bare its real function as a tool of colonial oppression. To him, the noble savage is a surly, ignorant, wasteful child who must be kept in place and controlled. The tenants of the estates are the worst of colonial subjects: "Would you expect it of a black man? Ignorance, deceit, rent evasion, begging." He is dealing with "primitive man," but this wild species is ungrateful and treacherous, "travesties of the beautiful countryside."

"I insisted all houses have chimneys. But the chimneys are gone. The chimneys are knocked down and the holes blocked up. What for? Is it that the fairies don't like heights? Or was the banshee getting caught up in them in her frequent entrances and exits? Or was it the Pope?"

The tenants are "the monkeys roaming the hills out there." Captain Shine's vision of the native Irish is of a primitive people animated by superstition and popery into irrational acts of viciousness and deceit. But there is another answer to the question of why the chimneys which Captain Shine constructed have been knocked down. It is, as Father Horan points out, that "The rents was ruz because of the chimneys!" It may be that we are dealing, not with primitive man, but with economic man.

Famine poses this question and dramatises the relationship between men and their world which is the essence of economics. The most obvious and immediate fact about John Connor is that he is a good man. He has a highly developed sense of morality, a keen sympathy for the people around him, a concern, above all, to do what's right. But *Famine* shows the possibility that this might not be enough. From the opening scene of the play, *The Wake*, we are clearly witnessing the breakdown of the social order which makes sense of Connor's values.

The wake is a traditional way of dealing with death, the communal marking of a private catastrophe, made all the more significant in this case by the fact that the death is that of a chieftain's daughter, a loss to the entire society of the village. But this traditional social ritual is at odds with the reality of the world outside. Though Connor does not yet realise it, it is already an anachronism, its sense of community, its extravagance as a gesture of tribute to the dead, its use as a confirmation of the Connors' standing in their society, all out of keeping with the new times. The Wake is the triumph of tradition over reason, for the Connors, as Liam insists, "cannot afford it for life or death." The Wake is part of John Connor's faith in doing what's right, a duty that is both social and religious: "We can't send them off mean ... She was regal ... And-we-won't-send-them off mean. In spite of — In spite of — Whatever! Welcome be the holy will of God. No matter what He sends 'tis our duty to submit."

But underlying the futility of his gesture is the anxious wait to see whether the second crop of potatoes will, like the first, fail. The vigil over the corpse in the house is set against a vigil over the field outside, a vigil that has its own macabre form of entertainment in the attempt of the men to outdo each other in the recollection of misfortunes, a contest which prefigures the laughing competition in *Bailegangaire* which reaches its peak when the subject of merriment is "Misfortunes!"

"Well, I remember in '17 — and the comical-est thing — I seen the youngsters and the hair falling out of their heads and then starting growing on their faces."

The dignified, formal ritual of the keening of the dead is undermined by a grotesque ritual of keeping vigil over the fatal field, forcing Connor, in order to retain some semblance of belief in his daughter's wake, to end the tension over whether or not the potatoes will be blighted. He digs into the field with his bare hands and uproots some plants, showing them to be blighted. The individual death of Connor's daughter becomes the communal death of the village and of the values which the wake represents. Mother's final keening for her dead daughter becomes a knell ringing out over the entire village. By the end of the scene, Murphy has created an identity between private sorrow and communal tragedy, a dramatic world in which there is no gap between the public and the personal. This is in itself a rare achievement and one which is exploited throughout the play. For as the play goes on, we see this unity crumble in the face of famine.

Famine is essentially a play about freedom and its limits. It sets up two competing forces, embodied by Connor and by Mother, one of an abstract moral notion of right, the other of economic necessity. The central question is that which Mother confronts Connor with when he insists that "I'll do nothing wrong anymore. It's only by

121

right that we can hope at all now." "What's right?" she asks. " What's right in a country when the land goes sour? Where is a woman with children when nature lets her down?"

Connor, buoyed by the dignity of his ancestry and the ideal of responsibility which he derives from it, sees freedom in the power to stand against a hostile world, to live by his own good lights even when all around him is darkness. Mother, on the other hand, is more concerned with necessity than with freedom: "These times is for anything that puts a bit in your mouth." Connor believes that "There's more ways to live besides food."; Mother knows that man cannot live without bread. Dramatically, this tension subverts our expectations and disrupts our natural tendency in the theatre to identify and sympathise with the characters, to be on the side of the good and against the bad.

For Connor embodies goodness, generosity, responsibility, care for his fellow man, and yet, we know he is wrong. His courage and dignity in holding to what he believes can only lead to his own destruction and that of his family. When he calls the villagers together to discuss what is to be done, he insists that they should have food and warmth in his house even though there is not food enough for his own children, and turf, if preserved, can be sold in the town to buy flour. Mother, on the other hand, is carping, mean and ungenerous. She begrudges everything that the neighbours get at her house, and suspects them of hoarding food and turf. She is not moral or righteous and, later in the play, she commits a terrible crime, stealing a neighbour's turf and in the process indirectly causing his death. But she is right, for everything she does is an attempt to preserve her husband and her children. When generosity is folly and viciousness is wise, it cannot be men and women who are wrong. It must be the world in which they live.

Famine therefore makes its audience consider, not individuals, but the world as a whole, and one of the tensions which it dramatises is a tension which exists very strongly in the world of the Ireland of the 1960s. The central tension between Connor and Mother is a tension between two notions of human responsibility. Connor's sense of responsibility is communal and traditional. He feels himself inescapably cast in the role of a chieftain who is responsible for his tribe's welfare, who must think for them and keep them together. His tragedy is that that sense of communal responsibility is no longer compatible with his sense of responsibility to his own family.

The play dramatises a growing disjunction between the public world of shared values and responsibilities and the private world of family affections and duties. Connor loves his wife and his children but he cannot encompass that love within his sense of his overall role in the community. Near the start of the play we see him pondering the dilemma of the community faced with disaster. We hear the villagers say of him that "he'll think of something brave for us yet ... The Connors would do the brave thing always," casting on him the expectation that he will live up to his role as their chief. At this moment, his son Donaill tugs at his coat and Connor turns around angrily to "squash the boy into the ground." In this short piece of action, the contradiction between Connor's sense of responsibility to his community and his role as a father to his own children is dramatically incarnated.

One of the things that is being dramatised here is that shift that was so much a part of the resonance of *A Whistle in the Dark*, the replacement of the extended family with the nuclear family. To an extent *Famine* tells much of the same story as *A Whistle in the Dark*, lifting it out of its immediate time and place and giving it the distance of history in order that its full meaning can be made clear. And just as *A Whistle* sets Michael's loyalty to a tribal family against his responsibility to Betty, so Connor's loyalty to the tribe is placed in a fatal tension with his loyalty to his own family.

The more Connor immerses himself in the role of tribal leader, the more we see him turn on his own wife and children. After his harsh reaction to Donaill, we see him verbally attack his daughter Maeve, again at a time when he is most under pressure in his role as tribal elder, attempting to hold the village together when it threatens to disintegrate during a wild, vicious assault on Mickeleen led by the priest Father Horan. Later again, when, as elder, he holds the meeting of the villagers in his house, the children are pushed away from the fire and food. In the end, his bond with his children is completely destroyed; Donaill used, grotesquely, to try out the false-bottomed coffin on which he and Dan are working, and Maeve becoming more and more bitterly alienated from her father until she is his enemy, berating him harshly and stealing his bread. For Connor, a gap has opened up between the private world and the public world, and he is tragically caught in it.

And this disjunction between private values and public virtues is also something which would have a deep resonance for a modern audience, something which speaks to the twentieth century from out of the play's nineteenth century setting. For at the time when the play is written there is precisely this disintegration of shared traditions and values, the common ideology of Catholic and nationalist Ireland, and their replacement by an individualist ethic. In the Ireland of the 1960s and afterwards, ideals of duty, shared notions of what is right, the appeal to the authority of the past — all of the things which characterise Connor's response to his world — are replaced by the personal standards of the individual consumer.

In *Famine,* the demands of survival lead most of the characters other than Connor to break with social ties, traditions and taboos, in favour of immediate responsibility to themselves and their families. Mother sacrifices her neighbour to the survival of her own family by stealing his turf. Liam joins the Agent's eviction gang, turning traitor to his responsibility as a member of the village community. Mark goes against both his loyalty to Connor's leadership and his love of his own village by accepting emigration to Canada because "I can't watch any more of them die on me." When the play is written, Ireland, in order to survive, is breaking with its traditional loyalties and values. In this way, the twentieth century is present in the play.

Connor's tragedy is that he puts his faith in the public world at a time when everyone else is abandoning the public world for private survival. Connor himself, as "King Johnny," belongs to the public world, deriving his status from the agreed social conventions of his village. He believes that this world will not fail him, that if he trusts in God, the politicians and the government, they will eventually deliver salvation. Himself intensely loyal to what is "expected of me," he thinks that the same must be true of others in authority. His faith in politicians and those in power comes not from an abject or craven attitude, for he is man who is often courageous and dignified, but from the sense that there is an objective moral order in which, if he keeps his side of the bargain, they will keep theirs:

"It'll depend on — Important things. The Government, the Deal, the Policy, Business, the Policy ... It wasn't given to us to understand. A bitter man, or a hungry man, or a dying man doesn't understand. But they're there, and for our good, and it's better we understand that. They have rules that they must follow, and we have one: to live and be as much at peace as we can with them, as with God ... Well that's what I believe. I believe that. Help will come, because it's right. And what's right must be believed in if we're to hope."

Connor is still caught in a feudal world in which duty, rank and place are absolutes, in which each element of society must fulfil its obligations towards the others, while the world outside has adopted the laissez faire values of capitalism. Connor's way is not the way of the coming world. His dilemma, and his response to it, are strikingly reminiscent of those of Okonkwo, the village big-shot in Ibo tribal society in Chinua Achebe's novel, *Things Fall Apart*: a man and a world doomed by their inability to understand that their frame of reference is not that of the colonial power.

In a sour and hostile universe, the primary duty is to survive, the primary motivating force of human behaviour is hunger rather than right. Connor believes that he can share in a fixed and ultimately just order of things, but the play shows that the order of things is shaped by circumstance. While Connor persists, others adapt, learning the harshness which is the legacy of the nineteenth century to the people of Murphy's plays.

The starkest image of the way in which humanity is deformed by the world is Mickeleen, the hunchbacked man who has been shaped in the image of a cruel time. His hump is not the handiwork of nature, but an ugliness inflicted by his father "that put this (hump) on me with his stick." And just as his physical nature mirrors his world, so too does his behaviour. He insists from the start that the village is doomed and that the others will come to be like him, making his physical deformity an image of the emotional deformity that will afflict them all. He embodies the way in which the lowest of the low can assimilate the values of those in power, the vicious values that govern his society. When his brother Malachy assassinates the well-meaning Justice of the Peace, Mickeleen at first tries to stop the shooting, then, having failed, kicks the dying JP as he pleads for help. "Humpy slaves" he says "can be tyrants too! " He has taken on the deformities of his time.

It is Maeve, Connor's daughter, who most fully represents this shaping of the human soul by the material conditions of life. We see her digging with her hands in the desperate search for a few miserable potatoes that might have survived the blight. We then see her taking a leading part in the hysterical attack on Mickeleen, urging on the crowd that is becoming a mob. Connor asks "What's coming over you?" and we know that what is coming over her is her adaptation to the world in which she finds herself, to all of its cruelty and harshness.

In the ironically entitled Love Scene, we see the effect of the famine on her emotions, the squeezing dry of whatever capacity for love and generosity she may have inherited from her father. Her manner with Liam is ferocious, and she is devoid of all sentimentality in relation to Glanconor or to the traditions which her father reveres. She talks of a family which is headed for America: "Crying and whinging when they should be laughing." Liam says of her that "I fear you're not affectionate." And she replies "Christ-jays, there's a lot to give me cause." Her interest in Liam is preserved only by the fact that he has food. The food which he gives her, however, transforms her. As she eats a sour apple "progressively she becomes a sixteen-year-old girl again," shedding the manners of a bitter old hag and beginning to talk freely and to laugh. There could be no more clear image of the material basis of human emotions, of Connor's contention, which Maeve reports to Liam, that "we'd be different people if someone came along and put the bit in our mouths." Revitalised by the food, Liam and Maeve begin to kiss and even to sing. But just then, the moon comes out and reveals the corpses of a woman and her two children, with the dying body of a man nearby. The pleasure of young love turns to the horror of a starved family, a violent image of the blighting of relations between men and women in a world of material deprivation. Maeve is the future generation, the bearer of the desiccated determination to survive even at the expense of emotional starvation into the twentieth century. The last scene of the play lies with her and her contention that "There's nothing of goodness or kindness in this world for anyone. But we'll be equal to it yet."

If Maeve and Liam and Mickeleen are the unfree creatures of blind necessity, there is at the same time some grim kind of freedom which survives in the play. Connor's defiance of the world leaves him, as Mother says "still engaged, defying all, standing in the rubble of what you lost," while she must "keep stealing from the dying." But at the same time she understands his pride, though she cannot share it. And she comes to see the world, not as afflicted with a natural calamity, but as divided between slaves and masters. She sees history as a continual process of slavery and famine: "always the slave of a slave, day after day, to keep us alive, for another famine," and she sees these famines as man-made:

"Jesus Christ above, what's wrong at all, and all the clever persons in the world? Biteens of bread are needen only. Life blood of my heart: hunger, childre, pain and disease! — What are we going through it for?"

She understands her life as a life of dependence, on Connor, on God, on the "them" who are in charge of things. The one freedom that remains is the freedom to die outside of their whim, outside of God's blind application of fate. She goads Connor into the only free act that is possible — the killing of herself and of his "heir," Donaill:

"They gave me dependence. I've shed that lie. And in this moment of freedom, you will look after my right and your children's right, as you promised, lest they choose the time and have the victory. Take up the stick."

Connor does as she bids, having promised her early in the play that "if a time comes when something better is to be done, for you or childre, I'll do it.", and kills his wife and son. It is a final act of defiance, a sign that not everything in the world has to be shaped by the necessity of conforming to the demands of the times. It is a bleak kind of hope, as bleak as Liam's tentative aspiration which ends the play "Well, maybe it will get better. And when it does we'll be equal to that too."

Tom Murphy, Dublin, 1984 (Eamonn Farrell).

Tuam Christian Brothers School, 1947-48. Tom Murphy is in
the second row from the back, second from the right. Noel
O'Donoghue is first from the left in front row.

Donal McCann (centre) in *A Crucial Week in the Life of
a Grocer's Assistant* at the Abbey, 1969.

The Abbey's production of *A Crucial Week in the Life of a
Grocer's Assistant* in 1988.

Niall O'Brien in the Abbey's 1992 production of
On The Outside / On The Inside

Druid's production of *Famine* in 1984.

Dan O'Herlihy (as the Kennedy lookalike, JJ Kilkelly) and Maire Ni Dhomnaill in *The White House*, The Abbey, 1972.

Philip O'Flynn and Dan O'Herlily in *The White House*, The Abbey, 1972.

Michael Duffy as James in *The Morning
After Optimism* at the Abbey, 1971.

Michelle Forbes and Tony Doyle in *Too Late for Logic*,
The Abbey, 1989.

Deirdre Donnelly as Roscommon in *The Blue Macushla* at the Abbey, 1980.

Tom Hickey (left) as JPW King and Godfrey Quigley as the Irishman in *The Gigli Concert*, The Abbey, 1983.

Cast of *The Patriot Game*, The Peacock, 1991.

Cast of *The Patriot Game*, The Peacock, 1991.

Maeliosa Stafford and Pat Leavy in Druid's
production of *Conversations on a Homecoming*, 1985.

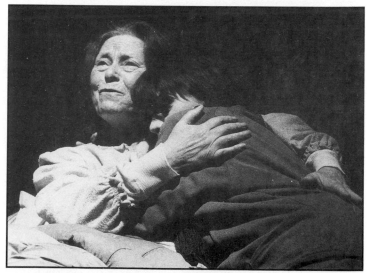

Siobhan Mckenna and Mary McEvoy in Druid's production of
Bailegangaire, 1985.

Famine is remarkable as a play which manages to unfold a historical story that is grotesquely different from the everyday life of the time in which it is written and yet convey a continuity between one and the other. It gives us a world that is a hostile place, uncongenial to humanity. But that hostility is not, as it might be in a historical setting, made to seem universal and timeless. Rather the world is hostile because of economic and political conditions, and those conditions can be changed. In the hands of an absurdist writer, famine and pestilence are images of the implacable and innate meaninglessness of the world for man. In *Famine,* on the contrary, the viciousness of the world is a human creation, and man's dependence is a lie which can be shed. This is important for Murphy's later work, for it means that the vision of the world in those plays, a vision which sees it as an essentially evil place, is rooted, not in metaphysical or theological abstractions, but in history. The emotionally starved characters of Murphy's theatre are the victims of a real famine.

To understand this distinction it is necessary only to compare *Famine* with work from the same period which it superficially resembles. The most important theatrical event in London in the years before Murphy wrote *Famine* there was Peter Brook and Charles Marowitz's Theatre of Cruelty season at LAMDA and Brook's subsequent production of Peter Weiss's *Marat/Sade* in 1963 and 1964. Both were heavily influenced by the writings on theatre of Antonin Artaud and, at first glance, *Famine* would seem to have much in common with that Artaud-Brook strain of Theatre of Cruelty. This would seem to be even more clearly the case with Brook's subsequent production of *The Ik* (1975-6), another play about famine and its effects on human society.

Murphy's famine does have something in common with Artaud's notion of the Plague in his famous 1933 lecture *Le Theatre et La Peste,* which used the image of plague as a scourge with "liquifies" all social structures and permits the emergence of a theatre of extreme and pointless gestures. Equally, *The Ik*, based on the work of anthropologist Colin Turnbull with a starving tribe in Kenya, and dramatising his conclusion that values like love, compassion and generosity are not inherent in human nature, might seem close to the spirit of *Famine*. In fact, though, while Artaud and Brook address themselves to the "human condition" as if it were timeless, Murphy does something quite different in *Famine*, showing human nature as the product of history and economics, as the result of political conditions and decisions. Famine is not, in Murphy a force like Artaud's Plague which liberates human creativity, but one which destroys it. Hunger is not a subject for anthropological study from a distance — and it is hard to gainsay Robert Brustein's remark that *The Ik* in New York was a "parade of human misery before an audience helpless to do anything about it" — and *Famine* constantly reminds its audience of precisely its lack of distance from the events on stage, of the connection between this physical hunger and our emotional hunger.

In doing so, *Famine* avoids an easy absurdity by playing on the double sense of hunger, as a horrible lack of food but also a condition of radical openness to the world, a void which makes Murphy's characters, however alienated, still hungry for life. For an Irish playwright, and for a playwright of the command which Murphy had now attained, it was possible to take a central current of 1960s theatre and divert it into a richer, more concrete and more humane vein of his own. Doing so may have placed him outside of the fashionable trends of 1960's avant garde theatre, but it also allowed him to create a play that has not dated and that remains as an extraordinary achievement.

V

Man and the Moon

The *Orphans* is undoubtedly a weak play, certainly the least successful of Tom Murphy's works. Written during his exile in England, and first produced for the 1968 Dublin Theatre Festival, it is a play which both shows the signs of a writer working in a vacuum, and carries the marks of the failure of its author to find an audience in the theatre for fully seven years. Murphy's three previous stage plays, *A Crucial Week in the Life of a Grocer's Assistant*, *The Morning After Optimism*, and *Famine*, three major plays by any standards, were still awaiting their first stage production when *The Orphans* was written. Those three plays were formally and thematically adventurous, *A Crucial Week* mixing dream and reality, *The Morning After Optimism* dealing with a fairytale world and an extraordinary theatrical language, *Famine* evolving a form somewhere between epic and tragedy. But none of them had been produced, let alone acclaimed.

By 1967, Murphy had dealt with virtually all of the ramifications of the Irish industrial revolution, of his own upbringing and of his exile to England. He was ready to try to place all of this in a broader philosophical context, to deal with the situation of man in the world at a more abstract level. But his failure to have a whole series of plays produced encouraged him to see whether he could work in a more palatable, more naturalistic form. In *The Orphans* he wrote a well-made play about the homelessness of man in the world, and the result is predictably cramped and static, a big genie in a very small, very uncomfortable bottle. *The Orphans* is interesting as a reminder of how triumphantly successful the form of later plays like *The Sanctuary Lamp* and *The Gigli Concert* is, in the way that it manages to contain flights of philosophical imagination while remaining funny and theatrical. *The Orphans* explains why Murphy could not be a naturalistic writer.

The Orphans has the feeling of a late nineteenth century play, of Ibsen and Chekhov. The Chekhovian air comes from its setting in an English country house, a place which has the same relationship to London as a Chekhovian country house has to Moscow, and from the general paucity of outward action, the sense of a group of people frozen in time and space, hovering on the edge of some great catastrophic event in the outside world. The house belongs to Kate and Roddy, brother and sister, the orphans of the title. Kate lives there with Dan, Roddy comes to visit with his pregnant wife Moggie. As in Chekhov, there is a servant, Beryl, who has the run of the house and who interferes in the conversation with enigmatic asides. And there is Mr Kyne, Dan's Irish father, who comes to visit, and hangs uneasily about the house.

The whole thing has a purgatorial feeling of souls deprived of a vision of the face of God. The characters might as well be dead, except that, like those in Purgatory, their souls live on. The opening speech of the play is Beryl's image of a dead body that is still somehow alive:

"But here, this poor man died. And whereas he died, the cancer in his body was still alive. And now an eminent clergyman from the Midlands has made a statement. Yes. That it is wrong to bury the body because the soul might still be alive in it ..."

This is not just a parody of theological absurdity, setting the tone for a play which treats religion as something of an absurdity in itself. It also defines the atmosphere of the house in which there is no direction or purpose, but signs of life persist. As the play opens, Kate is painting a picture of Roddy, Moggie and Beryl, and Moggie remarks "Wouldn't it be awful to be caught like this forever?" The image is of frozen lives, souls in aspic.

Murphy was indeed reading Chekhov when he wrote *The Orphans* but the play which had most bearing on the work was Ibsen's *Rosmersholm*. *Rosmersholm* is by no means a model for *The Orphans*, and there are no direct correspondences between them, but Ibsen's attempt to use a naturalistic form and invest it with symbolic weight is strongly influential on the Murphy play. *The Orphans*, like *Rosmersholm*, is dominated by an emptiness in the middle of the action, with everything held in tension by the pull of the past. In Rosmersholm everything holds its breath waiting for the final revelation that Rosmer's wife Rebecca West had pushed his previous wife towards suicide, so that she might supplant her. In *The Orphans*, everything holds its breath but there is no revelation.

The problem with *Rosmersholm* as an inspiration for a Murphy play is that it is not dramatic enough, indeed, as Georg Lukacs has argued, it is not dramatic at all. Lukacs says of the scene in which Rebecca West explains that she pushed Beate into suicide one small step at a time that it is in novels and not in plays that things happen one small step at a time: "Here, with the unflinching honesty of a great writer, Ibsen declares why *Rosmersholm* could not become a real drama: at the decisive moment, we see that the actual drama, namely Rebecca West's struggle, tragic collision and conversion, is, as far as subject-matter, structure, action and psychology are concerned, really a novel, the last chapter of which Ibsen has clothed in the outward form of drama with great mastery over scene and dialogue. Despite this, however, the basis of the play is still, of course, that of a novel, full of the undramatic drama of modern bourgeois life. As drama, therefore, *Rosmersholm* is problematic and fragmentary; as a picture of the times it is authentic and true-to-life."

All of this could have been written about *The Orphans*, which is true-to-life in its reflection of the aimless sixties world of LSD and permissiveness, but is full of the undramatic drama of modern bourgeois life, and comes across as the last chapter of a novel. Unlike in *Rosmersholm*, however, the rest of the novel is missing, and we can piece it together only in strange, disconnected fragments. In drama, people and their actions must converge at some point, but in *The Orphans* there is a lattice of conjoined characters, a world of relationships rather than of individuals, and those relationships struggle to express themselves in any kind of action.

There is, however, another aspect of *Rosmersholm* which is more fruitful for *The Orphans*. It is a play which considers the dialectics of change, and the consequences for the people concerned in it. Rosmer is a man who has improving designs on his fellow man, but his faith in progress is unavailing in bringing him happiness. *The Orphans*, too, is a play about change, specifically the technological change of modern progress, and it is concerned to show its characters dwarfed and immobilised by that change. Murphy's previous plays are all about people struggling to cope with a changing world, drawing their immediacy and their substance from the actual change which is taking place in Irish society. The general thrust of those plays has been supportive of that transformation, but *The Orphans* marks a point of rest, a stasis before Murphy goes on to launch a new critique of the emerging society and to develop a richer and more dramatically powerful notion of transformation.

The Orphans is concerned with a change which is very pertinent to what is happening in Ireland in the late sixties, the decline of religion and the rise of a new religion of technology. It examines the conflict between instinct and reason, the fear that emotion will be replaced by a science that is just as distant and oppressive as the old God. These tensions are real enough; the problem is that Murphy has not constructed a dramatic story which is sufficiently strong to contain them. For the only time in his work, the sense of helplessness in the face of change takes over, giving us a play that is as frozen in the gulf between the mind and the body as are its characters. Ideas do not result in physical actions, and where this is the case, there is no drama.

The Orphans is set in 1969, one year after its first production, and gambles, correctly as it happens, on there being an attempt to land on the moon in that year. The moon landing is the great public event which hangs over the play, from Beryl's announcement near the start that they're "landing on the moon in two weeks time" to the final scene in which the count-down to lift-off is heard on the radio. Beryl's question is "Does it help against stagnation?" and the triumph of technical progress is set against the childishness of the characters, their inability to form proper relationships, their petulance, the sense that they are lost even in the confined narrow world of the house, never mind in the great world outside.

The house itself is "a doll's house," a childhood refuge topped by an "early Victorian roof with its turrets and cupolas and what-nots," making it sound like a fairytale castle. Kate and Dan have lived there for four years after Dan left the priesthood. Both Roddy and Dan's father opposed their union, and now all have gathered in an attempt at reconciliation. They are caught in an uncomfortable world of forced happiness, trying to convince each other how well they are doing. It is an era of progress and they should be developing. Kate says to Roddy:

"And I was wondering how we poor earth-bound provincials should equate our home-preserves with the brave new world of ideas you would bring home. 1969, Rod. We're evolving. Redundant ministers and registrars are being redeployed. New ethical codes, heaven is here and now, we are landing on the moon. Defecting priests are growing prize-winning marrows."

Technology is the new religion, but it brings God no closer. Moggie remembers coming round after a delirium: "It was dark; I don't know where I was. But then I saw the light. Hah-haa! In a corner. And in this patch of light was a sort of man doing whirlings, and tubes sticking out of him all over the place. And I thought, if you can catch one of his tubes you can pull yourself up to heaven. Otherwise, you'll sink, Baby. And then I realised what it was. And do you know what it was? The telly! You could see it had been left on for days. You could see that. And a great big bloody astronaut chirping away for himself in space. And the announcer talking about the strides the modern world was taking. Christ I said! But, Christ!"

This is a world abandoned by God in which religion has ceased to have any meaning. Dan is the living symbol of this decline, a Catholic priest who has deserted the church and taken to growing marrows with Kate. The Church has been reduced to irrelevance:

"Dan used to say that the effort of the Ecumenical Council was like an attempt to amalgamate the branches of village smithies all over the world. You know: the futility of trying to re-organise something that no longer matters."

But this collapse of religion has not been a liberation. Kate and Roddy are literally orphans, but also spiritual orphans, left without a place in the world. Because science has taken the place of religion as a domineering force, the people of the play are still full of yearnings.

Kate and Roddy are incomplete, he living in the city, where he runs a trendy, swinging London restaurant, but haunted by this house in the country, she living in the country but afraid that she may be missing out on life. Beryl is driven to inventing her own beliefs, convinced that there is another world "down there" with people "not like us." Dan's leaving of the priesthood is no more a matter of conviction than was his joining: "I don't believe I'm here. I forget why I joined the priesthood. I can't remember why I left it." In spite of his country refuge with Kate, he feels that "I'm a fugitive here." And Dan's father is like a man in purgatory. Having spent his working life in England, he refuses now to return home to Ireland because Dan has left the priesthood.

The collapse of religion has left them all in an unhappy limbo. But the technology which has replaced religion is, in the play, sinister and nightmarish. Its invasive nature is symbolised by the disruption of biological processes. Beryl talks of "the pair bonding species . . . being destroyed by the pill" and of test tube babies. Roddy, in surreal, nightmarish gibberish talks of "our sixteen mil supermatoza screen started plup-plup-plup-plupping, bubbling over on to the floor. Gyrating, coming towards me."

Moggie has had two abortions. Human reproduction is breaking down, as in Moggie's ramblings about her father: "I never worried about my daddy until this relation suggested that my daddy was a fairy. But I said he fertilised me, didn't he. But she said fertilising wasn't foolproof. But I said foolscap, dutchcaps, dildoes, freddies, frenchies, coils, tubes, pills, suppositories — I'm not vulnerable. But she said statistically nine out of every ten men in England are queer. So what could I say?" Sexuality has become technological, and Roddy's image of London is of "automobiles mounting mobiles, tube trains going in and out of holes, screaming jets chasing each other across the sky with smoking genitals." The body is becoming a machine, and the soul has nowhere to go.

Within this framework of lost and confused humanity, cut off from God and from its own instincts, *The Orphans* is very much a play of Murphy's own exile, for its sense of frustration and yearning is set within a dialectic of Ireland and England, home and abroad. Both Kate and Roddy are caught between the house and London, the sanctuary of home and the big world outside, where Kate once thought that "away from this place people were giants." But more pointedly, Dan and his father have a painfully ambivalent relationship with Ireland. Given Murphy's childhood background in which part of his family was in England and part in Ireland, it is hardly surprising that Ireland and England should appear in his plays as two incomplete parts of the one whole, incapable of achieving a healthy unity unless they are somehow, symbolically, brought together. *In A Crucial Week in the Life of A Grocer's Assistant*, the image of exile is that of being "half-men here or half-men away" and in *The Orphans*, Ireland and England are two halves, each lacking and unsatisfactory.

This is incorporated into the wider theme of the play by identifying Ireland with instinct and England with reason, Ireland with the physical and England with the mental, the two sides of human nature which have been divorced from each other in a technological age. Kate talks of the fear that mankind has become "A body without the instinctual urges that have held good for millions of years; a mind cluttered in a nostalgic daze of things that no longer matter." In the play, England is trapped in a body in which the instinctual urges have been replaced by biotechnology, but Dan and his father perform physical work, and Roddy refers to Dan as a genetic mutation that has been introduced to save the family from extinction: "The family needed a mutation, you said, if we were going to survive." Dan and his father, however, have their minds "cluttered in a nostalgic daze of things that no longer matter."

Roddy taunts Dan with the reminder that "Cromwell is dead a long time. The bogmen should get with it." and affects a stage-Irish accent to annoy him: "Sure'n 'tis an awful thing entoirely I do be afther doin'!" Dan slips into nostalgia for a rustic childhood: "Do you remember that piece of con-acre we got one year down near Gurrauns? We used to get mushrooms in the tufts of grass on the sides of the ridges ... Well I'd like to go home." His father cannot face the new ways of the world, and sees Dan's desertion of his priestly calling as a judgement of God on the family's pride. Roddy and Dan, England and Ireland, impotently lash at each other, throwing ludicrous national stereotypes in each other's faces: " Pray to Victoria, Pray to that ponce of a Pope! Tell him to let you go!", "Victoria is screaming between heaven and hell now! " "Cause the pope won't take off his chastity belt!"

Ireland and England in confrontation become like two little boys calling each other names. The clash between Dan and Roddy is a clash between a static and sterile rural nostalgia and an equally static and sterile urban sophistication. We see Dan in his country retreat, pottering in the shed, growing marrows, fixing the rafters, a vegetating man. Roddy, on the other hand fancies himself as a successful businessman with his car, his flat and a restaurant called "Happenings." Dan is seeking the "happiness of the compost heap," still muttering about "Rotten English oppressors! What they did to us! Rotten Protestant bastards!", while Roddy is so confused and aimless that much of his conversation is reduced to sheer, meaningless sound. In this, *The Orphans* continues Murphy's attack on the sentimental Irish traditions, while entering a large caveat about just how genuine the "progress" of the sixties is.

The tussle between Dan and Roddy is played out over the affections of Kate and Moggie, and neither of them can win. Kate "belongs" to Dan and Roddy tries to win her back for himself. In the end, both of them have lost her. Moggie is Roddy's wife, and Dan tries to win her away, even offering her confession and absolution for her sins. But in the end, she, too, leaves both of them. Dan is left in limbo, Roddy with nothing but a pathetic vision of an ideal family which constitutes his attempt at writing a novel:

"Angie, intelligent, beautiful, lay on the rug, her eyes fixed on Teddy with love and understanding. How wonderful in the end of all to be together. Being with one's own was love. Over the intercom that lay on the rug beside her came a cluck and two coos. The baby was well in the nursery. She smiled up at Teddy."

In fact, as he reads this, Moggie is just leaving, bringing with her their unborn child and leaving the house in childless sterility.

As a play, *The Orphans* collapses under its own weight, since it is so dense as to be almost incomprehensible at points. A mark of its density is the fact that there is something of practically every Murphy play written after it contained within its ferment of words and ideas. The idea of man as orphaned by God and the search for a replacement to religion is central to *The Sanctuary Lamp*. Its juxtaposition of a great public event announced over the news media, the landing on the moon, with the daily details of small lives prefigures the first half of *The White House*, in which the assassination of John F. Kennedy is set against the events of the same night in a public house in the West of Ireland. Also containing the seeds of the central device of *The White House* is Roddy's reference to his business partner, Henry Smeed: "what gets me is the way he likes to think he has this John F. Kennedy thing about him." In *The White House*, JJ Kilkelly, owner of the pub which gives the play its ironic title, also thinks of himself as being like Kennedy and cultivates the image with smatterings of Kennedy's speeches.

The house in *The Orphans*, preserved as a refuge from the outside world, and Dan's flight to it as a sanctuary, is part of a series of refuges stretching through *The White House, The Blue Macushla, The Sanctuary Lamp,* and *The Gigli Concert*. The roles of Irishman and Englishman assumed by Dan and Roddy, the one all instinct and yearning, the other all pained and overwrought, is a prototype for the Irishman Francisco and the Englishman Harry in *The Sanctuary Lamp*, and for the Irishman and JPW King in *The Gigli Concert*. And Kate is an embryonic version of Mary in *Bailegangaire*. Like Mary, who looks after the ancient Mommo, Kate has looked after her rambling 86-year old aunt, and, like Mary, she has been

140

away in London and has returned to the house in search of some memory of peace and happiness.

If it is itself a failure, then, *The Orphans* was to prove remarkably rich seed-ground for Murphy's later, and infinitely more successful work. It effectively marks the end of Murphy's attack on the old pre-sixties Ireland, and the beginning of his attack on the world that has replaced it. Taken together with *Famine*, it shows man as the victim of history, still outside of the course of great events while being affected and imprisoned by them. It implies the need for a leap beyond progress, a step into a new realm of human existence which inaugurates a new world. That step is made in *The Sanctuary Lamp* and in *The Gigli Concert*, but first Murphy had to develop a critique of Ireland since Whitaker, a sense of how little had changed below the surface of great events.

VI

Be Like Americans

You know you are approaching Tuam when you pass, on your right, the streamlined modern bottling plant and the huge sign on its front wall which says "Drink Coca-Cola". Until the 1960s the bottling factory was in town, a few hundred yards up from the house on Church View where Tom Murphy was raised. Then, it was Egan's plant, bottling the local product, Egan's mineral water. But as the Irish economy began to expand with the injection of foreign capital after 1959, and with the new spirit of American-inspired optimism and enterprise, the cosy, unambitious Egan's was bought by a man who had a sense of mission about him. Tom Naughton took over the plant, discontinued the production of Egan's mineral water and got the franchise to bottle Coca-Cola from the American parent company. He was so successful that within a few years he had to move to a larger and more modern plant that now stands just outside the town on the Galway road.

Tom Naughton's enterprise was a model of the sixties spirit, turning the company from an indigenous, sleepy industry, to a go-ahead Irish version of a dynamic American success story. For many people in Tuam, Tom Naughton was the Sixties. He was not only a successful businessman with his finger on the pulse of a new era, but also the embodiment of that spirit of enterprise from across the Atlantic which seemed to offer such hope to a depressed people. He was a man of culture and of vision, encouraging writers and artists, full of hope for an end to the dark days of ignorance and intolerance.

People said that Tom Naughton looked like John F. Kennedy, and, in fact, he modelled himself more than a little on the young, apparently heroic President. If he was not the model for, then he was certainly the inspiration behind JJ Kilkelly, the central figure of *The White House* and the ghost who haunts *Conversations on a Homecoming*, who also represents the Sixties spirit and also models himself on John F. Kennedy.

When Kennedy visited Ireland in 1963, he came as the living symbol of the new national self-confidence. As symbols go, he was tailor-made: young, glamorous, energetic, he summed up America in all its glory and modernity. But, for a country which was still fiercely Catholic and which clung desperately to the national pride which had seen it through the years of frustration since Independence, he was also an ideal image. He was Irish, Catholic, apparently saintly, one of our own who had made it to the most powerful job in the world. For the Irish, his image was broad enough to combine piety and sexuality, youth and ancient tradition, the ould sod and the brave new world. As he stood beside the increasingly decrepit Eamon de Valera, President of Ireland and presiding deity of Irish politics and nationhood for five decades, who went to meet him at Dublin Airport, the torch seemed to pass to a new generation. National self-confidence, battered by the complete collapse of the ideal of self-sufficiency, soared.

Kennedy spent just three days in Ireland, but it was enough to crystallise the national mood of a turning to America. At a garden party for celebrities, officials and business people in the Phoenix Park, Kennedy was mobbed like a film star, touched like a faith healer, his clothes torn by the cream of refined Irish society. At public addresses in different parts of the country, Kennedy would call out the names of different cities in America and ask the members of the crowd whether they had relatives there. Everyone put up their hand for every city. Self-assertion and self-abasement went hand in hand, as people paid homage to Kennedy, seeing in him an image of their better selves. In Kennedy, Ireland and America merged, and it was as if the pain of generations of emigration had been healed by this homecoming son.

One of the peculiarities of Irish nationalism and of the culture which surrounded it had always been the fact that while it was hyper-sensitive to possibly pernicious influences from England, it had no such sensitivity to America. Mass Irish emigration to America long predated mass emigration to England, so that, even in the most backward of peasant societies, there was a knowledge of American places and of American life from letters home and, later, from returned emigrants. While England was the traditional enemy, America was always regarded as a moral ally, and Irish republicanism took many of its concepts and forms of organisation from the Irish in America. With the movies came more images of the good life in America, and with the destruction of traditional music and the construction of dance halls came American-style dance music.

Murphy was one of the first writers to note the identification of Americanisation with material success in the figure of Mickey Ford in *On the Outside*, but as the sixties progressed and the very ideology of Irish nationalism was modified to take account of American influence, the process which he had spotted in 1959 was speeded up. Throughout the sixties and into the seventies, rural Ireland in particular adapted its own self-image to American models, so that the thatched cottage was replaced by the hacienda-style bungalow and the popular music of the Irish countryside became a peculiar hybrid of sentimental Irish ballads and American country-and-western, often sung in lounge bars in a mock-American accent by bands dressed in cowboy suits. Irish nationalism had so little difficulty in accommodating to this change, that Fianna Fail, the party of mainstream nationalism and the party of the Sixties, became closely associated with the country-and-western industry itself.

In a series of plays, Murphy has reflected this development. Having gone utterly against the grain of the old nationalism in his early plays, he continued to reflect on its decline, and then on its accommodation to new forms. As essentially a playwright of southern society, he has not reflected directly on the explosion of violence in Northern Ireland since 1968, but a bitterness at the re-emergence of nationalist militarism is evident in his work of the Seventies, and an attack on the hypocrisy of the southern political order in relation to that militarism is very much to the forefront of *The Blue Macushla* and just under the surface of *Conversations on a Homecoming*. What there has been in Murphy's work is a steady erosion of the myths of nationalism followed by an examination of its present, bastardised, condition. This process of reflection on nationalism has gone hand-in-hand with a tracing of the Americanisation of southern society, as the two sides of the one coin, and the two are brought decisively together in *The Blue Macushla*.

The Blue Macushla is related, not so much to any of Murphy's other original stage plays, as to two works, one a television play (subsequently re-worked for the stage), the other an adaptation of a novel, with which it forms a loose trilogy. *The Patriot Game*, written for the BBC as a commemoration of the fiftieth anniversary of the Easter Rising of 1916 in 1966, and re-written as a theatre piece for the 75th anniversary of the Rising in 1991; *The Informer*, adapted by Murphy from Liam O'Flaherty's novel of the same name, and dealing with the period of the War of Independence; and *The Blue Macushla,* showing the activities of a modern-day nationalist splinter group, together trace the disintegration of Irish nationalism and the rise of Americanisation. They cover three crucial periods of armed conflict, much as O'Casey's *The Shadow of a Gunman, Juno and the Paycock* and *The Plough and*

The Stars, do. None of the plays is exclusively political, and indeed all three show the way in which Murphy's characteristic themes of disillusion, the search for forgiveness, and the possibility of redemption, arise out of history and politics.

The Patriot Game was commissioned for BBC's Wednesday Play slot in 1965, to be broadcast the following year, with Christopher Morahan directing. Because of its scale, however, the cost of the production was reckoned to run to a figure of around £10,000, very much in excess of the £6,600 budget allowed for the Wednesday Play. After various attempts at altering the script in order to scale it down, it was eventually abandoned and the BBC broadcast instead Hugh Leonard's *Insurrection*. In 1966, the play was taken up by Phyllis Ryan's Gemini Productions as a possible stage production for Dublin, but by then it was too late to stage it for the anniversary year, and the idea came to nothing.

As a television script, it is a somewhat uncomfortable mixture of drama and documentary, with an often didactic narration and the use of W. B. Yeats' poem *Easter 1916* along with the poetry of the rebel leaders, but it is remarkable for its view of the Rising as a bizarre ritual, a considerably less heroic and more jaundiced view of the central event of modern Irish nationalism than was being expounded in the ecstatic celebrations in Dublin. The very title, taken from Dominic Behan's bitter song of the same name about the price paid by a young IRA man for believing the romantic illusions of his elders in the IRA's farcical Border campaign of the late 1950s, implies a sardonic distance.

The original television version of *The Patriot Game* opens, not with the hoisting of the green flag over the General Post Office or the reading of the proclamation of the Republic, but with Dublin in ruins. The scene is O'Connell Street after the Rising: "Buildings in ruins, still smouldering: corpses and silent mourners, dead animals:

men standing with their hands in their pockets, trying to look casual (as if ashamed of the cameras), perplexed, trying to comprehend it all: women unsympathetic, vindictive, looking for an outlet." This attitude of perplexity and anger with which we are led into the story of the Rising is about as far as it is possible to get from the official pride and awe. And what is more, this same scene is repeated at the end of the play, reinforcing it, and also giving to the whole thing the air of a ritual, framed as it is by exactly similar sequences.

And this feeling of ritual is precisely the way in which the Rising is presented, as a ritual which goes wrong and tumbles into calamity. The Narrator remarks of Patrick Pearse and Thomas McDonagh that "war is some kind of poem to them," and the literary nature of the rising itself is stressed; "Poets, sure, an' the tragic fates waitin' for them around the corner." The Rising, when it is finally agreed, begins, not with shots but with a priest at Mass declaring "Christ is Risen!" It is invested with the air of a religious rite, a search for redemption through sacrifice.

But this ritualism is set constantly against the sordid realities of Dublin life. The first voices of the television play are those of the Dublin populace abusing the rebels as they are being led away. In the crowd for Pearse's oration at the graveside of O'Donovan Rossa are a starved-looking woman who complains of leaders "featherin' their own nests" and a young man who says he is thinking of joining the British Army "but I might get shot". During the Rising itself, the looters and drunks get into a fight with the rebels. And to all of these voices from outside of the process of ritual sacrifice, Murphy has the narrator add a reminder of the Northern Protestants: "An' up in Ulster there, the Proddies were sayin', we want none of it; Home Rule means Rome Rule. An' they could be right."

Murphy's view of the Rising is tinged with the cynicism induced by the knowledge of what kind of Ireland it helped to create. Unusually for a commemoration of the Rising itself, *The Patriot Game* concentrates on the build-up to Easter Week, the slow teetering into calamity which becomes a headlong rush. And in that portrayal of Ireland before the Rising, there is no sense of a single, unified people waiting to emerge into nationhood. In the most skillful and intricate scene of the play, a kind of expressionistic montage in which Asquith, Connolly, Pearse, Redmond, Eoin MacNeill and an evangelist all address a crowd "lookin' for men for their revolutions, or wars or whatever," there is a cacophony of competing voices:

Connolly: Ireland is rotten with slums. Nations that know not the powers and possessions of Empire have happier, better-educated, better equipped men and women than Ireland has ever known, or can ever know, as an integral part of the British Empire.

Evangelist: An' sizzle an frizzle an roast. An yiz'll join yer hands down there, and yiz'll look up to heaven up there, and yiz'll say —

Asquith: I have only one more word to say —

Redmond: Trust the Old Party.

Pearse: Redmond has dined too long at English feasts.

MacNeill: What's going on?

Asquith: Though our need is great, your opportunity is also great.

Redmond: Remember, Home Ru- Autonomy is on the way, you'll see.

Connolly: That pitiful suspended abortion, hung on a nail.

Asquith: There is no question of compulsion or bribery.

Evangelist: Aw but sure God, we didn't know.

And even within this confusion, some of the main protagonists are themselves shown as confused, Connolly, according to the Narrator, "an internationalist ... trying to battle against the narrower nationalist side of his nature,"

Pearse an "unfortunate man," tormented and unhappy. For his portrayal of the Rising itself, Murphy plays up the hesitations and contradictions of the leaders. First Connolly bluffs Pearse into an alliance and into preparing for revolution; then MacNeill countermands the orders to the Volunteers and the revolutionaries are all but paralysed with confusion. As poets, their only release is in language:

Plunkett: Orders, countermanding orders, orders confirming countermanding orders, orders flying hither and thither like...

MacDonagh: Dying leaves astray on the wind. (He smiles at Plunkett).

Plunkett (returns the smile): Something like that.

Dublin Castle is no better organised than the rebels themselves, full of indecision and unsurely scrutinising the tealeaves for evidence of Irish intentions.

The Rising becomes a mixture of absurdity, heroism, blood-letting and repression. Connolly's humanity helps to sustain the rebels; the British begin large-scale measures of repression; a nurse comes down the stairs of a darkened building and is shot simultaneously by rebels and soldiers who are pursuing each other around the corridors. The Narrator becomes increasingly desperate in his efforts to interpret it all:

"Wouldn't we be free sometime? Whatever that is, whatever that is. It's a long time since any country was free, victor or vanquished. And we don't really hate the English, we don't really. But Jesus Christ above, let there be a conqueror or no conqueror. And if it be yes, let him rule so hard and so well that there can be no rebel and no faithful and no questions and no concessions. Jesus Christ above, make us mightier yet to shoot a million horrible nurses and maybe someone will be free."

And within this desperation is a comic absurdity. A young Volunteer shouts "Up the Republic, up on your sister, me hand on your drawers, God save Ireland" as his oath of loyalty. Rumours abound:

"Jim Larkin is marching from the west with one million even American soldiers. The Volunteers' reserve forces have taken London. The English are bringin' in artillery to level Dublin. Patrick Pearse and James Connolly are both dead — fought a duel on the roof of the post office. Twelve German submarines in the duck pond in St. Stephen's Green."

But in the midst of this melange of nonsense, one rumour is true: artillery does indeed come to level Dublin. Reality has become so grotesque that it is indistinguishable from the absurd. Murphy gives us a mad and horrible world rather than a glorious struggle.

The Patriot Game is not a debunking of the Rising as a nationalist shibboleth, but neither is it a celebration of freedom. Instead it draws attention to the fact that the world remains unredeemed after the Rising. "The struggle was over" says the Narrator at the end. "And where was the redemption they were talkin' about? The sacrifice mustn't have been great enough." Nationalism and war, in the play, are not roads to freedom in an unfree world. In nationalist thinking, the Rising is an act of salvation comparable, and specifically likened, to the crucifixion. But in Murphy's theatre, neither the crucifixion nor any other act of salvation located in the past can redeem his people. They must win their own salvation.

The 1991 stage adaptation of the play for the Peacock Theatre (where it played in tandem with *The Plough and the Stars* upstairs on the Abbey stage as the Abbey's marking of the 75th anniversary of the Rising) keeps this balance between human sympathy for the rebels and refusal of hero-worship intact. In it, the play is integrated more fully within Murphy's work as a whole, and comes, curiously but significantly, to resemble his great 1985 play, *Bailegangaire*. The resemblances provide a reminder both of the formal and psychic concerns which Murphy brings to a political/historical subject, and of the layers of political allegory that are buried within a personal play like *Bailegangaire.*

In the first place, the stage version of *The Patriot Game* clarified the extent to which Murphy's approach to the Rising is consistent with the interplay of illusion and disillusion in his work as a whole. Throughout Murphy's work, illusion is seen as deathly, and in 1966 *The Patriot Game* would have helped to undermine illusions about the glory and brilliance of the Rising. But equally, in Murphy's work, there are negative illusions — the refusal to acknowledge the past, the repression of traumas which blocks off the future. In 1991, the danger in the Irish Republic was as much one of "repressing" the Rising from national memory as of glorifying it into a national illusion. The political purpose of the play therefore became one precisely of acknowledgement. In an author's note in the programme for the Peacock, Murphy stated his belief that "nationalism is an elemental emotion and a dangerous one, intrinsic to us all. But I believe that it is more dangerous not to acknowledge it or to pretend otherwise." In the introduction to the published version of the play (Methuen, 1992), he remarks of the Rising "It happened... It was the birth of the Irish nation."

This need for the trauma of the past to be acknowledged is also the wellspring of *Bailegangaire.* Re-inforcing this link between the two plays is the use, in the novel *The Seduction of Morality* (1994), itself occupying very similar territory to *Bailegangaire,* of some of the patriotic texts used in *The Patriot Game.* In the opening section of the novel, snatches of quotations that conjure up the revolutionary period run through the ironic context of a family gathering to divide up inherited property. Connolly's "man is a slave and woman is the slave of a slave!" is uttered by a solicitor "quoting someone, though not knowing quite what he meant by it." The "jingle-poem" "Bide your time, your worst transgression Were to strike and strike in vain" appeals to Mary Jane because "it made business sense." The satiric distance between the quoters and the quoted marks the utter degeneration of the revolutionary ideals in the gombeen republic. This sense of generations becoming deaf to one another's words is central to both *Bailegangaire* and *The Patriot Game*.

And the process of acknowledgement is much more explicit in the stage version of *The Patriot Game* than in the television script. The Narrator now is a young woman in a leather jacket, clearly a figure located in 1991. With her at the start is "Pearse, a young actor," both the Narrator's brother or boyfriend, and, in the play, Patrick Pearse. The Narrator's attitude to the story of the Rising is that "it doesn't exist." And, as the stage fills with young actors who play out the roles of the protagonists in the events of 1916, the sense of detachment, of distance from the story, is palpable. As in *Bailegangaire*, there is a play-within-a-play, or, more precisely, a story-within-a-play. An old, old story (in this case that of 1916) is proceeding endlessly, careless of the younger generation for whom it has no meaning. What follows is, as in *Bailegangaire,* a process of surrender to the story, of a release into the narrative that is also the means of getting the story to end.

Like Mary in *Bailegangaire*, the Narrator is at the mercy of a story being told. Unlike *Bailegangaire*, however, it is the story, and not the character, which must be acknowledged. By the end of the play, the Narrator, angry, sceptical, hurt, is yet forced to acknowledge the implac-ability of the narrative, just as Mary in *Bailegangaire* gains recognition by making the story her own. She is compelled to utter the words "Up the Republic," and, when she does so, she is addressed directly by the Pearse actor who tells her to "Come on home." The play, like Bailegangaire, ends on that word "home," a stark reminder that the "home" envisaged in Murphy's work is political as well as metaphysical, historical as well as spiritual. In this play that home is a Republic of Ireland that has acknowledged its own messy, inglorious origins.

Nothing in the 1991 version of *The Patriot Game* implies a softening towards nationalist illusions. On the contrary one of its most powerful scenes is a speaking of Pearse's poem, written in the borrowed voice of his mother, by an actor playing that mother. The male heroic voice of romantic sacrifice dissolves in the mouth of a woman, the rhetoric becoming bitter, incredulous and grief-stricken. The words remain the same, but the pitch and rhythm are changed, providing a superbly theatrical moment of the familiar transformed. Thus,

The generations shall remember them,

And call them blessed.

becomes in the mouth of the mother:

The generations shall remember them,

And call them — blessed?

Typically, Murphy allows neither the amnesia about the origins of the State, nor the rhetoric of national resurrection to hold the stage. He takes his stand with what was and what is, so that, in remembering, the country might still move on to what may yet be.

Murphy's version of Liam O'Flaherty's *The Informer* is much more than a mere adaptation of the novel for the stage, and it is in many ways closer to being an original Murphy play than it is to O'Flaherty. It is imbued with religious imagery and language, and, just as *The Patriot Game* turned the 1916 Rising into a ritual, *The Informer* makes of O'Flaherty's story of the betrayal of a revolutionary by his comrade, a search for redemption and forgiveness in "a rotten aul' world." But its use of this imagery could not be more distant from the symbolism of the nationalist revolt, in which the informer is the ultimate pariah. In Murphy's plays it is the outsider who can achieve salvation, and he makes of O'Flaherty's informer Gypo Nolan a soul on a progress through a vicious and barren world towards forgiveness. Gypo carries the burden of guilt which all of Murphy's central characters bear, and his voyage into confusion, despair and rejection ends with his being relieved of that guilt.

Whereas in the language of nationalist mythology, the informer is the one bad apple who spoils the common cause, the guilty individual cut off from the rest of the people, Murphy goes to great pains to make Gypo, not an evil individual, but the beast of burden who bears the guilt of the world on his shoulders. Gypo's act of betrayal is not a knowingly committed sin, but something which torments him as being blind and inscrutable. The question which tortures him is "Is there no one to tell me why I done it?" He gives Frankie McPhillip, his old comrade with whom he has engaged in a wild act of terrorism, shooting the head of the Farmer's Union, up to the police for a reward of twenty pounds, but he gives most of the money away, and his act of betrayal is far from being a simple one. For Frankie, cleverer than Gypo, who is compounded of instinct and suffering, with very little of intelligence or nobility in his nature, practically goads Gypo into betraying him, in order to relieve him of his own world-weariness and disillusion. Frankie is already sick, and will probably die anyway. He stresses to Gypo that "I told you I don't much mind anything no more," and we sense that he understands the thoughts of betrayal that are going through Gypo's mind and actively encourages them. Even Gypo senses this: "Yer not playin' games with me, are yeh, Frankie?"

But what really makes it clear that Gypo is the bearer of the common guilt of humanity is Murphy's introduction of the figure of the Evangelist, whose street sermons introduce and punctuate the action. The Evangelist opens the play with the words "What is sin, what is sin, sin is meanness, sin is smallness, sin is selfish" and the world we see is a mean, small, selfish one. It is the world which has to be guilty for its distorted and crippled state, not Gypo as an individual. The Evangelist later asks:

"What am I guilty of, what am I guilty of, what am I guilty of? Here comes in confession. Now what's to be done, what's to be done? Well the first thing is to be sorry. That will be something. Once I begin to feel I'm sorry, I begin to think of that Other whom I have betrayed. Moreover, the thought of that Other, that great Friend, betrayed, crucified on the cross, his bleeding wounds, his awful death, well, by contrast with him I'll be able to measure my meanness properly and see myself as a scamp."

This religious language of guilt and betrayal makes Gypo not a pariah but a scapegoat, the one who bears the common guilt. Gypo is a physical giant, towering over everyone else on stage and in his size, strength, and brutish intelligence, he is reminiscent of Frankenstein's monster, the innocent creation of a bad world. (All of this was emphasised in Liam Neeson's magnificent performance in the role.) Dan Gallagher, leader of the Revolutionary Organisation, says of Gypo that "He's an animal, reacting and responding to the calls of nature, that's all," and what he has to react to is poverty, privation and need.

Murphy populates the stage with the crippled, the disfigured, the maimed, from the dirty, dope-crazed bed-ridden hag Louisa in the first scene, to the addled old man hunted out of the cheap hostel where Gypo meets Frankie, to the silent, crippled figure of Uncle Mick at Frankie's wake and the hideously scarred Phyllis at Aunt Betty's brothel. And the source of this disfigurement is poverty. Murphy makes the story take place in a very specific setting of urban deprivation and class division. Gypo is a creature of the world of *Famine*, where the human spirit is pared down to the bare instincts of survival. His aspirations are for two things: food and a bed, the essentials of sustenance and shelter which every animal needs.

The first scene in Louisa's room is one of dire squalor, with three adults trying to sleep in or around one filthy bed. Mary, Frankie's sister, is later driven by the need to "get away from the slums" and we are shown on stage exactly what it is she is trying to escape. And this poverty is not universal but socially determined. In the McPhillips' house for the wake, the neighbours discuss their coughs and diseases: "Them auld houses in Clontarf: they're wicked cold to be down on your knees scrubbin' the floors o' them." And after his betrayal of Frankie, Gypo moves across the river from his usual stomping ground of tenement slums to a more comfortable and respectable world. The whore here is high-class: she approaches him, "sees that he is a working-class man" and says "Forget it, Duckie."

In the pub, Gypo encounters "a nouveau riche couple," Mr and Mrs Cassidy. Cassidy is an image of the coming Ireland of political independence in which his class will be the new ascendancy. He buys drinks for a poet at the bar who reciprocates with rhetorical hagiography: "The industry of your bricks and mortar, joined with the magic eloquence of my as-yet unfinished novel will see our New Ireland, in word and deed, take its resplendent place among the nations of the earth!" Cassidy wants to insist that the revolution is over, won by himself and his likes. To a blind musician playing the patriotic ballad "Kevin Barry," he shouts "Oi, segosha, the troubles is over, the topic is changed." Here, the nationalist revolution has served its purpose, and Gypo, on the fringe of a fringe group of revolutionaries, must bear the guilt of an unchanged world. The New Ireland is hell on earth, and Gypo is a soul damned into that hell. "God's love" the Evangelist says "builds Hell, but man's treachery, meanness, hatred and betrayal lodges him there forever."

The fact that the religious language of the Evangelist is used to give depth to the central currents of the story does not mean that he represents some sort of locus of truth in the play. On the contrary, Murphy manages to build slowly but inescapably an identification between the Evangelist and Gallagher, the sinister revolutionary leader who is hunting Gypo down. The Evangelist talks of a vengeful God, and Gallagher is animated by "revenge." The Evangelist talks of the guilt of betrayal, and Gallagher sets out to punish that betrayal. And both are incapable of human emotion, as they reveal in counterbalanced speeches, one hilarious, the other chilling.

"At this stage" the Evangelist says "some of you may be thinking to yourselves that I'm not the jolliest of boys, that I'm just a grumbler, just a grouser, that I know no joy in life and that I'm particularly determined to see that no one else does either. That is not so, for when I'm feeling out of sorts through self-denial, I whistle, I whistle vigorously, and that I can tell you relieves my feelings remarkably, that lets off some steam."

Nor is Gallagher the jolliest of boys when it comes to admitting humanity into his scheme of things: "What has pity to do with a revolutionary? Pity is a ridiculous sensation to a man of my nature. Do you see pity in the violence and corruption of the State? Would you call it pity, the one-sided hysteria of the press? The wrath of our great Church upon those who simply complain against rack-rent landlords or exploiting employers?"

Both Gallagher and the Evangelist within their own systems of language understand the world in its corruption, its viciousness and its implacability. But neither has the humanity to get beyond it, however much their analyses may explain it. In the end, Gallagher begins to speak the Evangelist's language, completing the identification between them: "Pity! And as we are told there is no single drop of water, of hope, to alleviate the suffering of the poor in hell, there is no single drop of water for the tormented and parched animals on earth." Gallagher's political imagery and the Evangelist's religious imagery intermingle, but without pity neither can offer a drop of hope to the world.

What Murphy does in *The Informer* is to take the religious language of the Evangelist and turn it upside down. In the course of the play, Gypo, the outcast sinner, becomes Christ, the lamb of God who takes away the sins of the world. The Evangelist says that "Christ could not die on the Cross at Calvary without testifying the awful magnitude of human guilt," and Gypo is the embodiment of that guilt. In his state of sin, he goes through the world dispensing alms to the poor. He gives the scarred Phyllis the money to return home from Aunt Betty's brothel, both a healing of the sick and a saving of Mary Magdalen from sin. He performs the miracle of the loaves and the fishes by buying fish and chips for "practically the entire population of Marlborough Place." He is brought before the judges of the Revolutionary Organisation's court as Christ is brought before the High Priest and Pilate. In his hour of crucifixion, after he has himself been betrayed by Katie Fox, turning him definitively from Judas to Jesus, he asks Gallagher who is interrogating him for water, as Jesus on the cross cries out for water, and is refused. He is shot and, metaphorically, dies, descending again into the purgatorial underworld of Katie and Louisa's den, where Katie, seeing him, thinks he is already dead and that this is his ghost. But he rises again, and encounters Mrs McPhillip, Frankie's mother. In the scene of the wake for Frankie she has already been identified with the Mother of God, through the praying of the Rosary and the Hail Holy Queen. In this final scene, she accepts Gypo as her son, and embraces him like Mary taking Jesus down from the cross "Aw, Gypo, me poor son, what have they done to yeh?"

As Christ, Gypo is the image, not of God, but of broken, forlorn humanity, crippled by poverty and outcast in the world. Gypo is a Christ who cannot forgive but must himself be forgiven and redeemed, and it is Mrs. McPhillip who does this, uttering the words of forgiveness of Jesus on the cross, "Father, forgive them for they know not what they do": "I forgive yeh, Gypo, son. Yeh didn't know what yeh were doin'."

Much of this parallel between Gypo and Christ is present in embryo in O'Flaherty's story, but Murphy deepens it immeasurably, both bringing out the clear lines of the structure, and adding important new details to it. Murphy's Informer dramatises the inadequacy of post-revolutionary Ireland, setting the world of political terrorism against the infinitely richer transformation of man in which the world is redeemed. His achievement in the play is to create in Gypo a figure who goes beyond being an individual character to become representative of humanity without ever ceasing to be a beast-like, hunted, inarticulate creature. Its fusion of religious and political imagery brings the two worlds into collision and results in a vision which is to do with the apocalyptic sweeping away of things as they are. In this, the play looks forward to *The Gigli Concert*, on which Murphy was working at the same time, as well as being closely related to the image of nationalist politics as a form of gangsterism in *The Blue Macushla*.

The Informer also indicates a distancing from traditional Irish orthodoxy in its form as well as its content. O'Flaherty's novel is heavily influenced by American pulp detective fiction, and it is that, as much as the story it tells, which distances it from the conventions of nationalist discourse. Murphy preserves this formal distancing from orthodoxy by using suggestions of an equivalent of detective fiction — the melodramatic gangster movie. His script is almost cinematic, intercutting sharply from one scene to the next, from outdoors to indoors, from crowd scenes to close-ups. Often the rhythm of the play is visual rather than verbal as it moves from day into night and back towards the dawn. Its pubs, brothels and dives are reminiscent of Chicago speakeasies, its revolutionaries often like hoods deferring to the boss, Gallagher. Kitty is like a gangster's moll. And towards the end, there is the stylised use of a movie technique, voice-over, as Gypo, delirious and running for salvation, hears his own voice speaking to him of freedom. Murphy's original play *The Blue Macushla*, first staged at the Abbey in 1980, takes these movie parallels further, presenting itself as an obvious parody of American gangster movies. It also makes the critique of militant Irish nationalism much more explicit, setting the action in " late seventies Dublin" and getting much of its sting from the conjunction of the Americanised, corrupt pseudo-patriotism of the business-men who came up through the Sixties, and the obsessional conspiratorial world of contemporary republican terrorism.

Its hero Eddie O'Hara is a self-made man, a man of the Sixties, "a poor kid from the gutter, now likes to put on a show and play the big shot", who is haunted by the old nationalist patriotism which will not leave him be to enjoy his hard-won prosperity. In the world of *The Blue Macushla*, half way between the exaggerations of gangster movies and the realities of Irish politics, all of those in power in a corrupt and disintegrating state are in debt to the shadowy nationalist splinter-group, Erin Go Brath. Ireland slides into America, gangster melodrama into political satire, reality into a stylised formula.

Yet it is important to remember that the reality beneath the formula was not that far from this stylised world in which the businessmen have debts to the Mob. At the time of Murphy's return home to Ireland in May 1970, the sensational Arms Trial in which the dismissed Minister for Finance, Charles J. Haughey was charged with conspiracy to import arms for the IRA (he was acquitted) was in progress. By the time of the play's premiere at the Abbey, he was Taoiseach (Prime Minister). "Nothing", as Murphy puts it in his introduction to the published version of the play (Methuen, 1992), " was transparent in the Republic... I knew that gangsterism in movies did not spring gratuitously out of the ground, that it had come out of American culture; I don't remember when it was that I realised I had discovered in it an apt metaphor for a play about Ireland in the 1970s." That metaphor, in any case, did not spring gratuitously out of the ground.

The opening scene of the play presents a parody, not just of kid-from-the-gutter element of the gangster movie, but also of the Catholic sacrament of confession, establishing the typical Murphy mix of social and religious imagery. Eddie, tense and seemingly desperate, is talking to a priest, who is bound in a chair and gagged, having been kidnapped by Erin Go Brath and hidden in Eddie's nightclub, The Blue Macushla. Eddie's patter also presents a vision of a vicious class divide in urban Ireland, an image of deprivation and exclusion which remains as a contrast to the nationalist aspirations to a united country:

Both from the same area, "Rathgar, posh, huh? And yous come from big family too, I was readin'. Can't remember 'xactly how many o' us there was. But you didn't have 'nadress like Lady O' Perpetual Succour Mansions. Why with 'nadress like that, even before unemployment became unemployment, an' you 'proached a place lookin' for a job, you was 'rested for loiterin'. So none o' us workin' 'cept Mom, Mom was a trier." (The published version of this speech is slightly different. I have kept to the original production script, except where there are major changes.)

Eddie's childhood reflects the Dublin of the time in which the play is written: scourged by drugs and unemployment. According to Eddie, "most o' my family's junkies now, mainliners, huh?" His is a family which has ceased to exist, one a "zombie", one "retarded", one a "pusher", one up for killing a cop, another dead from an overdose. His mother is in an institution, and "the only sane brother I got left is crazy". In this monologue, Murphy keeps a balance between comic exaggeration and bitter truth. Eddie's story is so bleak that it is a parody of the tough childhood, but there is also enough truth in it in relation to the actual

Dublin of its time, and it is delivered with such a strong sense of tension and menace, that it cannot be dismissed. The connection between the movie parody and the reality of Ireland is established and maintained.

The critique of modern Ireland is not just in the content of what Eddie says, but also in his language, an extraordinary blend of Chicago mobspeak and Dublin idiom. The language of the play makes clear the extent to which the country has been colonised by American patterns of speech and thought. The idea of a Dublin gangster movie is in itself a comment on this phenomenon, but it is strongly re-inforced by the references to Saint Patrick's Day, on which the bulk of the play takes place. Saint Patrick's Day is itself an American creation, celebrating an American conception of Ireland which has been accepted as home-grown. (Murphy's attitude to it was plain enough from as far back as Mush's remark in *A Whistle in the Dark* about the Irish economy being destroyed "since the demand for Saint Patrick's Day badges fell.") Mike, the loyal but dumb doorman, looks out at the parade outside:

"Just look at those   - Wow! what you call 'em? - majorettes. Wow! Dese 'Merican girls . . ."

Eddie has Mike prepare green Guinness, decorated with miniature Irish and American flags, for the club's Saint Patrick's Day party: "everything's gotta be like Americans". The Ireland to which loyalty must be given in the play is already somewhere else, an American fantasy which Eddie sums up as "a united little ol' Emerald Isle". And this romantic fantasy, with its attendant dream of a rural paradise, so often mocked in Murphy's work, is still weighing on the minds of an urban working-class for which it should have no meaning. Eddie's father, patriarch of a disintegrating family on the fringes of urban existence, "keeps talkin' 'bout patch o' grass down Tipperary ways."

Eddie's progress from the gutter has been a search for selfhood and in this he represents a nation looking for an identity with which it can feel comfortable. "I just wanted to become a person" he says, and the badge of personhood he has adopted is the ability to "be like Americans". Whereas the rural Irishman like Liam in *Conversations on a Homecoming* has adopted the rural American image of the cowboy, Eddie has taken on the urban American mantle of the gangster chief. This is the embodiment of power and selfhood with which he can identify:

"People come in that door out there, kid, the classiest. That's the boss they say, an' he just smiled my way. They know I come from nothing but it's 'Sure, boss, yeh boss, you're the boss, boss.' I kinda like it ... and the politicians ... the biggest! They come cruisin' up to my door in their armour-plated mercs, takin' the country for a ride."

Eddie is essentially an expressionistic character, not so much an individual with a detailed psychological history, as the representation of the psychic history of a country in search of a new self-image. He is the Sixties incarnate, the man who has come up from nothing to riches, and who needs an image to go with his new status. But he is haunted by the old nationalist identity which will not let him go. For Eddie is being blackmailed by Erin Go Brath, in whose name he carried out a bank-raid for his own benefit, and they are muscling in on his "little spot on earth", the nightclub. He has made use of the old nationalism when it suited him, and he now cannot escape it. "I ain't the boss no more. I ain't even a person again."

The *Blue Macushla* treats the entire period of the Sixties and its new found affluence as corrupt. Eddie and the people with whom he associates prefigure the Irishman in *The Gigli Concert,* who has made his fortune by graft and violence. Just as a film like *The Godfather* achieves its effect by treating crime as a normal, even quintessential, business enterprise, *The Blue Macushla* treats business as closely allied to crime. The small-time crimes in which Eddie and his partner Danny started their careers, and for which Danny has had to take the rap, are very deliberately chosen by Murphy. They are pig-smuggling and "subsidy rackets", both corrupt activities which are perfectly acceptable in most rural communities, and that only came to be publicly acknowledged as corrupt in the beef scandals of the early 1990s. Eddie and Danny are not criminals on the fringes of society, they are representative of the corruption that is endemic in the society itself. And Eddie later talks about a third area of corrupt business which is close to the heart of the political establishment of the Sixties, building:

"Let me tell you somethin' 'bout morality. Was at this big-shot shindig coupla months back, and there's this guy there called John who decides to do a maudlin' turn an' confess a murder to all present. He's big in development an' the buildin' game, see? an' he's got this well an' trusted 'sociate-friend called Martin, but they just wasn't gettin' along. So, one day, John climbs up on his crane and drops forty ton o' steel on Martin's head. An' yeh know what the party says to our murderer? They was bankers, professors, guys from government an' big business — the guys is changin' the world to the right way like you? Know what they say to our murderer? They says 'Don't let people see ya cryin' John'. Huh? They was 'barrassed. They was em-barrassed for our murderer."

Murphy creates a world in which every success has been based on corruption, in which every office desk has a dead body under it. Crime, Eddie tells Danny, not only pays, "It leads to greater corruption — Fortunes, money, riches, lolly, land, property, cabbage." But the evil of the past has now returned to claim its own. Not only is Eddie being held to ransom by Erin Go Brath, sinking further and further into violence and inhumanity, but his partner Danny returns from prison, expecting to be welcomed and given a share of the club for which, as Eddie's companion in crime, he helped to lay the basis.

Danny, too, is a stock character from the movies, the boxer who could have been a champ but turned to crime.

He believes in happy endings and thinks that he has come home. Danny is one of a long line of Murphy characters from the later plays who is searching for home. Homecoming has been a major motif of the plays since Murphy's own return to Ireland in 1970, with Danny in *The Blue Macushla*, Michael in *Conversations on a Homecoming*, and Mary in *Bailegangaire*, all returning from exile in search of a reconciliation with the past and with themselves. All are seeking sanctuary, and Murphy's later plays are full of such sanctuaries, from the church in *The Sanctuary Lamp*, to the dynamatologist's office in *The Gigli Concert*, to *The White House* in *Conversations on a Homecoming*. *The Blue Macushla* itself is such a sanctuary, an attempt to find refuge from the world. But, as in all Murphy's plays, the world is implacable, and cannot be escaped. Danny's would-be refuge is in reality a place of imprisonment — the priest is held and tortured there — a paradise which as it turns out, is bugged by the Special Branch.

Danny, indeed, is not so much a separate character — he says little about himself and does not develop through the play — as an alter ego for Eddie. He is Eddie's own past, the naive and hopeful side of his nature. Danny is full of aspirations, Eddie of regrets. Danny is looking to the future, Eddie imprisoned by the past. Danny sees the *Blue Macushla* as a home and a sanctuary, Eddie as a lost empire, slipping from his grasp. In the course of the play, Danny absorbs Eddie's realism, his sense of the fact that the world is a hostile place, and loses his belief in the Blue Macushla as a refuge. As Eddie declines, taking with him all of the sins of the past, Danny gains a freedom from illusion which allows him to walk free at the end, homeless but unfettered by impossible dreams.

The vehicle for this interchange between Eddie and Danny is Roscommon, the hard-bitten blonde singer with a heart of gold, who is lost by Eddie and won by Danny. Roscommon (her name, contrasted to her situation, is an ironic joke on the loss of innocence of the West of Ireland, like the whore in The Informer who is called Connemara Maggie) represents Romantic Ireland. She sings sentimental songs of Catholicism and nationhood like The Dear Little Shamrock and Countess Markievicz's Battle Hymn. She identifies herself, jokingly, as the daughter of a hedge-school master and a harpist, an ideal lineage for a fallen Cathleen Ní Houlihan, which is what, at one level, Roscommon is. In winning her, and escaping from *The Blue Macushla* with her, Danny is taking her away from Eddie and all that he has come to stand for.

Danny's escape, however, is equivocal, for the political world remains unchanged, the corruption intact. Erin Go Brath has been holding over the political and business establishment a little black book which contains the names of supporters "Prominent and public citizens, both from here and abroad." After Eddie's shoot-out with the gangster/terrorists, in which he and they are killed, the piano player Pete reveals himself as Special Branch man Tom O'Bannion and searches for the little black book. When he finds it he makes a phone-call to "the Minister":

"Names, dates, donations received, favours expected ... Abroad? Yeah, them ... yeh, the Congressman an' his crew ... an' the CIA guy ... some stuff 'bout NATO . . . At home? Yeah, his name's on it too ... yeh, the developer too: very gen'rous man ... Army? the commandant ..."

But Pete's job is not to reveal the contents of the book — rather the operation has been geared at getting it for safe keeping, to prevent it from falling into the wrong hands, to protect the guilty.

The Blue Macushla is not an entirely successful play, largely because its central device of gangster idiom is not used with enough suppleness and discrimination. Because everyone speaks in this same idiom, it becomes a convention which is quickly absorbed by an audience and therefore ceases to have much dramatic power. Eddie should essentially be a Mickey Ford from *On the Outside* or a Liam from *Conversations On a Homecoming*, a character infected with borrowed speech and a borrowed image. But when everyone around him speaks pretty much as Eddie does, the point that he is speaking an assumed, foreign language is lost. The fact that he is playing out an image is less clear than it needs to be. For in *The Blue Macushla*, it should be as if James from *The Morning After Optimism* had adopted the mannerisms and speech of the fantasy-image Edmund, as if the ponce had started wearing a Robin Hood hat. Whereas *The Morning After Optimism* was about the unmasking of the image of a romantic pastoral Ireland, *The Blue Macushla* unmasks the image of Americanisation which replaced it. In order to see the image clearly, we need some element of reality from which to view it. That reality is present in the play in the form of Eddie's opening monologue, but it is not present linguistically, which means that the play's central device is somewhat neutered. Nevertheless *The Blue Macushla* remains a remarkable combination of the ingenious and the scathing, a playful excursion into the deadly serious world of terrorism and its hold over respectable society in the Republic in the 1970s.

If *The Patriot Game* and *The Blue Macushla* struggle with the legacy of romantic Irish nationalism to contemporary Ireland, figures from the sacred writings of the great nationalist Patrick Pearse, leader of the 1916 Rising, also lend their names to the unmerciful burlesque of the Irish historical success story which is *The J. Arthur Maginnis Story*. Pearse's visions of beautiful boyhood, Iosagan and Eoineen na nEin, (Little Jesus and Little Eoin of the Birds) turn up as J. Arthur's sons, Iosagan and Eoineen na nOl (Little Jesus, son of Arthur, who is more commonly known in the play as Jaysus, and Little Eoin of the Drink). The send-up is one of many jokes at the expense of romantic Ireland in a play which is intended as a light-hearted romp but which nevertheless furthers Murphy's attack on the success story of the Sixties.

Though set at various times, such as "a typical Thursday in 1759" or "five to twelve in the early eighteenth century", it constitutes a madcap reflection on the social mobility of the Sixties. As the narrator of the travelling show which it presents announces: "And we're here to tell you the story of the trials, tragedies and triumphs of the fighting Maginnisses! Yes, a rags-to-riches story, folks, of one family's rise from the humble beerage to the mighty peerage." The reference is, of course, to the Guinness family and their fortunes, but the story of the play is one of peasants being transformed into nouveaux riches. We meet the Maginnisses huddled around a turf-fire, their costumes adjusted "to suggest peasant beginnings", barefoot, cold and hungry. What was enacted as tragedy in *Famine* is here re-enacted as not so much comedy as burlesque. Arthur is a humble wart-remover until he is visited by the Angel Seamus and told to brew the perfect pint, and the whole world of folk tradition and superstition is sent-up, with Seamus being the "seventh son of a seventh son" and the formula for Maginnis being found in an attempt to apply a traditional folk cure to a scald on Iosagan's flesh. The tale of the Maginnises is a parody of the struggle against constant misfortune of Irish history and the keeping alive of the old faith, as they carry on brewing dreadful beer which no one wants year after year until they find the right formula. As they begin to rise in the world, (their success in selling 572 pints of Maginnis in a year leads to their first great advertising slogan: "572 Paddies can't be wrong") Malady Maginnis, Arthur's wife is spurred by social pretensions: "When are they ever going to leave off this dust-rising, clod-hopping and stick-in-the-mud-comeallyeh singing? Not the thing at all for people rising in the world! (Sings) This is my lovely day . . ."

On the way to social standing, the Maginnisses remain priest- ridden with the lascivious Fr. Mathews Rose, the "great Cork-Irish coonic", based on the temperance preacher Fr. Matthew, attempting to close them down and their son Dan Wan seducing the sexy nun Elvira, intertwining the story of Don Juan (whose wife is also Elvira) in the increasingly chaotic action. The parody of Irish lamentation continues, with Eoineen na nOl apparently succumbing to the drink, and his mother mourning over him:

"Aaa, late have I loved thee, Eoineen na nOleen Maginnis, mo stor, mo treasure, mo first-born, mo little peata of a drunken punster! Aaaa, phy-phy-phy did ye die-die-die?"

When Arthur feels the lash of the clergy, Synge's *Riders to the Sea* is heard in mocking echo: "There was nothing more the Holy See could do to him now." Old Arthur, lamenting the deaths of Malady and Eoineen weeps "the craytures were buried on the same wet day, in the wan single cold grave. and in the one small coffineen. Aaa, they were hard times and ...", causing Iosagan to interject: "It was a fine day, it was a nice grave, and there were two coffins." *The J. Arthur Maginnis Story* mocks the sentimental mush which Irish historical woes had become, marking again the deterioration of the nationalist tradition and its appeal.

The play was originally conceived as a vehicle for The Dubliners folk group, who had acted in Brendan Behan's cabaret play *Richard's Cork Leg*, and it experiments with cliché, stock characters, songs, and, above all melodrama, in a way which makes it the precursor of *The Blue Macushla* in Murphy's work. In spite of its determined zaniness and its self-consciously awful jokes, it is not entirely separated from the main body of his plays. For J. Arthur Maginnis is a clownish version of Dada from *A Whistle in the Dark*, an outrageous patriarch who lives to 140, dominates his sons, is much given to sentimentality and refuses to give anyone else in the family credit for anything they do, claiming it all for himself. The refusal of this bullying patriarch to die is an ominous image of the failure of social mobility and success to kill off the ogre of the past that was Dada. The re-appearance of such a figure in a Murphy play of 1976 symbolises the end of any hopes there might have been in his work that the Sixties revolution might change the world in any real way for his characters.

The Patriot Game, The Informer, and *The Blue Macushla* collectively give a picture of the disintegration of nationalism and its adoption of new Americanised, bastardised forms. All three plays, however, deal with the birth and decline of an ideology in forms which are outside of the traditional Irish ones. *The Patriot Game* is conceived as a television play, *The Informer* is a theatrical version of a pulp detective novel, and *The Blue Macushla* is consciously based on American gangster movies. But could the process of Americanisation be dealt with in more traditional Irish stage forms?

In his first play after the return to Ireland in 1970, Murphy attempted to do so. *The White House*, staged at the Abbey in 1972, consists of two halves, the first (subtitled *Conversations on a Homecoming*) set in the present, and the second (*Speeches of Farewell*) in 1963, at the time of the death of John F. Kennedy, on whom the central character JJ Kilkelly models himself. The attempt was not entirely successful, however, and even after the order of the two halves of the play was reversed, it remained unsatisfactory. It was not until the play was re-written for a production by Druid Theatre Company in Galway in 1985, under the title *Conversations on a Homecoming,* with the first half, *Speeches of Farewell* subsumed into its structure, that its full power emerged.

At first glance, the play is very traditional indeed. With a detailed naturalistic set, a run-down public house, a "normal" indoor space of the sort not used in any of Murphy's plays since *The Orphans,* it seems to present us with one single world, jettisoning the ironies implicit in the juxtaposition of the two halves of *The White House* which were set a decade apart. But in fact, *Conversations on a*

Homecoming uses a naturalistic base to construct a sense of time out of joint. In *The White House*, the past and the present were apprehended seperately, invoking an overall irony at the end of the play in the contrast between one and the other. In *Conversations on a Homecoming*, the past and the present are on stage simultaneously, gnawing away at each other, making the ironies constant and infinitely more effective in dramatic terms. Real drama comes about when there is more than one world present on stage at the same time, and in *Conversations on a Homecoming* there is a world of hopes, aspirations and memories and a world of real disillusionment.

The signal that the times are out of joint is an almost sub liminal one. The passing of time as the friends gather in *The White House* pub to mark the arrival home of one of their number, Michael, from America, and then drink themselves into the night, is marked, not by the chiming of one clock, but by the chiming of two. As each hour passes, first the town clock sounds, and then the church clock, a few minutes later. This can of course be explained in perfectly naturalistic terms as a point of realistic detail, but it gradually creates the sense that one time period has been imposed on another and that the two do not quite fit. There is a gap between one world, the world of the past and JJ Kilkelly and the hopes of a generation, and another, the world of the Seventies and the broken dreams of a generation. In that gap lives the pain of disappointment.

While these two clocks measure the disjointed passage of time, the clock on the wall of The White House stays permanently stopped. It is all that is left of the past for Tom, the schoolteacher who was meant to go on and be a great writer, Michael, who should have been a great actor, but is clearly a failure in America, Junior, who is still, as his name suggests, the boy of the company, and Peggy who has invested much of her life in Tom without reaping the reward of marriage. On the wall is a dusty picture of John F Kennedy. JJ, who behaved like Kennedy, is off in another pub in the middle of a drinking binge. The White House which was meant to be "our refuge, our wellsprings of hope and aspiration," is a space defiled. When it was built, as Michael remembers, "This was all one room. Remember, Tom, one of your socialist ideas to JJ. We were all very impressed: that there should be no public bar, no divisions or class distinctions." But this image of the egalitarianism of the Sixties, has become, in the early Seventies in which the play is set, a symbol of division. A crude partition runs down one side of the set, dividing the White House into a public bar and a lounge area in which the action takes place. It is the work of Liam, the modern gombeen man who is set to inherit the place.

Liam is the true spawn of JJ's Kennedy-style idealism, even though he has nothing but contempt for JJ himself. For the naive adoption of American notions in the Sixties has benefitted no one but Liam, the mean little businessman who is being set up by Mrs Kilkelly to marry her daughter Anne — said to resemble JJ — and so inherit The White House. Liam is described by Tom as "Mr Successful-swinging-Ireland-in-the-Seventies" and he sums up the legacy of the previous decade. He is "a farmer, an estate agent, a travel agent, he owns property". He speaks with a "slight American accent." His adoption of American mannerisms goes hand-in-hand with a rabid nationalism, based on his belief that, as he tells Michael, "Property-wise, this country, A-one, Mick. This country, Mick, last refuge in Europe." He is prepared to fight for the northern nationalists, at least while he is in a pub, and talks of "A minority Catholic group being oppressed" and "Brave Irish Catholic men and women". He is entirely unaware of any possible contradiction between his own Americanised image and the traditions of Ireland, believing in "racial memory" and an ideal nation of Faith and Truth:

"And Truth and Faith and Faith and Truth inex-inextricably bound. And — And! — culture heritage

— you may not have heard of it — No border, boy! And cultural heritage inex-inextricably bound with our Faith and Hope and Hope and Faith and Truth! And some of us, and some of us, at least, cherish and — cherish and — and — are not supercilious, boy, with it — about it. Fella. I will not forget it! Last refuge in Europe."

In spite of his wealth he is insecure about money, needing to insist constantly on how well he is doing. And, like Eddie's father in *The Blue Macushla* he is still tied to a small farm, to the nineteenth century land hunger of the post-Famine Irish, clinging to the land above all else. Tom jeers him:

"This eejit, this bollocks, with his auctioneering and tax-collecting, and travel agenting and property dealing and general greedy unprincipled poncing, and Sunday night dancing — and he's still — Jesus! — still — Jesus! — watching the few acres of bog at home, still — Jesus! — caught up in the few acres of bog around the house at home."

Liam, the modern man of the 1970s has not advanced from the intellectual and emotional starvation of the nineteenth century. The Famine continues.

Liam's personal adoption of American mannerisms is widened in the play to take in the influence of Americanisation in general. Peggy says she is "in the running" for a job at a tourist office "they're hopefully going to open ... here next year. — Isn't that right, Liam? (a smile at Liam) ... if I know the right people." Later Michael tells Mrs Kilkelly that what she should do to improve business in the pub is to "get in a few of the natives telling funny stories for the tourists, and singing. And when things get going, you could move out with the family and live in the henhouse for the season." Like the Saint Patrick's Day parade in *The Blue Macushla*, Irish culture is coming to be defined for the Americans. Instead of producing a new flowering of intellect and culture, as JJ hoped in the early days, the Sixties has produced only a country and western culture. "What did the Sixties represent?" asks Tom, and answers his own question:

"...despite us representatives of the rising cultural minorities, aforementioned, what is going on now, this minute, below in Paddy Joe Daly's? 'Put th' fuckin' blanket on the ground'."

Tom sees this new provincialism as having built itself into a complete ideology: "the country-and-western system itself".

"Unyielding, uncompromising, in its drive for total sentimentality. A sentimentality I say that would have us all an unholy herd of Sierra Sues, sad-eyed inquisitors, sentimental Nazis, fascists, sectarianists, black-and-blue shirted nationalists, with spurs a'-jinglin', all ridin' down the trail to Oranmore."

Liam is so oblivious to this rhetorical attack, that, when he gets the opportunity to sing, his song is the cowboy anthem "There's a bridle hanging on the wall" There's a saddle in a lonely stall/You ask me why my teardrops fall" It's that bridle hanging on the wall . . ." One of the great dramatic strengths of the play, however, is that this easy adoption of American images, is caught in the undertow of Michael's edgy presence. Michael has been living in America, supposedly at the heart of American culture, the movie business. He is meant to be the paragon of the success of the American dream, proof of its vitality as a holy grail for the Irish ("Someone" says Tom "has to be doing well, and we're all delighted, we are, we are, we really are.") He enters like the archetypical returned yank: "Gee! Gee! Lots of changes round here." But his memories are too insistent, his answers about what he is doing in America too evasive. When he tells a story about a man at a party who takes off his clothes, jumps on the table, shouts, "No! No! This isn't it at all! This kind of — life — isn't it at all," it is clear that the man is himself. The revelation is allowed to pass until much later in the evening when Tom, under attack from Michael for his failure to fulfill his promise as a writer, slips in a killer punch from the blind side: "Would you ... take me from my great vocation and send me off to be setting myself on fire in the great adventure of the New World."

Michael has clearly come home not as the conquering hero but as a broken man in search of sanctuary. Instead of setting the world on fire, he has set himself on fire, and the pun provides a disturbing counter-image to Liam's glorification of things American. Michael's homecoming is an attempt to capture something of the hope of the early years. At first he tries to bring JJ back to life by intoning the Kennedy speeches which he used to deliver. Then, his fingers grasp more and more determinedly at Anne, JJ's daughter in whom, he convinces himself, he sees her father. He begins a courtship of Anne, showing an interest which she reciprocates, and asking her out for a walk the following day.

Michael and Tom are a typical Murphy couple, the one full of illusion and questing, the other full of disillusion and destructiveness. Michael still wants to see The White House as a refuge; Tom is determined that there should be no refuge for anyone. In the course of the evening, Tom attacks every member of the company, exposing their illusions to scorn and truth. He relentlessly demolishes Michael's belief in the myth of JJ:

"He hopped up on that load of American straw and he had so little going for him that when that load of straw went up in smoke, JJ went up with it ... He had so little going for him and we are such a ridiculous race that even our choice of assumed images is quite arbitrary."

In attacking JJ, Tom also attacks Michael's homecoming dream, for he paints JJ as a man who, at the beginning of the Sixties, limped home from an unhappy time in England and constructed for himself and others a fantasy image of success and liberation, just as Michael, at the beginning of the Seventies, has now limped home from America in a vain attempt to re-establish the same fantasy. And Michael is not the only victim of Tom's fierce drive to strip away false hopes. He attacks the inoffensive Junior with the reality of his situation, the fact that his father will not leave him the garage in which he has worked all his adult life: "One of the young bruthers will have that." He taunts Liam with his failure to secure for himself the few acres of bog that constitute the coveted patrimony: "Because your attempts, and the details of your attempts, and the details of the failure of your attempts to upset them and evict them off the nine-and-a-half acre O'Brady estate are widely discussed and reported upon, in this town." And he attacks and insults Peggy, whose hopes and dreams are entirely bound up in him, literally banishing her to the exterior darkness outside the pub.

Tom takes the role of the teller of unpalatable truths and in the process reveals himself as still bound up in the tyrannies of small-town gossip. Since John Joe's great revelation of everybody's business at the end of *Conversations on a Homecoming*, nothing has changed: John Joe's hopes for an end to material and spiritual poverty have not come to pass in spite of all the radical transformations of a dynamic decade. For what Tom reveals about himself and about the others is that they still belong to the category of over-grown children who inhabited Murphy's earlier plays. The dominance of the father in *A Whistle in the Dark*, of the Mother in *A Crucial Week*, have still not been broken. Michael has had to get money from his mother's post office savings to spend around the town in the accustomed manner of the returned yank; Junior is slaving away in his father's garage which he will never inherit; Liam, in spite of his material success, is psychologically tied to the piece of land that represents his family and ancestors, and is, according to Junior, unable to get married because he still lives at home with his mother and sisters and "couldn't go bringing a woman into the house where there's three of them already". And what is more, Tom himself, the great revealer of other people's illusions and dependencies, belongs most emphatically to the same category. His prolonged and sterile courtship of Peggy, which has failed to emerge into marriage, is a stark image in the play of the failure to achieve adulthood.

Tom is still in thrall to his parents, with whom he lives: "My mother, Jack, for Christ's sake, and my father, Jack, for Christ's sake . . . I can assure you they're both still alive." Liam, under attack from Tom, counter-attacks with the question "Why don't you get married?" and provides an answer himself: "Afraid of his Mammy and Daddy. And, d'ye know, he has to hand over his paypacket to his Mammy intact, every week, into her hand." Tom denies the details of Liam's allegation — he is, he says, paid monthly and by cheque — but in the process effectively confirms their substance. What is significant is not only that these adults in their thirties are still dependent, but that, particularly in the case of Junior and of Tom, this dependence is economic. Junior is tied to his father's garage by the fact that he works there. Tom is unable to marry Peggy because he cannot afford to do so, having handed his wages over to his parents. In this way, the dependence of some of the play's characters on borrowed images of identity and selfhood is linked to economic dependence, mirroring the way in which the Sixties' process of Americanisation had its roots in a new economic dependence on American multinational capital.

The play's images of dependence, of prolonged childhood, of the failure to develop adult relationships, are social and political as well as personal. When Mrs. Kilkelly repreatedly refers to the group as "boys", she is providing a reminder of the state of stunted growth which is both individual to these people and general to their country. In this light, the attempts by both Michael and Tom to establish relationships with women are attempts to push at the boundaries of their confinement, to become whole and adult. But each attempt is infected with the despair that grows in the gap between illusion and reality. Just as

JJ hangs over their failures in other areas, so his absence from the White House on the night of the play, the resigned concern mirrored on the faces of his wife and daughter, provides an overhanging image of the failure of the relationship between men and women. Anne's exit near the start of the play, when she is clearly going out to look for her father, instils the sense of an unhappy home, an incomplete family, and a failed marriage into the play, and it hangs there like a pall of stale cigarette smoke imbuing the action with a faint but acrid tang.

Peggy's yearning for a home with Tom is set within this context of palpable failure. Her and Tom's attempt to emerge into adulthood through marriage is contaminated by the failure of those who have gone before, the sins of the father-figures visited on those who are still sons. Michael's yearning for Anne is, on the other hand, not so much an attempt to emerge into adulthood as a continuation of his search for the mythical promise of the past. For what he sees in Anne is not so much herself as JJ in a youthful female form, a focus for his diffuse and confused love of JJ's memory: "Its not a jiggy-jiggy job. JJ's daughter. A walk in the wood, a breath of fresh air."

This is why, in the end, Tom colludes in warning Michael off Anne by reminding him that she is Liam's territory. Tom knows that Liam will take over the White House through Anne and that he will sell it off, breaking at last its residual reminder of the sanctuary it was supposed to be, making illusions such as Michael's impossible. Tom wants to end the power of the past to haunt him, even if that means recognising the fact that Liam is now in control. Michael recognises that his dream of an idyll with Anne is merely the vain attempt to resuscitate a dead past, and in that recognition all hope of finding a sanctuary to come home to is gone. He has no alternative but to leave again.

Michael and Tom are referred to as twins and as the two who together might make up one decent man, but in *Conversations* there is not, as there is in, say, *The Gigli*

Concert or *The Morning After Optimism*, a symbolic absorption of one by the other in order to create one character with the possibility of wholeness. This is because, in a play which reflects Irish life and politics so directly, such a leap into a comic resolution of the tensions of the play would be untrue to reality. Whereas in Murphy's last Tuam-based play *A Crucial Week in the Life of a Grocer's Assistant*, a comic resolution is possible because Ireland, at the time in which the play is written, is on the brink of an apparent transformation, by the time of *Conversations on a Homecoming*, that supposed transformation has taken place and has proved a failure. The play is full of the sense of the right-wing Catholic backlash of the Eighties in Ireland from Tom's memory of the priest's warning to JJ— "We, the poor conservatives — troglodytes, if you will — have seen these little phases come and go. All we have to do is wait." — which has now proved to be bitterly true, to his later reference to the "current swing to the right of the majorities, and the crusades of the christian fundamentalist majorities, promoting mediaeval notions of morality and reality, begod — ". In such a context, it would be a lie to have Michael and Tom emerging into a new and triumphant consciousness, banishing Liam and all his Americanised ways. Michael has not found the home he was looking for. Tom is stuck in a home that is not his own, with only a very dubious chance of finding some happiness with Peggy.

But yet there are counter-images to this dose of relentless realism, and both of them are, unusually, female. In a play which is concerned with an overwhelmingly male world, and which takes the form of one of the great Irish male institutions, the drinking session, female images of hope can work in a quite significant way. If it would be a lie for a sudden image of hope to emerge from the ordinary — male — world of the play, it is not the same for an image of hope from the peripheral, underground world — a female world — that is on its fringes. The images which provide this counter-current of hope come from Anne and from Peggy, not from either of them as characters in the predominatly naturalistic level of the play, but from their passage into the realm of pure symbol. For one thing, Anne is never developed as a character and is therefore allowed to continue as a symbol of a new generation, of youth and of hope. In her, JJ's nonsensical mimicry of Kennedy's rhetoric of how "the torch has been passed to a new generation" is, in a typical Murphy reversal, given some kind of muted meaning, for she it is who holds the stage at the end of the play when all of the rancour and rambling has passed, "smiling her gentle hope out at the night".

A more direct image of hope is provided by Peggy. From early in the play, she is urged to sing, with Junior making attempts to get *All in the April Evening* going, and she herself doing a deliberately off-key version of the song. But after she is banished to the darkness by Tom's insults, she sings the song seriously, creating a moment of stillness and beauty, of simple and true expressiveness, at the heart of the play. At the time in which she sings, she is deliberately placed outside of the lounge, in the doorway, giving her song the force of an intervention from the outside, a deus ex machina providing a glimpse of a more benign and harmonious world than the present one. Typically, the language of the song is religious, representing not a pious aspiration to Christian salvation, but a shift into a metaphor of human redemption and the transcendence of the present. In a play which is characterised by a constant flow of talk, orders, interruptions, shouts, arguments, Peggy's song represents a standing still of time, a momentary escape from the mocking chimes of the two clocks which mark the passage of the play. In these two images of Anne and Peggy, the play reaches beyond the present towards the possibility of another life. And significantly, both of the images are entirely non-literary, depending on the pure theatricality of performance, using the distinctive characteristic of the theatre which is its alchemical power to transform leaden reality into an elusive glint of gold.

These images of another realm of possibility leave *Conversations on a Homecoming* as perfectly poised between despair and hope as it is between social realism and a kind of secular spirituality. Within the conventions of something that looks like naturalism, Murphy gives us a world that is not unlike the hellish God-forsaken room of Sartre's *Huis Clos,* with JJ functioning as the God who has abandoned the mortals whom he created. But Murphy moves beyond that existential absurdity too. The cramped space of *The Orphans*, to which, as stated, earlier *Conversations* has obvious links, is made, not large but deep, avoiding the claustraphobia of absurdity. Figuratively, we are in a bar room for the entire play, but imaginatively the space acquires three layers of meaning. It is a shambolic pub in Tuam. It is a bathetic version of Kennedy's Camelot/White House. And it is a poor man's Purgatory, where God in the broken-down shape of JJ will not show his face, where Michael avoids the fires of Hell with which he tried to burn himself in New York, and where Tom lives out his long, suspended adolescence. That these layers of metaphorical space co-exist so coherently and without strain or heavy-handedness is a mark of how superbly developed Murphy's gift for theatrical compression had become.

And yet, all of this was achieved without losing out on directness and social realism. The extent to which *The White House* and *Conversations on a Homecoming* touched the raw nerve of social change in Ireland by illuminating the fact that the king's new clothes were a cowboy suit was clear from the reaction which the plays provoked. When *The White House* was screened by RTE television in 1977, it met a response which was the modern equivalent of the riots which greeted *The Playboy of the Western World* and *The Plough and the Stars*. It was the occasion for a resolution condemning "the recent permisive trend in RTE programmes" which received the unanimous support of Midleton Urban Council, and for a resolution protesting against the "scandalous filth of RTE programmes" passed unanimously by Youghal Urban Council. Tipperary North Riding County Council unanimously condemned *The White House* as "scurrilous and filthy" and one of its councillors called for the sacking of those involved in putting it on the air. The West Donegal executive of Fine Gael, the country's second largest political party, condemned the play as a "blasphemy" and as "a gross insult to Christian principles". In Cashel, it was condemned both at Catholic masses and by Protestant clergy. Cork County Council regarded the play as "obscene" and "absolutely disgraceful" and an editorial in *The Cork Examiner* attacked the play. The illusions about Ireland which the play attacked persisted to the extent that the play itself was regarded as a gross distortion of Irish reality.

It is clear, then, that in his most directly political plays, from *The Patriot Game* in 1966 to *The White House* and *Conversations on a Homecoming* in the Seventies and Eighties, Murphy has charted the dissolution of an ideology which, in a sense, explained and unified the world in which he grew up, and the replacement of that ideology with a set of acquired mannerisms which were no more than a desperate attempt to accomodate the old ways to the new world. This process of dissolution forms a sort of subtext for Murphy's greatest plays. In a world in which shared beliefs and values, and even the common public language, are patched-up and without conviction, it is hardly surprising that Murphy seeks truth through the outsiders, through those who are most firmly excluded from that public language of ideas and values. This is not to say that Murphy's major works are determined by or confined to the reflection of Irish reality, merely to say that the immediate form of the universal breakdown of public language, of shared beliefs and values in the western world in this century, is, for Murphy, found in the contemporary history of Ireland. What has happened in Ireland, particularly in Ireland since 1959, gives a shape and a force to Murphy's exploration of a loss of meaning which is felt throughout the western theatre. But the sharpness of Murphy's relationship with contemporary Ireland also means that that sense of meaninglessness is not made abstract and absurd. In the extent to which he is open to the historical process of change lies the key to Murphy's achievement in moving beyond absurdity to a new sense of meaning.

VII

Beyond Tragedy

In 1970, the International Commission on the Use of English in the Liturgy, a working group established by the Bishops of the English-speaking world to adapt the rites and sacraments of the Catholic Church to the demands of Vatican 2 that all services should be conducted in the vernacular language, met in Dublin. While there, some members of the commission went to the Abbey Theatre where they saw Tom Murphy's *A Crucial Week in the Life of a Grocer's Assistant*. They were so impressed that one of their number contacted Murphy to say that he felt he could make a great contribution to their work if he were willing to join them. It was not, ordinarily, an invitation which he would have felt inclined to take up, but at that moment it struck him as something that might hold out hope. He was tired of his own bitterness at the repressiveness of a Catholic upbringing, weary of all the late night recollections of educational atrocity that are so much a part of Irish conversation. He was willing to try to confront Catholicism constructively, holding out "a naive hope of salvation." In agreeing to involve himself in this way in the workings of the Church, he was also taking a hand in one of the great influences on the modernisation of Irish society, for Vatican 2 was, along with television, the greatest cultural force in the changes in Irish life which followed the economic revolution.

In this way, he was immersing himself not only in his own Catholic past of childhood religion, but in the present and future of Irish life. For any writer to be so involved in the creation of a new language for Catholicism was extraordinary, but for Murphy, whose work had been already so imbued with Catholic language, it could not but have a profound effect. He told Father Jack Shea, who had invited him to join the Commission that he was not a Catholic and that he would not wish his Catholic background on anyone. He was invited to be an observer at the Commission's next meeting, at which he said that "God" was now "a dirty word" and should be replaced in prayers with "Father." He was, nevertheless, invited to become one of the Commission's ten clerical and two lay members. At meetings in Rome, Washington and Toronto, he helped to shape the prayers which millions of Catholics around the world utter every day. He sat under a lapis lazuli dome in Rome and argued that the Church should not bamboozle its faithful with words and sounds that were closer to riddles than to prayers. He put forward the suggestion that "Dust thou art and unto dust thou shalt return" should be changed to "Remember, man, you will return to dust."

He immersed himself in the language of religion. But it did nothing to bring back the faith of his childhood. He felt as he had felt in the classroom at Mountbellew before he had resigned, that he was shaping things for others which he did not himself believe. He found that there was no salvation in the church. Having failed to transform the old religion to his satisfaction, he went on imaginatively to try to create a new one.

At the same time as this experience, there occured in Tuam what he remembered as a "holocaust of death." In 1972, for no apparent reason, the death rate in Tuam rose to twice the national average. People died in road accidents, of diseases, of old age. Church View, the street where he was born and raised, seemed to suffer particularly badly, becoming "a street of widows." Three of his own uncles died. So did one of his brothers-in-law, aged 32. One of his closest friends was killed in a car accident.

He remembered seeing a woman kissing the corpse of a loved one and saying to the dead man "I'm sorry." This combination of death and guilt, along with the failure of his hopes for some kind of religious salvation, sent him into a deep depression. But it also contributed to the making of *The Sanctuary Lamp*, a play which plunges into death and guilt and religion and seeks to exorcise them.

The play took shape from two immediate and random impressions, one of the voice of Jack Doyle, the boxer and singer ("the man who boxed like John McCormack") who was Ireland's most glamorous man when Murphy was a child, but who was close to being a down-and-out when Murphy met him in The Hoop pub in Notting Hill in the late Sixties. Doyle's slightly military and upper-class British affectations of voice, his faded celebrity propped up by assumed images of dignity, stayed in Murphy's mind and became a part of Harry, the central character of *The Sanctuary Lamp*. The second impression was of hearing Father Patrick Peyton, the international Rosary crusader, telling of how, when he went to America as a young man he got a job sweeping up in a church, and every night before he locked up he would peep in to say goodnight to the sanctuary lamp, the symbol of the presence of God which burns constantly in every Catholic church. The image reminded Murphy of a childhood memory of locking the hens up in their coop for the night, and singing to them to comfort them. The thought "It was man who lit that lamp, not the Church" is the core of *The Sanctuary Lamp*.

These two images triggered the opening of the play in which Harry arrives at a church and gets a job sweeping up, with duties that include the tending of the sanctuary lamp. They began to make concrete the images of death, guilt and religion which had been in Murphy's mind. But even more important in shaping the play was Murphy's reading of the *Oresteia* of Aeschylus, a renewal of his engagement with the tragic consciousness of the Greeks. *The Sanctuary Lamp* is more directly engaged with the

Greek drama than any of Murphy's other plays, asking many of the same questions about God and man. It is an attempt to travel through tragedy and to emerge beyond it, bringing a Christian sense of redemption to the Greek sense of desolation.

"So how are you going to get forgiveness from that lot? Have you ever thought who's going to forgive them? Who's going to forgive the gods?" Francisco's mocking question to Maudie in *The Sanctuary Lamp* is a question that has been with the theatre from the start. Greek theatre may have started out as a religious ritual, but it came to be a statement of the inadequacy of the gods to man's needs. Tragedy, for the boldest of the Greeks, Euripides, is the realisation that man has outgrown the gods, that human anguish is no longer contained within the bounds of their moral imperatives. In Euripides' *Hippolytus* tragedy reaches its height when a man, an innocent man dying a cruel death because of the wilfullness and stupidity of the gods, forgives the goddess Artemis for what has happened to him. It is a vision of man as morally greater than the gods but it is a vision also which is of very little use to man. The gods may be blind and irrational, but they still control the universe. Hippolytus may forgive them, but the world is still absurd. Murphy's Francisco is not so quick to forgive the gods. He prefers to beat them at their own game.

The vision of absurdity implicit in Greek tragedy is one which has returned in the twentieth century theatre. Much of modern European theatre, in the wake of Auschwitz, takes as its starting point a sense of the uselessness of God, bringing the theatre back into the same oppositional relationship to religion which it had at the time of the Greeks. In Beckett, Genet, Ionesco or Pinter, it is a sense of man's relationship to God, or rather the lack of any such relationship, which animates the drama. As Ionesco put it, in an essay on Kafka, "Absurd is that which is devoid of purpose . . . Cut off from his religious, metaphysical and transcendental roots, man is

lost; all his actions become senseless, absurd, useless."
Man is lost because he can no longer trust God. It is a new
version of the Greeks' tragic vision. Just as in *Antigone*,
Creon comes to see man as an unwelcome stranger in this
world, so Camus, in our century, defines man as "a
stranger" in a universe without God's guiding hand. "His
is an irremediable exile, because he is deprived of
memories of a lost homeland as much as he lacks the hope
of a promised land to come." Tom Murphy shares many of
the basic preconceptions of both the Greek tragedians and
of the modern absurdists, and the roots of *The Sanctuary
Lamp* lie in a poem (one of very few he has written) in
which he laments the loss of God from his world:

> *Where are the angry mountains,*
> *The winds that whispered with revengeful solace,*
> *Long ago in Catholic childhood,*
> *When I could quench my pain*
> *In the burning fires of Hell,*
> *When fear was food to my existence,*
> *Was mystery and was meaning to my soul?*

But his theatre pushes towards a transcendence of
tragedy, and searches for that which Camus believed to be
impossible — the hope of a promised land to come. By the
power of theatrical alchemy, he transmutes the tragic into
the apocalyptic.

Murphy's plays take place in a universe which should be
tragic. They combine the Euripidean sense of a world in
which God still exists, but only as an absentee landlord
playing poker with the fruits of humanity's labours, and
the absurdist notion of man as a stranger in the world. In
The Orphans humanity finds itself in a nightmarish limbo
in which God has been replaced by a new deity, technology,
which is even more inscrutible and wilful in its operations.
In *The Sanctuary Lamp* Francisco asks "God made the
world, right? ... What has he done since?" In *The Gigli
Concert* JPW reckons that God has "cut your losses on this

little utopia of greed and carnage some time ago." In
Bailegangaire, man is a flaw in God's creation, an anomaly
which God is too careless to put right. God stays in his
Heaven and all is wrong with the world.

The way all of this is expressed and made concrete in the
plays is through the image of the family, and in particular
of the disintegration of the family, the dismemberment of
blood relations implicit in the metaphor of the orphan. The
plays are full of literal and metaphorical orphans, the
characters being either the children of dead parents or the
spawn of a dead God. Roddy and Kate in *The Orphans*,
Dolly and Mary in *Bailegangaire*, Anastasia, James and
Edmund in *The Morning After Optimism*, Maudie in *The
Sanctuary Lamp*, are all orphans, while nowhere in
Murphy's work are there happy families. His families are
broken by violence, loss, cruelty, by the inability of men
and women to cross the divide of the sexes. With this image
of the dismembered family so deeply rooted in his work,
and with the intention of writing a play about the
relationship of God to man which might go beyond the
tragic and the absurd, it was natural that Murphy should
look to the *Oresteia*.

There are three things about the *Oresteia* which make
its story dovetail with the one that Murphy had to tell. In
the first place, it uses, as he does, the image of a family
torn apart, the doomed House of Atreus in which father
kills daughter, wife kills husband, and son kills mother, as
the embodiment of the terrible turmoil in the relationship
of man and God. Secondly the *Oresteia* is unique in that it
is the only surviving trilogy by a Greek tragedian, and the
trilogy contains tragedy while going beyond it. The first
two parts of the *Oresteia*, *Agamemnon* and *Choephori* are
tragic, but the third, *Eumenides*, ends in reconciliation and
forgiveness. It is therefore an example of a vision which
does not overlook the tragic absurdity, but which sees a
way beyond it. And thirdly, the *Oresteia* is a shape which
includes within itself theology, psychology and politics. It

finds a way to bring together the intimate world of sons, daughters, mothers and fathers, with the great world of the state and of God's relationship to man. In all of these things, the *Oresteia* coincides with Murphy's theatrical concerns. He uses its shape and reaches after its monumental scale of achievement, but he does not merely follow its story.

For one thing, the religious world which Murphy is confronting is not that of the Greeks but that of the Irish and universal Catholic church. Murphy builds the imagery of Catholicism into the play. It is set in a church, and the first figure we encounter with Harry is an elderly priest, the Monsignor, a clearly disillusioned man, more interested in reading Herman Hesse than in tending to his clerical duties. Harry himself, as we discover, is an English Jew, possibly, because of his exaggerated assumption of English mannerisms, of foreign origin, but he has sought sanctuary on Catholic territory. We learn that he is fleeing from his entanglement with Francisco and Olga, tricksters in the same circus in which he has worked as a strong-man. Olga, Harry's wife, has left him for Francisco, and Harry has abandoned the pair of them with a performing dwarf, Sam. This trio Harry later calls "a right Holy Family — A right-looking Holy Family." The window of the church at the back of the set depicts the Holy Family, setting Jesus, Mary and Joseph against the family of a foul-mouthed juggler, his contortionist assistant and a performing dwarf, blasphemously identifying one with the other. The sacred has been reduced to the profane; there is no God left, only man. Underlining this use of Catholic imagery is the fact that in the first half of the play bread is eaten and in the second wine is drunk, counterpointing it ironically with the holiest sacrament of the church. Similarly, the last scene takes place mostly inside a confessional that has been laid on its side, making it a skewed version of the sacrament of Penance in which forgiveness is granted to the sinner.

Imbued as it is with the language and imagery of Catholicism, though, *The Sanctuary Lamp* takes much of its theatrical shape from a re-arrangement of the *Oresteia*. That re-arrangement is crucial. For while the Greek trilogy starts with the horror and moves slowly to the reconciliation, Murphy incorporates the three stages of the trilogy within the last part, the play of reconciliation, *Eumenides*. This not only allows Murphy to use the story without being imprisoned by its structure, it also stakes out the theatrical terrain as being the search for hope, reconciliation and forgiveness through the overcoming of tragedy.

It is the setting which identifies the opening of *The Sanctuary Lamp* with *Eumenides*, for *Eumenides* is set in a "church," the Temple of Apollo at Delphi, from where the scene changes to the shrine of Athene, another "church" which is also, very specifically, a sanctuary. In *Eumenides*, Orestes has sought shelter in the shrine, having been driven mad by the Furies who pursue him there. Harry, like Orestes, has sought sanctuary at the shrine, and like him is pursued by Furies. Harry's furies are internal, the grief and guilt of the death of his daughter Teresa and the pain of his desertion by Olga. In *Eumenides* the first character to appear is the priestess of the shrine, the Pythia, who lights the brazier which guards the inner shrine. In *The Sanctuary Lamp*, Harry's first encounter is with the Monsignor, who tells him to tend to the sanctuary lamp.

Having placed the action in the final play of the Greek trilogy, *The Sanctuary Lamp* then moves back to the world of Agamemnon and Choephori, the tragic world. In Scene Two, which corresponds generally to Agamemnon, Harry addresses the lamp, and identifies himself as a man who, like Agamemnon, has had his wife taken from him by another man (Francisco). And, as *Agamemnon* has lost his daughter Iphigenia, he has lost Teresa.

"You know Francisco? Juggler actually. Well, he was my friend, I took him in. Then he usurped, sneaked my wife. And now he lives — my greatest friend! — quite openly with her. And we had brought a child into the world ..."

In this address to the lamp he also takes on something of the air of the Watchman whose speech opens *Agamemnon*. The Watchman, waiting for the light of the beacon, tells how his songs to keep himself awake through the night vigil has turned to weeping, because of the curse on the House of Atreus. Harry, too, keeps vigil before the lamp, making a bargain with it: "Supposing in exchange for the accommodation I engage to make good conversation — break the back of the night for you? Alleviate the holy loneliness."

The play uses these Greek parallels, but it does not use them in a crude, static way. Harry is identified in this part of the play largely with Agamemnon, but he is also the weary watchman and the haunted Orestes. And the heroic parallels are undercut — the modern equivalent of Agamemnon's warrior-king, possessor of superhuman strength and performer of great deeds is a circus strong-man. Harry the strong-man, Francisco the juggler, Olga the contortionist, Sam the performing dwarf, are all performers of extraordinary actions, heroes and champions in their own way, but, in an unheroic world, these marks of the extraordinary and the superhuman place them outside of society as freakish vagabonds, little better than beggars. In this, Murphy manages to imbue them with a great richness: they are at once heroic and outcast, superhuman and on the fringes of human society. Nor, of course, are the parallels static, since they change as the play moves through the three phases of the trilogy.

In his long speech to the lamp, Harry is the father haunted by guilt at the death of his daughter and the husband bereft at the unfaithfulness of his wife. He has not, like Agamemnon, killed his daughter himself, but he is pursued by guilt nevertheless and prays for forgetfulness:

"Help me to forget! You who rule the heavens and the earth, stretch forth your mighty arms therefore: help me to forget."

But in the course of the speech he moves from being the guilty father and wronged husband to being the Avenger, Orestes, who, in the *Oresteia* kills Clytemnestra and her lover Aegisthus in revenge for their murder of Agamemnon. Harry's attempts at revenge, however, have been pitiful. He thought of killing them with his penknife, but stopped because "I do not want to be like them, I believe in life!" Instead, he waited until their next engagement as a performing troupe and left them in the lurch. "And to punish them, I walked away. Well, sloped actually, to let them down ... I sloped away!" This awareness of the inadequacy of his retaliation stings him into becoming again Orestes the Avenger. He prays "Oh Lord of Death, I cannot forget! Oh Lord of Death, don't let me forget! Oh Lord of Death, stretch forth your mighty arms, therefore! Stir, move, rouse yourself to strengthen me and I'll punish them properly this time!"

This marks the movement of the play into the second part of the trilogy, the *Choephori*, for this prayer to the Lord of Death is the opening line of that play, spoken by Orestes — "Hermes, Lord of Death, Be with me now" — and repeated by both Electra and the Chorus later. After he utters this prayer, Harry hears a creak and thinks it may be Francisco. Again the avenger, he takes his penknife, thanks the lamp for, as he thinks, answering his prayer, and moves off to stalk his prey. It is not, however, Francisco he has heard, but Maudie.

Maudie, a sixteen year-old girl who has run away from her grandparents and home, brings Harry back from the thoughts of revenge to his earlier search for forgiveness and forgetfulness. An abandoned child, she has been haunted by visions of what she believes is her dead mother, first frightening her, then, according to her grandmother, granting her forgiveness. Maudie, like Harry, is haunted by the guilt of death, but she believes that Jesus can give "forgiveness." She identifies with the baby Jesus ("I like him best"), while Harry identifes with Joseph, the lost father in whom no one had any real interest ("I've always felt he must have been a bit lonely."). In this, Harry metaphorically adopts Maudie, caring for her as a substitute for his own lost child. When she gets cold, he places a priest's vestment around her, making her an image of the power of religion reduced to a frightened, vulnerable child. This matches Harry's vision of Jesus, whom he sees as a much reduced figure:

"A veritable giant of a man, if you want my opinion, but between one thing and another, his sense is gone a little dim. And who would blame him? Locked up here at night, reclining — y'know? — reflecting his former glory".

Later he takes up this image again, when Maudie asks him whether Jesus sits on a throne: "No, more like a wheelchair, if he's sitting on anything ... " In this, Harry is constructing an image of Jesus which reflects his own position. He, too, is "locked up here at night," crippled and dimly reflecting his former glory. For Harry is a strong-man who has lost his strength. He has tested his strength against the pulpit, trying to lift it, and has failed. Rather than God making man in His own image, Harry makes a God who conforms to his own weakness and decrepitude. It is the first step in the making of a new, human, religion towards which the play builds.

Maudie's adoption by Harry is made possible by the fact that she, too, is a performer, a member of the family of outcast show-offs. She tells Harry of her proficiency at climbing lamp-posts, putting on a show for the other children in her street:

"Sometimes I would climb even higher than the light. I would catch the iron thing on top and pull myself up over the top, and sit there in the night. And sometimes, if I waited up there long enough, everything made sense."

The performer in Harry recognises this experience and is a little jealous of it. For he, too, is looking to make sense of things through performance, to lift the pulpit as a symbol of his return to manhood.

Harry is an Orestes figure, but he is a mixture between two images of Orestes from Greek drama, the Orestes of *Choephori*, impelled to a dark deed of violent revenge, and the Orestes of Euripides' *Orestes* and *Iphigenia in Tauris* who has, as Gilbert Murray puts it, "the shadow of madness and guilt hanging over" him and who describes himself as having "ranged a homeless world, hunted by shapes of pain." Harry is pulled between his desire for violent revenge, his compulsion to kill Francisco and Olga, and his need to emerge from a state of homelessness and madness, to have his guilt forgiven.

He is both literally and metaphorically homeless. The arrival back into the church of the Monsignor, who catches Harry still there and lets him know that he has found out that Harry is in flight from his home, reminds us of his literal homelessness. But he is also a man not at home in the world. The world, for Murphy's people, is a hostile place, an inclement environment. Happiness, the easy accommodation with the world, can only be bought at the price of soullessness, for, as Harry says, "You never feel your soul when you're happy." Harry is tormented by the madness of the Furies, but these Furies are siren voices luring him to flight from the world. He says of madness that "I don't mind telling you I keep it as a standby in case all else fails." But it is a standby he resists, as he continues his search for a home in a homeless world.

Harry's real test will come in his confrontation with Francisco, who enters at the end of the first act and opens the second with a long speech on religion. Francisco is the

Aegisthus whom Harry must kill, the usurper who has stolen his wife. But the prey is stalking the hunter. Instead of Harry pursuing Francisco, he has fled from him, and Francisco, prepared to dice with death, living on the edge of self-destruction, comes to meet Harry's promise of revenge. For Francisco is the character in the play who carries the burden of religion on his shoulders. He is clearly the play's only Irish character: Harry being an English Jew, and Maudie with her speech mannerisms of "Do you know?" and "were" (as in "I knew she were dead") is also English and non-Catholic. So Francisco is an Irishman in exile, carrying with him the twisted passions of a Catholic upbringing, closer to God in his obsessive rejection of him than is the Monsignor in his resigned cynicism.

Francisco is at war with God and with the Jesuits who have educated him. In order to escape their attempt to pre-determine his life ("Give me a child until he is seven they say, and then you can have him back! If there's one thing my life disproves it's that.") he has made his life an unpredictable walk along the edge of danger and destruction. He has become a preacher against God, answering his own question as to what God has done since he created the world: "Evaporated himself. When they painted his toenails and turned him into a church he lost his ambition, gave up learning, stagnated for a while, then gave up even that, said fuck it, forget it, and became a vague pain in his own and everyone else's arse."

Having taken Harry's wife, Francisco tries to seduce his "adopted" daughter, Maudie, attempting to lure her back to the house which he and Harry and Olga had shared. As Harry returns, and the act progresses, Francisco's attempt to win Maudie's allegiance round to his side becomes a re-enactment of his usurpation of Harry's place with Olga.

This stings Harry back into the role of Orestes the Avenger. He begins to threaten Francisco with the penknife, but settles instead for punching him, sending him sprawling and then flattening him. He accuses

Francisco of believing in nothing — "and when you have nothing and you believe in nothing, you have nothing at all." — unlike himself — "I always believed in things." The fight is between the believer and the unbeliever, the seeker after forgiveness and the seer of a blasphemous vision of salvation. Harry believes because he does not know the truth, the message which Francisco has brought and which he holds in reserve, that Olga is dead.

Before Francisco tells Harry of Olga's death, he tells him of the "last engagement" of himself, Olga and Sam, the one which Harry walked out of in order to punish them. Francisco subtitles this story, which takes up much of this section of the play "is there not always a kind of melancholy attaching to the glory we attain in this world?" This question is the one which is asked so insistently and so often by Aeschylus and the Greek tragedians. The story of the *Oresteia* is about the retribution of Nemesis on unrighteous prosperity. Deeply imbedded in the myth is the notion that prosperity — Agamemnon's victory at Troy — brings with it the fall, because prosperity is a temptation to wickedness. Francisco's story of the last engagement admits this notion in the context of the unrighteous prosperity of the new Ireland of the time the play is written.

For Francisco's story brings the world of the nouveau riche into the play. The engagement, he says, is to "sow the seeds of merriment at the mansion of a mighty man who writes only for the most important papers and who even has his own television show." This mansion of the mighty is also a den of corruption full of Wedgewood furniture, and "VSOP ten year-old Napoleon Bonapartes." He does not tell this story in ordinary conversation, but declaims it from the pulpit, where he has gone to escape Harry's threats. He has become a preacher, scathing of the unrighteous prosperity of the world:

"But the patterns of man's sins will be the pattern of his punishment. See the depraved ones, who so loved their own pleasures, now bathing in black, hot, bubbling pitch and reeking sulphur! See the gluttonous pigs, now parched and hungry!"

Olga's death has been at the hands of this unrighteousness, and Francisco implicates Harry in it, because he did nothing to save her:

"Know what I mean, Har? The ones who didn't lift a finger — but who now claim they know better ... There was no one but myself to kiss away the tears of that poor, unhappy, lost, unfaithful wife."

This forced recognition that he too, bears guilt, though he does not yet fully understand for what, gives Harry back his lost strength. He rushes at the pulpit and lifts it, with Francisco inside. Like Orestes in *Choephori*, he has performed his great, heroic deed. But like Orestes, he is not free. He is pursued still by guilt and madness. He will not be free until the Furies have been banished.

The final section of the story, *Eumenides*, now takes over. The play is moving from the tragedy of death into the possibility of reconciliation and forgiveness. *Eumenides* breaks the cycle of tragedy by moving beyond the blind exposure of man to the will of the Gods. It is, in effect, a play about the foundation of a new *religisn*, a religion of man, whose justice is greater than that of the Gods. And the foundation of this new religion is also the foundation of a new political order, in which moral justice prevails over the dark forces of violence. This is precisely what happens in the last section of *The Sanctuary Lamp*. In *Eumenides*, the Furies try to wreak vengeance on Orestes for his killing of Clytemnestra and Aegisthus, but Apollo intervenes to save him and the matter is referred to Athena, goddess of the city, who entrusts it to the judgement of the citizens. Apollo on the one side, and the Furies on the other plead their respective cases. This is a clash between an old religion, that of the Furies, and a new one, that of Apollo,

whom the Furies revile as one of "the younger gods," the
religion which is seeking to succeed them. Aeschylus'
Furies are the survivors of dark irrational forces, the
ancestral ghosts and spirits of the dead. To banish them is
to banish death, and Francisco, *The Sanctuary Lamp's*
Apollo, seeks to cast out the Furies and exorcise the spirit
of death which has hung over the play.

The Furies of this part of the play are the priests of the
Catholic church. Furies are the creatures of night and
darkness and Francisco describes priests in the same way:
"Those coonics! They're like black candles, not giving, but
each one drawing a little more light out of the world."
Furies are black-cloaked and ugly and Francisco uses the
same imagery for the priests:

"Black on the outside but, underneath, their bodies
swathed in bandages — bandages steeped in ointments,
preservatives and holy oils! — Half mummified torsos
like great thick bandaged pricks!"

He then makes the identification explicit: "these
violence-mongering furies." And he paints the priest/furies
as they are seen in *Eumenides*. Apollo ordering the Furies
out of his shrine, identifies them with violence and
bloodlust:

"This house is no right place for such as you to cling upon;

But where, by judgement given, heads are lopped

And eyes gouged out, throats cut, where the sex of

Young boys is crushed or cut away, where mutilation

Lives, and stoning, and the long moan of tortured men

Spiked underneath the spine and stuck on stakes."

Francisco uses the same image of bloodletting and
torture for the priests:

"Founded in blood, continued in blood, inquisitioned in
blood, divided in blood ... Peace, Ecumenism? — I doze,
father, I doze! They cannot agree among themselves on the
first three words of the Our Father. Get the police in! Get
heavy mounted police in with heavy mounted batons and

disperse them, rout them, get them back from the round tables before they start the third and final world war we've all been dreading!"

Francisco builds into this "old religion" all of the forces of death in the world, broadening the individual deaths of Olga and Teresa, and of Maudie's dead son Stephen, into the entire nightmare of history from which Murphy's people are trying to awake.

The link is made through the story of the last engagement, where the humiliation which precipitates the death of Olga from an overdose is, according to Francisco, Christianity in action. In the story, the performance of Francisco, Olga and Sam for the assembled guests turns to a rout after Olga is "had" "half way on-and-off the Sir Basil Wedgewood kitchen table" by a friend of the host's who is then discovered in flagrante by his wife. In the row which follows, Francisco, Olga and Sam are ignominiously ejected from the party and their money pushed out the letterbox after them. This banishment into the exterior darkness, Francisco associates with Christianity, turning on its head the Christian promise of salvation.

And so, Francisco, in founding his new religion and proclaiming it from the pulpit, reverses the Christian order of salvation and damnation. He propounds the vision that is at the heart of Murphy's theatre, the vision of salvation coming only to those who are disaffected with the world as it is:

"I have a dream, I have a dream! The day is coming, the second coming, the final judgement, the not too distant future, before that simple light of man: when Jesus, Man, total Man, will call to his side the goats — 'Come ye blessed!' Yea, call to his side all those rakish, dissolute, suicidal, fornicating goats, taken in adultery and what-have-you. And proclaim to the coonics, blush for shame, you blackguards, be off with you, you wretches, depart from me ye accursed complicated affliction! And that, my dear brother and sister, is my dream, my hope, my vision and my belief."

Francisco's new religion is one which banishes God in the second coming of man. It is a vision which moves beyond the tragic to the apocalyptic, sweeping away the world of absurdity and suffering and proclaiming the resurrection of mankind. It is essentially a vision of human utopia.

This resurrection of mankind brings back to life all of the dead who have haunted the play. Harry and Francisco elaborate their visions of an afterlife in which the pain of the world is healed. Harry, who now finally accepts that Olga is dead, has earlier in the play imagined himself and Teresa, his daughter, together.

"In silhouette — that's it, that's it, in silhouette. Little girl and a man, standing black on the edge of the world, the edge of it all, looking out at all the sad, slow-moving mists of time and space."

He now elaborates this vision into an image of the reunification of the broken family:

"The soul — y'know? — like a silhouette. And when you die it moves out into ... slow-moving mists of space and time ... Loved ones. That's it. And one is implanted on the other. And the merging — y'know? Merging? — merging of the silhouettes is true union. Union forever of the loved ones actually."

The dismembered family which provided the image of man's plight in a godless, homeless world is made whole again. The House of Atreus is exorcised of its curse.

The fruit of a family made whole is in children, and in this apocalyptic ending, the children are also restored and resurrected. Harry has been haunted by his dead child, Teresa. He has been tormented by memories of her nestling under his jersey "like a little bird." He has danced as she danced out of her cot towards him one morning. Maudie has remembered how in hospital a nun had told her that her baby Stephen was dead. She cannot stop thinking of him. Now, Maudie says that "You don't get children back. They're gone. You get other ones." Francisco's vision of the afterlife, however, is of Limbo, of a place where babies could be happy without the fear of God:

"Imagine, the only snag to Limbo was that you never got to see the face of God. Imagine that. Now, what baby, I ask you, gives a burp about the face of God. No, the only thing that babies feared was the hand of God, that could hold your little baby body in his fist, before dipping you into the red hot coals of hell. Oh but Limbo, Har, Limbo! With just enough light rain to keep the place lush green, the sunshine and red flowers, and the thousands and thousands of other fat babies sitting under the trees, gurgling and laughing and eating bananas."

The pain of death has been banished, replaced, for Francisco, by the "pain of not having died" before he was baptised, thus being deprived of the passport to Limbo.

In the last moments of the play, the quests with which it began are completed. Maudie has looked for forgiveness, the existence of which Francisco has denied, but Francisco himself is forgiven by Harry, who blesses him. Harry has looked for forgetfulness, which at the end has been granted to Francisco also: "Oh my God I am heartily sorry for having offended thee and I ... See? I can't remember. I've beaten them." Each of the three characters has been unable to sleep: Harry remembers being awake with the dying Teresa, and has stayed awake with the sanctuary lamp; Francisco says that he "can't sleep sometimes because I can't stop thinking"; Maudie's sleep has been haunted by dreamings. So their final state in the play, with all three falling asleep in the confessional is a further image of the healing of their minds and souls. At the end, too, Harry and Francisco are re-united as ego and alter ego. Harry has told Francisco that "Without me you are nothing," and now Francisco tells Harry that "We'll go together, right?"

As a version of the *Oresteia, The Sanctuary Lamp* does what no other twentieth century version of the play manages to do. Since there are three other major attempts to re-tell the story in the modern theatre, Murphy's relationship to the others helps to place him as an international modern dramatist. Each of these has dramatised a strand of the entire story. Eugene O'Neill's *Mourning Becomes Electra* follows faithfully the structure of the trilogy, but it replaces gods and heroes with the sub-conscious, following through a fatalistic Freudianism to its logical conclusion. O'Neill achieves neither the final resolution of the *Oresteia* in which tragedy is transcended, nor the sense of the religious which is central to the story. We are left with a play which draws sustenance from the narrative thrust of the Greek original while bringing out only one element — the psychological — of its sweeping synthesis.

Jean-Paul Sartre in *The Flies* also uses the story of the *Oresteia*, along with its basic characters, making of it a political and moral allegory, with Orestes emerging as the authentic existential man in times of war and crisis. Sartre does not so much get beyond tragedy as argue his way around it. For him, the religious or anti-religious question of man's relationship to the gods does not really exist at all, which makes the final reconciliation impossible, again failing to achieve the full sweep of the *Oresteia*.

The third attempt at a use of the story, T. S. Eliot's in *Murder in the Cathedral*, which is an oblique version of Agamemnon, and The *Family Reunion*, which has echoes of *Choephori*, comes nowhere near a full engagement with it, since Eliot's bleak Christianity is far removed from the tragic vision. Eliot does not even attempt a *Eumenides*, a reconciliation of the warring forces, since such a reconciliation lies for him in the hands of God.

Murphy's is therefore the only modern version of the *Oresteia* which, without in any way being a prisoner of the original, includes its political, psychological, and religious themes, and, more importantly, achieves the same reconciliation of the three which Aeschylus does. This makes *The Sanctuary Lamp* a European play of considerable importance.

The least obvious of these achievements is the political one. The story of the *Oresteia* tells of the founding of a new political order, the discovery of the "springs of justice in the world." This new politics is founded on a new religion which banishes the blood-letting of the old. Although it is by no means a primarily Irish play, belonging instead to the broader western tradition, *The Sanctuary Lamp* reaches for the same apocalyptic sweep in relation to Irish politics and society. For it attacks both the ascendancy of the new middle-class, and the old religion which supports it. Francisco's assault on the "depraved ones," made specific in the story of their last engagement, is reminiscent of the assaults of the Biblical prophets on those in power, and of John the Baptist's denunciation of the decadence of Herod's court which heralds the arrival of the Messiah and the new religion. Francisco is indeed a John the Baptist, for he heralds his own Jesus — "Jesus, Man, total Man" — along with the sweeping away of the old order, just as Harry is also a Biblical Samson, shorn of his power but rising again to shake the pillars of the unrighteous. And Francisco's vision is followed by the final image of utopia, of the perfect kingdom which is the goal of all messianic movements. This desire to sweep away the order of things is political in the broadest sense, and it has a specific resonance in relation to the Irish society of Murphy's times.

For politics in the theatre is no mere matter of political statement or reference. The problem of politics is the problem of how to change the world. That the material conditions for such change exist is clear. What is not present is a belief in the possibility of change. Political action therefore requires an imaginative commitment to the possibility of transformation in the world. The theatre, no matter how overtly political, cannot provide images of this transformation of the world unless it presents us with more than one world on the stage, bringing into collision things as they are with things as they might be. This is what *The Sanctuary Lamp* does. It presents the anguish of man's estate in the world, his abandonment by God, his homelessness on earth, with all of the bleakness that tragedy can muster. But it brings that bleakness into collision with a visionary sweeping away of the world as it is, an apocalypse which is followed by the Kingdom of Man on earth.

Francisco's vision of the salvation of the goats rather than the sheep, Harry's statement that "You never feel your soul when you're happy" are counsels to despair, but it is a despair which is the precondition for changing the world. Unless the world as it is, is despaired of, it can never be changed. Unhappiness in Murphy is the state which gives access to knowledge about the world and the possibility of leaping into some new wholeness.

In this, *The Sanctuary Lamp* and *The Gigli Concert* are not unrelated to Catholic mysticism, which, after St. John of the Cross, postulates the necessity of unhappiness before a greater state of grace can be achieved. In the three stages of mystical purification, the Dark Night of the Senses, the Dark Night of the Spirit, and the Dark Night of the Soul, the soul on its way to purification is deprived of all physical gratification, of all spiritual consolation and finally even of faith itself. It loses its love of the world, its intellectual light, and its love of self, but emerges closer to God in the end. Francisco mocks at this process: "Die to self? I doze, father, I doze!" But Harry's trials do bear some resemblance to mystical purification. The difference, of course, is that whereas the Catholic mystic emerges with a renewed faith, in *The Sanctuary Lamp* the old faith is abandoned altogether. Murphy uses some of the shape and the language of Catholicism, but only to invert them.

The theatrical focus of this subversion of reality and its replacement by a new reality is Harry's attempts to lift the pulpit. Running through *The Sanctuary Lamp*, and keeping it together even through its most complex and dangerous moments, is the simple movie melodrama of the strong-man who has lost his strength through sadness. Rooted in the Biblical story of Samson (and, along with Francisco's guise as John the Baptist, acting to keep the play firmly on the terrain of religious imagery) Harry's story is also reminiscent of a children's tale in its outward sentimental simplicity, making him, as it does, the sad giant (Franscisco refers to him as "the tardy-footed giant") whose power has left him because of a broken heart. This also makes his eventual rush at the pulpit in which he lifts it and Francisco from the ground, into something from the impossible world of the fairy tale or the Biblical story, where the chains of reality are broken and a greater truth takes its place. Harry's lifting of the pulpit is a transformation of the world before our eyes. It prepares the way for the full-scale assault on the city of reality which was to come in *The Gigli Concert*.

Before the 1985 Abbey Theatre production of *The Sanctuary Lamp*, Murphy made substantial revisions to the text, particularly to the opening section of the play. These revisions resulted in the dropping of three scenes which come before the first meeting of Harry and the Monsignor in the church in the original version: a silent scene of Harry dancing Teresa's dance, which is incorporated into the revised text later on in the play, a scene of Harry singing and begging for money; and a scene in which a trendy young priest gives a crass sermon on the Biblical story of Mary's visit to Elizabeth who has become pregnₐnt in spite of her advanced age, to the accompaniment of furious heckling from Franscisco. While the image of the child leaping in Elizabeth's womb from the Biblical reading in this latter scene is one which fits well with the imagery of the play, the revisions make the play more compact, strengthening its correspondence to the Oresteia, and also remove the dated topicality of the trendy priest, broadening the range of the play's attack beyond the specific banality of one priest or one period. In this, immediate "relevance" is lost and the play's politics are considerably strengthened. For Murphy was now making plays which are images of transformation rather than mere reflections of reality.

VIII

Apocalypse Now

Politics and magic might seem to be irreconcilable opposites, the one concerned with shaping and changing the everyday world, the other with escaping from it into a realm of mysticism and mystification. Politics is above all rationale; magic seems irrational. And yet political change itself is not entirely a rational phenomenon, for the idea of changing the world implies the ability at least to imagine a different world, one which operates according to different laws. Tom Murphy's plays are full of the tragedy of rational men. According to the way he understands the world, Dada in *A Whistle in the Dark* behaves rationally and logically, even though, because we understand the world differently, we see his behaviour as grotesque. John Connor in *Famine* is not just rational but moral, for he does what he believes to be right in the world as he knows it. Yet he is doomed and his actions appear wilful and blind. Writing in a period of change, when one world-view has all but superceded another, Murphy has been keenly aware that reason is in the eye of the beholder. In his plays there is no use in simply understanding the world, when the world is wrong.

And this is where magic comes in. Magic, as the anthropologist Bronislaw Malinowski has argued, is to be expected and generally found when man comes to an unbridgeable gap, a hiatus in his knowledge or in his powers of practical control, and yet has to continue in his pursuit. "It ritualises man's optimism." When the limits of the known world are as tight and as oppressive as they are in Murphy's plays of the Sixties, and when the consequence of being bound by those limits is tragedy, the recourse to magic is a theatrical ritualisation of optimism. *The Gigli Concert*, a play whose central character is a magician and whose theatrical achievement is nothing less than making the impossible happen on stage, is about changing the world by escaping from what seems like the iron grip of necessity.

Magic, however, is of no use unless it is brought into a direct collision with reality. The great age of magic was the period of the breakdown of the old, fixed order of the universe, when astrology, alchemy and natural magic sat side by side with science and with radical politics in the ferment of ideas which broke down the hierarchical notion of the world in the sixteenth and seventeenth centuries. As the historian Christopher Hill has pointed out "Side by side with Protestantism, the cult of magic, so popular in the sixteenth and early seventeenth centuries had also offered man, through mastery of the secrets of nature, liberation from the consequences of the Fall ... (Francis) Bacon extracted from the magical-alchemical tradition the novel idea that men could help themselves — mankind, not merely favoured individuals."

A wonderfully downbeat vision of alchemy at work for the dispossessed is contained in Murphy's novel *The Seduction of Morality*. Finbar Reilly, a disreputable man living in the disreputable New Estate of a 1970s Irish town, makes a living of sorts by selling holy medals. He discovers a scam whereby he can make cheap tin medals look like good quality metal, the old alchemists' trick of turning base metal into gold, by using solder and vinegar. The high black arts of alchemy and the philosopher's stone are turned into a characteristic mix of low comedy and spiritual quest:

"He dipped the medal in flux, to promote the fusion, yeh see. Where's me grease gone, he says. Dab of grease from the sprocket-wheel of the bike onto the face of the medal.

209

Et cum spiritu tuo! Now, lo, he baptises the medal in molten solder, dips it, one, two, three times... What's this, he says? Lo, two small black dots appearing in the stone, appearing to come from the surface of the stone."

Just as magic contributed to the overthrow of the feudal order, so it constituted a threat to the stability of the new bourgeois world. "Stable laws of nature" says Hill "went with a stable society. Now that God was located within every human heart, it was inconvenient to have him intervening in the day-to-day running of the universe. Both popular magic and Catholic magic upset the ordered cosmos". The form in which this tension between magic and the ordered society of bourgeois civilisation has entered European culture is in the legend of Faust. *The Gigli Concert* is a version of the Faust story, one which again brings magic into a dangerous and destabilising contact with reality.

Because it uses magic in this dangerous and powerful way, rather than as mere escapism, *The Gigli Concert* is brutal and direct in establishing just what reality is. The play is set in the office of JPW King, an adherent to the cult of "dynamatology" whose leaders sent him to Dublin and have left him there, abandoned and forgotten. As a peculiar kind of church, JPW's office is a theatrical space analagous to the church of *The Sanctuary Lamp* or the forest of *The Morning After Optimism*, half real, half a place in which anything could happen, in which dreams or nightmares can be tested against reality. But once the second protagonist of the play, The Irishman, enters, he brings with him a crisp and clearly defined view of what the outside world is like.

The Irishman is the archetypal Irish business success of the Sixties, a builder and property developer. He could be Harry from *A Whistle in the Dark* twenty years on, having made enough money in England to stake himself for the boom times in Ireland and ridden the Sixties fantasy all the way to two million pounds in the bank, or the builder in *The Blue Macushla* who confesses to a party of politicians and bankers that he murdered his business partner. He describes himself as "a self-made man" and he is unflinching about the rules which govern the society outside of JPW's office:

"There's too many facts in the world. Them houses were built out of facts: corruption, brutality, backhanding, front-handing, lump labour and a bit of technology."

And while he has made his money, the ultimate outsiders of twenty years before, then called "tinkers" in *A Whistle in the Dark*, now refined to "itinerants," have continued to exist and to haunt him. The new Irish middle-class of the Sixties and Seventies was stricken with the terror of returning to the poverty and ignominy from which it arose, and the Irishman feels himself persecuted by the travelling people who have camped on his land. He tells JPW of how he went out to kill them:

"So, I decided I'd deal with the itinerants. The place is a shithouse, it's everywhere. Why did they choose me. Hmm? And I know the doorsteps where it belongs. The disrespect, to choose me, camp beside my territory, and the fuckers in this country. So. Went out. To kill them. But someone — the wife! — had called the police and they stopped me. Would've killed them otherwise."

In this fear and disgust, the Irishman is the typical middle-class self-made man of the Sixties. And to escape it, he has decided that he wants to sing like the Italian tenor Beniamino Gigli. He has picked on JPW to help him do it.

If the social and economic reality of the world outside is sharply defined, so too is its emotional landscape. It is the familiar Murphy territory of an idealised Family, and real, unhappy families, again a direct and distinct reflection of modern Ireland. JPW is wedded to the ideal of domestic bliss, holding to a comically absurd notion of family life, and obsessed with the typical Irish housewife Helen ("So we met. A hurried meeting. She had even forgotten to take her apron off which I glimpsed beneath her overcoat and which tugged strangely at my heart strings.") whom he phones at regular intervals. Although he obviously lives alone in disarray in his office, he tells the Irishman that he is married to "a saint":

"Irish colleen, apron, you know?, darns my socks, that kind of thing. I am very fond of her and she is very fond of chintz."

JPW is so blinded by this ideal that he does not realise until too late that he loves Mona, a woman whom he met in a supermarket and who visits him occasionally for sex. But beneath this picture of domestic bliss, the glimpses into the Irishman's family life are of a brutal and violent institution. The Irishman torments his wife and child, showering her with obscenities and burning the child's toys:

"The house is silent though there's a child in it. We were blessed with a late child. But I always managed to keep obscenities out of the house until lately. Now they're the only things that break the silence."

And the family of his childhood is yet more brutal:

"But my father, sick and then dying, and my eldest brother had took over, and he became a sort of tyrant ... Mick frightened us all. Shouting, kicking his bike ... And Danny was always trying to teach me — cunning, I think. Street sense. He used to tell me never trust anyone, and everything is based on hate. He used to tell me that when I got big, if I was ever in a fight with Mick, to watch out, that Mick would use a poker."

This is the vicious, tribal family of *A Whistle in the Dark* again. With this image of the family, and with the Irishman's understanding of the political economy of his time and place, *The Gigli Concert* is more directly reflective of social reality than almost any other Murphy play. And yet, it is also his most daring and most magical play, using this reflection of reality as a grounding for a leap beyond it. The fact that the world, twenty years on and in spite of all the changes, is still fundamentally as it was in *A Whistle in the Dark*, means that change must now be radical and complete, an utter transformation of the world.

The Gigli Concert establishes a highly specific reality only in order to sweep it away in a great apocalyptic gesture which has few parallels in the modern theatre. As the play progresses, JPW comes to share the Irishman's obsession with singing like Gigli, to focus on it all of his own reawakened striving for wholeness. He becomes a magician and he makes the magical leap of singing like Gigli. Appropriately, since in Murphy's plays the family is always the focus both of loss and of the search for health, his triumph is also a resurrection of the family. In his obsession with Helen, his symbol of the ideal family, he has refused to go home when his mother, believing that she is dying, called for him. At the end of the play, having shed his illusions about Helen, he, in turn, calls for his mother, believing that he, too, is dying. In this way, the magical leap which JPW makes is closely linked, even at its height, to the family which is the central embodiment of the world for Murphy. For all its philosophical and theological connotations, JPW's triumph in achieving the impossible remains the triumph of a very ordinary and recognisable humanity.

The play is, however, shaped both theatrically and philosophically, by a turning on its head of Christianity. It is, in a precise sense an anti-Christian play, for instead of attacking Christianity, it inverts it through its use of the myth of Faust. Both in form and content, it is intimately engaged with Christian tradition, but engaged in a way which overturns the language and the key concepts of Christianity. Not only is the shape and direction of its action counter to the movement of Christianity, but the entire aesthetic of the theatre which it implies is one which goes against the influence which Christianity has had on western thought and western theatre.

The play takes the Faust story but disrupts and destroys its traditional Christian meaning. The myth of Faust tells of striving, sin and damnation. Whether in the post-mediaeval morality of Christopher Marlowe's *Doctor Faustus* or in the cosmological forgiveness which ends Goethe's *Faust*, the story is meant to illustrate Christian concepts of salvation and damnation, and in doing so to fend off the dangerous heresy of magic. In Tom Murphy's work, however, damnation and salvation are not irreconcilable opposites. The former, rather, is a precondition to the latter. Only those who have been damned can be forgiven and saved, as James in *The Morning After Optimism*, or Gypo in *The Informer* are. In Murphy's inverted theology, spelt out most directly by Francisco in *The Sanctuary Lamp*, the damned, the goats, the outsiders, are the ones who will eventually be called to Paradise. The sheep will be banished to exterior darkness; the goats will see the face of God.

If salvation and damnation are thus identified with each other, as two parts of the one whole, then the approach to the Faust story which we might expect from Murphy cannot be the traditional one. He may, however, have found a key to the story in Carl Gustav Jung's *Memories, Dreams, Reflections,* which contains a gloss on the Faust myth that is very much in keeping with Murphy's way of thinking. Jung does with the protagonists of Faust, (Faust himself and Mephistopheles, the devil who is his familiar and tempter,) what Murphy does with salvation and damnation, making them not separate entities, but two parts of the one whole:

"Faust, the inept, purblind philosopher, encounters the dark side of his being, his sinister shadow, Mephistopheles, who in spite of his negating disposition, represents the true spirit of life as against the arid scholar who hovers on the brink of suicide."

Substitute JPW King for Faust and the Irishman for Mephistopheles in this interpretation of the myth, and you

214

have a precise description of what happens in the course of *The Gigli Concert*. JPW is an inept philosopher on the brink of suicide, a man whose ragbag of theories on the way the world works ("the rearrangement and redirection of the orbits and trajectories of dynamatological whirlings") has not kept him from the brink of breakdown, manifested in his obsessional phone-calls to Helen, his passionate drinking and his anxiety about getting through the day. The Irishman is dark and sinister, his Gigli-style hat giving him the immediate appearance of a movie gangster, his hand toying with what JPW thinks might be a gun in his pocket. But he does also ultimately represent the spirit of life, the real world "out there" from which JPW has been cut off in his arid domain. And as the play goes on it becomes clear that the two are indeed two sides of the one being.

An important point about Jung's version of the Faust story, an interpretation which Murphy almost certainly had in mind, is that it absolutely precludes a Christian version of the myth. For central to Jung's view is the belief that Mephistopheles, the representative of the devil, is ultimately a force for good, that his negations contain within themselves the necessary seed of new life. This is essentially the same vision that Francisco propounds from the pulpit, the vision of an apocalyptic beatitude being won through waywardness and despair. In Jung's interpretation, Faust and Mephistopheles are different sides of the one being, an idea which is dramatised in *The Gigli Concert* through the transference of aspiration and personality between the Irishman and JPW. The roots of this identification between the Man and JPW are laid down early in the play when the Man says "In the mornings I say Christ how am I going to get through today," echoing, in precisely the same words, one of the first things that JPW says on stage. With this identification, they are another of Murphy's typical couples, the two halves who together might make one whole man.

Mephistopheles, traditionally, is the lord of darkness, the destroyer of life. In Goethe's *Faust*, the version of the story which is most influential on *The Gigli Concert*, Mephistopheles characterises himself as "der Geist der stets verneint" — the spirit who always negates, the spirit of absolute destruction whose desire is that the entire world return to nothingness. This accords with the Christian vision of the story, seeing, as it does, the devil as the embodiment of all negativity, seeking to destroy God's creation. In Murphy's plays, however, it is the denizens of darkness who are to be saved, those who despair of the world as it is, who wish like Goethe's Mephistopheles to see it destroyed, who are to inherit the new kingdom of heaven on earth. Murphy must therefore go against Goethe, and against Christian thinking, and make Mephistopheles both the spirit of destruction and at the same time the vehicle for JPW's salvation. The Irishman in *The Gigli Concert* is thus a deeply ambivalent figure, full of hatred and self-loathing while filled with the aspiration "to sing".

If Murphy departs radically from Goethe and from Christian interpretation in his treatment of Mephistopheles, he does, however, use Goethe's *Faust* as a paradigm for *The Gigli Concert*. In this paradigm, JPW corresponds to Faust, the Man and the voice of Gigli to Mephistopheles and the devil, Helen and Mona to the two versions of Goethe's Helena. These identifications are clearly signalled in the text. JPW is twice referred to by Mona as "my magician" and "my magician friend." At the climax of the play, as he prepares for his leap into the unknown, he remembers "The soul! Of course!" He offers it first to heaven: "Rather not. You cut your losses on this little utopia of greed and carnage some time ago, my not so very clever friend." He then turns towards hell, speaking to the floor: "Assist please. In exchange — ".

This is his Faustian bargain. JPW's identification with Faust is completed in the same speech by his half-quotation from the "This night I'll conjure" speech from Marlowe's *Doctor Faustus*, a speech delivered by Faustus in the original: "This night I'll conjure. If man can bend a spoon with beady steadfast eye, I'll sing like Gigli or I'll die." The connection between the Irishman and Mephistopheles is made musically, when the man brings his record player to JPW's office and plays him an aria from Boito's *Mefistofele*. JPW looks at the record sleeve. "'Mefistofele': Ah yes, he is the devil."

Even more interesting, however, is the connection between both Helen, the object of JPW's unrequited love who appears only on the other end of a telephone line, and Mona, JPW's lover, and the two Helens of Goethe's *Faust*. Goethe makes Helen appear twice to Faust, in two different sections of his play. The first Helen, conjured up as an illusion in the imperial court, is a mere chimera, intangible and unattainable. The second, the real Helen of the Walpurgis Night episode, becomes Faust's lover and they have a child, Euphorion, together. Euphorion is a golden-voiced singer, like Gigli. He strives too high and is stricken down into the underworld, to which Helen follows him, leaving Faust behind. In *The Gigli Concert*, JPW, having sung like Gigli, uses Euphorion's words from the underworld: "Leave me here, in the gloomy Void/Mother, not thus alone," when he says "Mama! Mama! Don't leave me in this dark." But again, the Faustian parallel is upset. Whereas Goethe's Euphorion, having sung and striven, is banished to the underworld and the dark void, Murphy's JPW, having sung and striven, rises again from the fearful darkness, lets up the blind on his office window and lets in the early morning light. And while Euphorion's song is silenced, JPW ensures that Gigli will "sing on forever."

Both Helen and Mona in *The Gigli Concert* are identified with Goethe's two Helens. As she is leaving Faust forever, Goethe's real Helen says "Bliss and beauty ne'er enduringly unite." JPW's Helen, when she meets him in a carpark to say "You are a remarkable man and goodbye," tells him "Happiness and beauty are not meant to mate." In general, however, Helen here can be identified more with Goethe's false Helen. She, and the accompanying dream of domestic bliss with two children in a cottage with clematis around the door, is part of the illusory world which JPW must despair of before he is ready to take his great leap into the unknown.

It is Mona who is JPW's real Helen, as he realises during their last encounter. Like Faust's beloved Helen, she is about to go into the underworld of death, in her case from cancer. And just as Faust's Helen mourns her beloved child, Euphorion, before she leaves Faust forever, so Mona mourns her lost child just before she parts from JPW for good:

"I had a little boy when I was sixteen. They didn't mean to, but now I know they pressurised me. They wanted the father's name. I wouldn't give it. They needed it to have him adopted. I wouldn't give it. Still they had him adopted some way. Things hadn't gone right, complications, and I was very ill. I only saw him twice. He was so tiny. He's twenty-two now. Somewhere ."

The loss of these two Helens takes JPW from illusion, to disillusion, to despair. It also makes it possible for him to sing. His first attempt at singing, after the Man has abandoned him in his quest, results only in "a few pitiful howls." The phone rings and it is Helen. She tells him that he is no more than an obscene phone caller and we know that he has finally lost all hope of her. Immediately after this, Mona arrives and in the next scene tells him that she is dying of cancer. The action relentlessly deprives JPW of hope, plunging him into deep despair. At his next attempt, JPW sings like Gigli. This is the importance of Mona in the play, and her role is underlined by the Faustian parallel.

All of these links with the Faust story, and with Goethe's *Faust* in particular, make it possible to consider *The Gigli Concert* as a version of the Faust myth. As a blasphemous version of the story, one in which Mephistopheles is the bringer of salvation, it is also founded on an ontology and a dramaturgy which are both in direct contradiction to the philosophical tradition of New Testament Christianity. To say this is not to impose an external consideration on the play but merely to look closely at the ideas about Christian thought which are contained within the play itself.

In preparation for the task of singing like Gigli, JPW arms himself with stolen books. He constructs a philosophy which is, on the one hand, comic gibberish, and on the other a genuine statement of the preconditions of his attempt to achieve the impossible. JPW's ideas are funny, not because they are not in some sense true but because, without the actual despair of the world which is the only basis for his leap of the imagination, they are meaningless and arid. In the ideas, however, there are the seeds of the action. Instructing the Irishman on the supposed path to initiation, JPW tells him that:

"God taking his stroll in the Garden, as we are told, and passing by innocent Adam, he would nod, and say, I am who am ... Whatever can he mean, said Adam, I am who am? And he waited until the next time God came strolling by ... And he put the question to God. But God said, out! out! ... Which is a pity. Because the startling thing, God had got it wrong. Because what does it mean, I am who am? It means this is me and that is it. This is me and I am stuck with it. You see? Limiting. What God should have been saying, of course, was I am who may be. Which is a different thing, which makes sense — both for us and for God — which means I am the possible, or, if you prefer, I am the impossible."

The choice of the phrase "I am who am" from the Bible, and the suggestion that it might be changed, are not innocent. The phrase is central, not only to Christian theology, but also to the whole of western philosophy stemming from the Greeks. It occurs in the Old Testament, when God appears to Moses in the burning bush and tells him:

"I AM WHO AM. He said: Thus shalt thou say to the children of Israel: HE WHO IS hath sent me to you ... This is my name forever, and this is my memorial unto all generations."

For Catholics, the Douay Bible spells out clearly what is to be understood by this divine pronouncement: "I am who am: That is, I am being itself, eternal, self-existent, independent, infinite; without beginning, end or change." But this particular burning bush, in the standard Christian translations, speaks with a forked tongue. What God actually says to Moses is "Eh'je ascher eh 'je." and on the translation of the phrase hinge two different ways of looking at history, theology and dramaturgy. For the proper translation of the phrase is not as a statement of presence — I am who am — but as a conditional promise, either as "I will be what I will be" or, as JPW has it, as "I am who may be." The difference is that between a philosophy of eternal presence, an anti-historical understanding of truth as a once-off revelation, and a philosophy of hope, of transcendence, of the great leap into the future. It is this difference, JPWs shift from "I am who am" to "I am who may be" which underlines not only the metaphysical quest in The *Gigli Concert* but also its fundamental nature as a piece of theatre. The difference between *The Gigli Concert* and plays which remain within the dominant conventions of western theatre is encapsulated in JPW's attempt to shift the meaning of that Biblical phrase. It is what defines Tom Murphy as an apocalyptic writer.

Christian thinking is profoundly anti-apocalyptic. Its fundamental premise is that of an act of salvation — the crucifixion and death of Jesus Christ — which is located in the past and from which all hope and meaning continue to derive. In Christian thinking, there is one point in history at which everything that is really significant occurred, and that point is in the past. In this fundamental form, Christianity is in line with the Greek and Roman mythologies, where the past is represented as an everlasting foundation. The Catholic translator of the Douay Bible who had God defining himself as "without beginning, end or change" was profoundly influenced by classical thinking. Conventional Christian thinking is bound together with those elements of Greek thought which are oriented to a static, all-embracing notion of "being" and which are profoundly anti-historical in the sense of not being open to change and development. The inscription on the Temple of Apollo at Delphi reads " El " — Thou Art — summing up an idea of God as an eternal presence.

Fundamentally opposed to this conception of God as eternal presence is the Hebrew God who says "I will be what I will be." Yahweh appears before the people as a promise of the future, open-ended and eschatological. In Hebraic thought, which is the basis for the idea of magic, the idea of God is singularly undefined and unsensual compared to the detailed, tangible Gods of the Greeks and of the New Testament, because God is not yet fully formed and is still waiting to be invented. Time is not a chain of cause and effect but a path leading to a final end.

The opposition of these two systems of thought has profound implications for the theatre, implications which are central to *The Gigli Concert*. With a philosophy of eternal presences, based on an act of salvation located in the past, you get a certain kind of theatre, a theatre in which the climax comes when the essential nature of things is finally revealed. This is a theatre of epiphany and against it it is possible to set a theatre of the apocalypse, the theatre to which Murphy and in particular the Murphy of *The Gigli Concert* belongs.

By a theatre of the epiphany I mean essentially the "well-made" naturalistic play of the bourgeois theatre, a theatre in which there is only one world, a monistic and deterministic universe, within which the action is contained. In this theatre effect follows cause, we are concerned primarily with motivation, and the climax happens on the same plane as the rest of the action, revealing the truth which has been determined by the past. Even in overtly non-Christian plays of this type, the form of the thinking is, in this sense, Christian. The theatre of the "well-made" play is essentially about remembering the past.

Apocalyptic theatre, on the other hand, implies the presence on the stage of more than one world. In all of Murphy's mature plays there are two worlds on the stage: fairytale and reality in *The Morning After Optimism*; the nineteenth century and the twentieth in *Famine*; the humans and the presence of the lamp in *The Sanctuary Lamp*; the characters and the voice of Gigli in *The Gigli Concert;* the world of the story and the world of the present in *Bailegangaire*. And in these plays there is a leap from one world into another: the killing of the fantasy brother in *The Morning After Optimism;* Harry's lifting of the pulpit in *The Sanctuary Lamp*; JPW's singing like Gigli; and the resolution of the story in *Bailegangaire*. Whereas, in the theatre of the epiphany, the climax is brought about by the relentless accumulation of event and detail, in Murphy's apocalyptic theatre the climax is brought about by the stripping away of unnecessary detail, the loss of illusion, and the climax itself is a leap into a different plane of action from what has gone before.

Time in *The Gigli Concert* is not sequential — actions are not determined by what has gone before, by the past. In this respect the play's burlesque of Freudian psychology fits in with its upheaval of Christianity. Both Freudianism and Christianity are posited on an event in the past which determines the future, in the case of Christianity the Crucifixion, in the case of Freudianism a particular mental trauma. In *The Gigli Concert* Murphy has JPW indulging in a parody of psychoanlytic sexual probing. Mona advises JPW that the way to handle his "patient" is to "keep on talking" and "shock them — if you can." When he gets too

far beyond his depth with the Irishman, JPW takes her
advice: "Only sexual matters now or I shall not listen!"
JPW's own description of his first sexual encounter in
infants' school is a parody of the psychoanalystist's
attempts to probe the meaning of infantile sexuality:

"I distinctly — distinctly! — recall being slow to
withdraw my hand. Now, question is, was that cunning,
gallantry, or aberrative behaviour? You see the posers we
professionals have to grapple with?"

Because the past in the play is not an absolute
foundation for the future, memory plays a contrary role to
the one it plays in naturalistic theatre. The Irishman is not
governed by his memories, he invents them. His memories
are a kind of prophecy in reverse: by subsuming within
himself the memories of Gigli's childhood, he is trying to
invent a new self:

"Then suddenly everything was alright and I sauntered
back and forth with me parasol singing 'Passigiando un
anno fa'. I couldn't hardly believe my ears that all the cries
of 'Bis! Bis!' were really for me."

In the extraordinary language of these "memories,"
Murphy makes the Man's voice blend with Gigli's own, the
rough colloquial inflections of the West of Ireland blending
with the formalised, memorised language of the singer's
autobiography, giving us the painful sense of striving. The
man's memories are drawn from the future, from what he
wants to be, rather than from the past, what he has been.
Even when we do learn of what he has been, in the
shattering recollection of his brothers Mick and Danny,
these real memories are quickly buried and denied at the
start of the next scene:

"Listen, I'd just like you to know for one thing, boy, that
I had a very happy childhood. You'd like to suggest
otherwise, but I'm up to you." Just as the man's memories
of Gigli's childhood are a fabrication of the past, so he tries
to suggest that his memories of his own childhood are
equally a fabrication, invented by JPW. The past has value

only as an invention which suggests what the future will be.

Because the past is a fabrication, and the future has not yet occurred, the present in the play expands almost to infinity. It is, as JPW says, "the point of origin in the here-and-now where anything becomes possible." As all is stripped away, Gigli becomes the focus of this possibility. As they listen to his voice, Mona asks "What's he singing, what's he saying now?" and JPW replies "You don't have to know, whatever you like." Gigli becomes for them the point of origin at which everything is possible — "You and I are alive in Time at the same time." Everything tends towards an enriched moment of pure possibility. Gigli's meaning is whatever they want it to be — "That everything ends"; "that, at least, we end up friends"; "A baby. That's what it's all about." This, too, is part of the Faustian parallel, for, in Goethe's version, Faust is to continue living until he is so engrossed in the present moment that he begs it not to pass away.

What Murphy is reaching here is something that is at the very core of theatre itself. Theatre at its truest is not repeatable — it is of the moment, existing in a present enriched by the future in which, in the words of Peter Brook "each moment is lived more clearly and more tensely." The essence of the theatre is that it reaches moments in which there is an awareness that the actor and the audience are "alive in Time at the same time," and that this moment is one in which "anything becomes possible." The action of *The Gigli Concert* may take a philosophical form but its logic is essentially a theatrical one. It moves towards a daring moment in which the impossible becomes possible, not as an idea, but as an action on the stage.

This notion of time in *The Gigli Concert* may itself be strongly influenced by Jung, who held that events were linked not only in a causal sequence, but also by their simultaneous occurence ("You and I are alive in Time at the same time.") Jung's interest in "meaningful co-incidence" led him to postulate the existence of a principle of connection between things and events which was outside of cause and effect but just as important as it. This principle of "synchronicity" may have little scientific basis, but it is highly fruitful as a way of thinking about the theatre.   If Jung, as suggested earlier, may have provided the key to the Faust story for Murphy, it is clear that certain central Jungian concepts help to put a shape on Murphy's upheaval of that story and of Christianity itself.

Jung's psychology is animated by the notion of an ideal state of integration towards which the human being is striving. Jung saw his patients as suffering from one-sided development, and therefore in need of another half in order to create the synthesis of an integrated personality, exactly the synthesis which Murphy's characters strive for. In order to do this he encouraged them to play out their fantasies, in which they would encounter archetypal figures. One of these figures was the Shadow, a personification of the least acceptable part of human nature, often symbolised by a dark, alien, "other" who is felt to be terrifying and sinister. In order to attain integration on this Pilgrim's Progress, the individual must recognise and differentiate himself from the powerful influence of such archetypal images. But the important points about the Shadow in Jungian psychology are firstly that it is an aspect of the integrated personality — "the sum of all personal and collective psychic elements which, because of their incompatibility with the chosen conscious attitude, are denied expression in life" — and, secondly and crucially in relation to *The Gigli Concert,* that, although evil, it can be a force for good, displaying "a number of good qualities, such as formal instincts, appropriate reaction, realistic insights, creative impulses, etc."

Remembering Jung's interpretation of the Faust legend quoted earlier, in which the Shadow is Mephistopheles, it is easy to see the Man in *The Gigli Concert* as a Shadow figure. In this light, the transference of aspirations between him and JPW can be seen as the emergence of JPW's own real aspirations, hidden from him by his attachment to illusions of peaceful domesticity.

It would, of course, be foolish to see Murphy's plays, and in particular *The Gigli Concert* as illustrations of Jungian psychology but the Jungian concepts do provide a framework for two absolutely central notions in Murphy's theatre. Firstly, Jung's belief that domineering archetypes must be confronted and transcended is the essence of almost all of Murphy's plays from *A Whistle in the Dark* to *The Gigli Concert*, plays in which illusions are seen as tyrannical and stultifying. Only when these illusions are despaired of does salvation become possible, thus the importance of JPW's descent into despair in *The Gigli Concert*. Secondly the notion in Jung of the integrated personality being formed of two perhaps contradictory halves, one of which, as expressed in the Shadow, may be evil, helps to give shape to the essentially dialectical impulses of Murphy's theatre in which salvation arises out of despair, in which only the outsider can have the possibility of achieving wholeness, in which the agent of the devil can be the bringer of eternal life. Murphy replaces the certitudes of Christianity with a theatre of transformation in which, before our eyes, base metal turns to gold.

The fact that elements of Jung's psychology have a bearing on the action of *The Gigli Concert* should not, however, mislead us into seeing the play as essentially a psychological drama. Early on in Faust, Goethe's Mephistopheles promises to show Faust both "the small world" of personal feeling and experience and the "great world" of history, politics and culture. Murphy's Mephistopheles brings to JPW both the small world of psychological need and suffering and the great world of "out there" — politics ("the biggest in the land"), economics ("corruption, brutality, backhanding, fronthanding, backstabbing, lump labour and a bit of technology.") and the affairs of the world ("Oh and your Empire: that's located somewhere now in — what's them little islands called?"). And after his leap into the abyss, it is precisely into this world that JPW is free to go, letting in the light from the outside and leaving the sanctuary from life which he has established for himself. JPW's leap is made on behalf of both the small world and the great world, as an act of psychological healing, but also as a transformation of the way things are in the world. And because it takes place in the theatre, in the presence of the audience, it is also a leap on their behalf, a concrete experience of change and hope which is a challenge rather than a consolation. It is not an escape, but an entry into a demanding new reality. "In everyday life," as Peter Brook has said, "'if' is an evasion, in the theatre 'if' is the truth".

IX

Moving Statues

The candles were hissing in the rain, throwing a shadowy
light on a statue of the Blessed Virgin that stood in the
middle of a field. The hum of prayer was rising as the
Rosary was joined by up to two thousand people who had
gathered at the spot where the Blessed Virgin had
appeared to two young girls. The farmer who owned the
field, watching the destruction of a few of his too few acres
by the nightly trampling of crowds, had tried to have the
whole thing stopped, complaining to the Guards and to the
priest. But to no avail. Every night in Glenamaddy, less
than fifteen miles from Murphy's home town of Tuam,
flocks of people gathered in search of some miracle, to pray
and to hope. On one such night, just before he left Tuam
for London, Tom Murphy went to the field in Glenamaddy
with Noel O'Donoghue. The field, people said, was the
place where a priest had been beheaded in Penal times
when Catholic practice was outlawed. Among the
apparitions seen by the worshippers who had gathered
there after the sighting of the Blessed Virgin was a troupe
of Cromwellian soldiers, tramping around in wellington
boots. Someone else had witnessed The Flight Into Egypt
("Via Glenamaddy," as O'Donoghue remarked to Murphy).
The local priest had said that if such things could happen
at Lourdes or at Knock, there was no reason why they could
not happen at Glenamaddy, but the bishop at Tuam had
discouraged the whole thing with the standard church line
that such events cannot be supported until they have been
thoroughly investigated, a process which might take many

228

years. In the end, after a number of weeks, the nightly vigils stopped, not through the discouragement of the bishop or the pleas of the farmer, but by the actions of an opportunistic thief, who robbed the post office in Glenamaddy one evening while the inhabitants were at prayer. The irruption of harsh economic realities banished the Virgin.

Murphy was there that night out of cynical curiosity, but he did see something which was to have an effect on his work much later on, and which lies obliquely at the back of one of his greatest plays, *Bailegangaire*. The two children who had seen the apparition arrived with their mother, a large pigeon-chested woman. When the time came for her to give out the Rosary, she declined, saying that someone else should do it because she was feeling hoarse. Murphy noticed her pent-up nervousness, manifested in her voice and in a physical tick. He learned that the woman's husband had died shortly beforehand, and the apparition began to make some sense as a manifestation of grief, a grief hidden and denied. This image of a woman and two girls, of a dead husband, of prayer and despair and the bitter economic reality which underlay it all is at the basis of *Bailegangaire*, a play which encapsulates all the grief of history, expressed in a language of peasant Catholicism and exorcised in a final moment of extraordinary theatrical grace.

Grief is present as a motivating factor in a number of Murphy's previous plays (*The Morning After Optimism* was originally subtitled *Grief* and its action is triggered by the death of James's mother; *The Sanctuary Lamp* deals with the avoidance and emergence of Harry's grief) but in *Bailegangaire* it achieves its most effective theatrical expiation. The prayer in *Bailegangaire*, "Hail Holy Queen. Yes? Mother of Mercy. Yes? Hail our lives. Yes? Our sweetness and our hope", with its plaintive demanding of an answer, is the prayer of that woman in Glenamaddy grieving for her husband and of all such people.

Bailegangaire is in effect two plays in one, the recollection of a long past event by the senile Mommo who sits in her bed in the kitchen of a traditional thatched house, and the actual events on the night of the play, involving Mommo's two grand-daughters Mary and Dolly. This complex and superbly effective structure, holding past and present in a terrible tension, evolved out of what was to be a trilogy of plays tracing the connection between grief and faith, the private sorrow and the public language in which that sorrow turns to aspiration. The first play, *Brigit,* has been written as a television script. The second, originally called The Challenge was written as a television script but became *A Thief of a Christmas*, staged by the Abbey Theatre in December 1985. The third play, never written, was intended to arise out of the events of that night in Glenamaddy and to deal with an apparition of the Blessed Virgin. The scheme of the plays was to move from Catholicism and its failure in *Brigit*, to the paganism which underlies Catholic faith in Ireland, and on to what Murphy calls "hysteria," the pagan superstition dressed in Catholic trappings which is the distinctive religion of rural Ireland, taking forms as diverse as belief in apparitions and the organised Charismatic movement. What is important about this scheme is that it is a way of probing the transmutation of private grief and despair into public worship, dramatising again the connections between the inner and outer, the psychological world and the ideological world.

The trilogy, had it been written, would have followed through the story of the death of Seamus, a small farmer and woodcutter in his sixties. In *Brigit*, Seamus and his wife are established in a way that interweaves the barrenness of their relationship with the search for a religious imagery, and their orphaned grandchildren Tom, Mary and Dolly are introduced. In *A Thief of a Christmas*, Seamus and Brigit are taken into an extraordinary world of folklore, becoming the protagonists in the dramatisation of a tale, supposedly true, which Murphy heard from Frank Hugh O'Donnell in the early seventies. The event is said to have taken place around the turn of the century in Milltown, a village six miles from Tuam.

As Murphy heard the story, and as it is dramatised in *A Thief of a Christmas*, a stranger arrived in the pub in Milltown, forced to take refuge from the bad weather which prevented him from reaching his home. Hearing the booming laugh of one of the local men he asked if it was a man by the name of Costello and, on hearing that it was, challenged the man with the words "Well I'm a better laugher than your Costello." A laughing competition commenced, lasting five or six hours. In the original story, though not in Murphy's use of it,

"The stranger stayed the night in Costello's house. In the morning, as he was just putting the kettle on the hook, Costello sank to the floor and died. The stranger waited for the funeral before going his way. It is said that the stranger never laughed again either."

Murphy makes Seamus this stranger and has Brigit with him during the contest. In the projected third play, Seamus, too, dies, and at his wake the children believe that they see the Blessed Virgin. In fact, however, all of these elements are daringly integrated into *Bailegangaire*. Just as *The Sanctuary Lamp* integrates a trilogy by Aeschylus into the structure of one play, moving from tragedy to redemption, so, *Bailegangaire* absorbs this entire trilogy of Murphy's own making into one play, making for a magnificently rich and resonant drama that incorporates a great depth of different levels while retaining the simplicity and directness of a folk tale.

The family whose story is told in *Bailegangaire* is given to us in *Brigit*, but thirty years before the action of *Bailegangaire*, which is set in 1984. In *Bailegangaire*, Mary is 41, in *Brigit* she is 10. This sets the action of *Brigit*, and of the story of the laughing contest which Mommo relates in *Bailegangaire* back in the early fifties, well before the advent of industrial society. This is the old world of a peasant economy, and, at the opening of *Brigit*, it is Seamus' concern with a simple economic transaction which animates the play. We see him waiting determinedly at the gate of his house in order to waylay the priest. He has not been paid for work which he has done in the church and, we learn, he has been keeping the children away from Mass in protest. Piety and harsh economics co-exist in this world, and it is the latter which makes the most pressing demand. Seamus is willing to risk damnation for the sake of £1, and this sense of poverty persists in the play, where money is haggled over, where every pound is precious.

It is a world where religion is contaminated with commerce: the story of the play concerns the commissioning of Seamus to make a statue of Saint Brigit for the convent chapel, a commission which the priest secures for him as part-payment for the work Seamus has already done. In *The Sanctuary Lamp*, Francisco says of God that "When they painted his toe-nails and turned him into a church, he lost his ambition" and the image is brought to life here. The Reverend Mother of the convent sees saints as a commodity which can be bought in the form of statues with painted toenails, and bemoans the fact that Saint Brigid and Saint Patrick cannot be bought:

"Our own, our own, our two top saints, and you could walk the shops of Dublin without finding either one of them."

When Seamus is given the job of carving a new statue of Brigit to replace the one which has been broken, the Reverend Mother stands in the convent chapel with the statues all around her and haggles like a crossroads dealer. The whole atmosphere is of religion squeezed dry by the mean-mindedness of money-grubbing. Seamus' keeping of the children from Mass for the sake of a pound is a metaphor for the failure of any sense of spirituality to survive the exigencies of poverty and economic repression. In *Brigit*, official religion is a dead thing, and the story is of Seamus's attempt at a personal replacement based on the more immediate life around him.

Seamus's statue is to be made of bog-oak and is, when we see it, a primitive and beautiful image, the image of the endurance and defiance of a people who have known immemorial poverty and exclusion. The family of Brigit, as *A Thief of a Christmas* and *Bailegangaire*, is so constructed as to draw attention to history. It is a family of two grandparents and three young children. The missing generation, the parents of Mary, Dolly and Tom, at once gives us an immediate sense of discontinuity, of a leap having been made in recent history, and at the same time carries with it the notion of a past, the grandparents, which is still intruding in the world of the children. In these plays the mothers and fathers with whom the Michaels and John Joes of Murphy's early work struggled, are gone. In the early eighties, when the plays are written, the immediate struggle with the past which Murphy dramatised in the changing world of the early sixties is over, but there remains a past with which there is not so immediate a connection, the past of all the voiceless generations of the poor who have suffered in silence. Thus parents are replaced by grandparents as the central familial image in these plays. And those grandparents are a specific link to that world of the voiceless generations. Seamus in *Brigit*, both in his character and in his statue, is an image of all that suffering and endurance. "There is an element of fatalism in his personality as if everything he embarks on will turn out wrong — misfortunes. But the stronger element in his character is his refusal to submit: he has a dignity, determination and defiance."

Seamus makes his statue in the image, not of a plaster saint, but of a widow woman who lives nearby and whom he studies, watching her features and her movements. In the overall story of the three plays this makes sense as a premonition of Seamus' own impending death, for the statue is linked with his own wife, who is also Brigit, and she, too, is to become a widow. It is also, more straight-forwardly, an image of Seamus' attempt to construct a religion which is more in keeping with his own world. He visualises Brigit as "a bigger woman" than Mary, the Mother of God, because "Brigit was one of our own. I mean, the Blessed Virgin was a foreigner, a Jewish." This attempt is predictably rebuffed by the official religion, and when he presents his statue, Seamus is told by the priest that, although it is admirable, the nuns would like him to paint it. He in turn refuses to do so and is left without the money which was so important to his wife. But she comes to see in the statue something of possible value: their relationship has been so cold that he has not called her by her name, Brigit, for many years. Though they are not brought together by it, the statue represents some kind of recognition. This theme of recognition is not developed in *Brigit*, but it is later central to *Bailegangaire*.

A *Thief of a Christmas* takes further this rejection of an official religion in favour of one fashioned more in the image of the life of poverty and oppression. The play enacts the laughing contest between Seamus, now the Stranger, and Costello, and builds towards a ritual of expiation which sets man against the gods in fierce defiance. It also makes the relationship between the economic and the spiritual yet more explicit, intertwining this anti-religious tale with a story of economic struggle. In the play, the defiance of the gods is a prelude to economic triumph in which the poor win out over the rich. The throwing off of spiritual restraint is also a victory over the forces of economic oppression.

The play is set firmly on the territory of the gombeen man John Mahoney, whose "pub-cum-general-store" becomes the arena for the contest. Mahoney is no innocent barkeeper, and his pub is very clearly a place of economic exchange in which he is always the victor. We see him controlling and manipulating his customers by giving them credit and then buying up their fields when they hit hard times. In this portrait of a pub-cum-general store man, Murphy is fulfilling at last a task that Synge was tempted to take on but didn't. Synge wrote privately that "there are sides to all that western life, the groggy patriot / publican / general shop man (that) I left untouched in my stuff. I sometimes wish I hadn't a soul and then I could give myself up to putting those lads on stage. God, wouldn't they hop!" In John Mahoney, Murphy puts those lads on stage, and does so without losing his soul.

As the play opens, the hard times are at their sharpest. The town is called Bochtan, from the Irish "bocht" meaning "poor," and its inhabitants are steeped in poverty. The day is the day of the fair in Tuam shortly before Christmas, but the fair is sluggish and the goods which the people of Bochtan have to sell are not in demand. John's wife remarks that "I never seen more stuff leave Bochtan for fair or market than I did today" and the exodus is not a sign of the town's bounteous productivity, but of the desperation of the inhabitants who are forced to sell everything they have in order to get some money for the coming Christmas. And the failure of the fair has placed them more in John Mahoney's power than ever. We see Bina buying her miserable collection of goods ("tobaccy, icing sugar, raisins, Bex Tartar ... matches") and the way in which Mahoney's shop controls her affairs. "Give me your pension book ... Your pension money now is for last week's and I have them articles down with the others that are outstanding."

Mahoney's operation is a text-book version of the typical gombeen man's economic hold over his community, and the play is careful to root the action in that reality. This is not merely the background to the action, but its mainspring. For the laughing competition, started as a whim, looks like petering out until it becomes an economic contest. John opens a book on the outcome, and on it comes to hinge the material well-being of the entire community, pitting his interests directly against theirs. John backs the Stranger;

Costello and most of the others back himself as the champion in unarmed combat of the poor against the rich. The bet is worked out in great detail and with formal solemnity and much signing of books — "Sure, if I win" says Costello to Mahoney, "what's £250 to you? All you're stakin' is your happiness and a lifetime of regret, bejingoes. An' if I lose, you have the finest holdin' in Bochtan, and that'll only keep your appetite whetted for more."

The motivation of the Strangers, Brigit and Seamus, is not primarily material, however. As they enter, we see that Seamus is wearing a black diamond on his sleeve, a symbol of mourning, while Brigit is sobbing and worrying over the three children waiting for them at home. "And sure we told them for sure we'd be home before dark. Misfortunes." They are a couple immersed in death and fear, haunted by premonitions of more death to come, symbolised by the three sticks of rock which Brigit clutches to her breast, one for each of the children, which get crushed and trampled underfoot during the first half of the play. It is this omen, this sense of endlessly continuing misfortune, which causes Brigit to push forward the challenge to Costello which her husband has been backing out of: "Yis, yis-yis, he's challengin' ye, he is!" Her challenge is made out of grief, and as the contest takes the ever more serious shape of a dicing with death, she comes to see in it a challenge to death itself, a defiance of the force that has robbed her of nine sons. The death of her sons has been caused by her own hardness, the emotional famine which has starved them, and in pushing her husband into a challenge unto the death, she also seeks to overcome that emotional blight.

Once she has pronounced that the challenge will be settled by "He who laughs last" there is a recognition of each other by herself and Seamus, a recognition in which, for the first time in many years, they speak each other's names. What they share is grief and sadness, but even in acknowledging this they gain some sense of a common destiny:

"She starts to laugh with him. They stop laughing for a moment and look directly at each other. Tears brim to her eyes; the sadnesses which they have shared showing on their faces the misfortunes of a lifetime."

They embrace and dance together for a few moments. What she sees in this contest is a common victory which will bring them together in the recognition of their grief. "We've been defeated in all our hopes. But you have him bet: this one thing we'll win." And as the contest resumes, based now on the subject she has suggested — misfortunes — we see the roots of that grief:

"I had nine sons! Hih hih hih — an' for the sake of an auld ewe was stuck in the flood was how I lost Jimmy and Michael — hih hih hih! ... An' the nice wife Jimmy left behind died tryin'to give birth to the fourth child was to be in it. Bate that! Hih-hih-hih!"

This misfortune is economic in origin, caused by the terrible fear of losing an economic asset like a ewe. We are back in the world of *Famine*, where the material poverty blights the emotions. (There is, in fact, a small textual link between the plays in that both have references to Peader Bane, an almost archetypal figure of poverty who, in *Famine* has the spade which is his only livelihood stolen, and in *A Thief* has only "one auld sheep,") But the defiance and endurance of John Connor which, in *Famine* were tragic, are here blackly and bleakly comic, providing the nub of the laughing contest as it builds into a collective recognition of the way the world is and a defiance of the gods to do their worst. The play moves out of any semblance of naturalism and into a mesmeric recitation by the crowd of the misfortunes of their lives:

Those lost to America!

Arms lost to the thresher!

Suicide and bad weather!

Blighted crops!

Bad harvests!

Bad markets!

How to keep the one foot in front of the other!

Per'tonitis!

An', fever, yellow, black and scarlet!

Chicken bones!

Briars to take out your eyes!

Or to bate the children with!

Put smacht on them when there's nought for their bellies!

Mi-adh, misfortunes!

An' there's more to come!

Send them!

We're waitin'!

We are!

We are!

This pagan ritual of defiance hurled heavenward is a catalogue of poverty's particulars, the furious voice of the voiceless of history. It enacts the classic Nietzschean gesture of man's defiant laughter in the face of death but reverses its political and theatrical meaning. For Nietzsche, that God-defying laughter is a mark of tragedy and of the hero's division from the unworthy crowd. For Murphy, it is a theatrical move beyond tragedy into black comedy, and the moment at which the crowd, the great unwashed of history, becomes collectively heroic. And instead of being merely a heroic aceptance of death, it represents in itself a sort of resurrection of the dead, a coming to life of all the nameless generations of sufferers to blast heaven. And it is followed by a more specific resurrection, achieved on behalf of the poor populace in general.

As the contest goes on, Costello is driven beyond endurance and collapses, apparently dead. The crowd drives the Strangers out of the pub. John Mahoney insists that, in spite of Costello's death his book stands, meaning that he, the gombeen man, has been victorious and will gain still more control over the community. But Costello rises for one last laugh: "Wo ho ho, I'm goin'. An' that's the last laugh." John Mahoney is, after all, defeated, and the people have a victory over their economic enemy. The play ends with an exuberant wake for Costello in which death is turned into a triumph. Symbolically, death itself has been defeated and banished.

If *A Thief of a Christmas* achieves a kind of resurrection on behalf of history, *Bailegangaire*, a richer and more formally beautiful play, seeks to include the present in that embrace. Where the world of *A Thief* is almost mediaeval, that of Bailegangaire brings together all of past history with a specifically delineated modern Ireland. Here, it is 1974, and Mary and Dolly are grown women approaching the brink of middle-age. Brigit is Mommo, their ancient grandmother still caught in the world of the laughing contest, telling over and over the same story but refusing to conclude it. Mary is another of Murphy's homecomers, herself an embodiment of the failure of success. She has made it in London as a nursing matron, but has given it up to return in search of "home."

In this, she is very much a creature of the disillusionment with the promises of prosperity of the sixties. And in the play, the world she has returned to is one in which that sixties dream is turning sour. Its fruits are to be seen in Dolly's new "liquorice-all-sorts-coloured house" with rubber-backed lino in the bedrooms and a carpeted lounge. The play is set in an old thatched house, but it is a thatched house which is down the road from a Japanese electronics factory. Throughout the play, cars pass by on their way to and from the factory, and there is a stray, useless piece of electronic gadgetry in the house. And this brave new world is hollow on the inside: the plant "is for closure," and ominous helicopters have been seen. The world is controlled by forces which are so distant and inexplicable that Dolly insists on calling the owners of the plant "the Chinese." Just as Mary has returned and found that home is no longer in existence, so outside of the house, there is very little that the locals can call their own. Alongside the pagan, mediaeval world of the laughing contest, Murphy places a precise portrait of modern Ireland.

What gives the play its formal beauty, though, is that this precisely-delineated social world is contained within a timeless mythic structure — that of the nativity play. The basic structure of both the contemporary action of *Bailegangaire* and of the story of the laughing contest which is intermeshed with it, and which is enacted in *A Thief*, is the nativity of Christ. The Strangers on a road on a winter night, forced to seek shelter where they may, and finding, ultimately, no room at the inn, are reminiscent of Mary and Joseph caught cold in Bethlehem. In *Bailegangaire*, the play builds towards the birth of a child and the re-birth of God. The somewhat grotesque Christ which Costello becomes in *A Thief*, laying down his life for the salvation of others, emerges tentatively but unmistakably into the "live" action of *Bailegangaire*.

The parallels, of course, are not taken on face value, and many of them are reversed in their meaning. There is a black Christmas as much as a white one. The visitation of the Strangers brings death, not birth. The prayers of supplication and thanks offered by the faithful at Christmas become shouts and howls of defiance delivered at God. The traditional image of Christmas as a time of plenty is a mockery for the Strangers and Costello — the very abundance at the fair in Tuam means that prices are low and their stock is unsold. And even the benign Christmas image of a Santa Claus who is coming to all good children is reversed in Costello's warning to the children in John Mahoney's that "someone is comin' anaways if ye all aren't good."

The link between these two worlds of modern Ireland and the Christmas story that gives *Bailegangaire* its unity of texture and structure is the imagery of the folk tale. Whereas *The Sanctuary Lamp* and *The Gigli Concert* draw much from the great public myths of the western world, *Bailegangaire* owes its life to the poor man's myth, the folk tale. While myth trades in a heroic world, the folk tale stems from the everyday struggle of ordinary people and constitutes a secret history of the fears and desires of the poor. *Bailegangaire* is explicitly a folk-tale — its subtitle is "The story of Bailegangaire and how it came by its appellation."

Bailegangaire means the town without laughter, and this places the play in one of the great categories of folk tale — tales about the origins of the names of individuals and places. Naming is the central metaphor of the play, with not only *Bailegangaire* having its name changed from Bochtan, but Brigit and Seamus in the story coming to call each other by name, and Mary looking for a recognition of who she is from Mommo.

But to say that the play is a folk-tale is not to place it in a category of escapist fantasy with Edmund and Anastasia of *The Morning After Optimism*. Rather, this is the world of the real peasant folk-tales before they were doctored for consumption by middle-class children. Real folk tales are a programme for survival, not a fantasy of escape. The world they contain is that of a struggle for existence in which the weak can survive only if they outwit the strong. In them, the village is a nasty place: neighbours are presumed to be hostile; they spy on you and rob your garden; you should never discuss your affairs in front of them, or let them know if you acquire sudden wealth, for they will certainly conspire to deprive you of it. And they end happily only after they were cleaned up during the eighteenth century — in the originals, as Robert Darnton has pointed out, it is the inexorable and inscrutable character of calamity and misfortune that is at their heart. Mommo and her story belong to this pre-literate world, a world full of widows and orphans, sudden deaths, cruel diseases that cannot be overcome, a vicious struggle for survival.

Folk tales are essentially about one thing: home and the struggle to get there. When the world is such a hostile place, peopled by giants, witches and nasty neighbours, home is not just a physical place, it is a metaphysical one, the embodiment of man's search, the goal of all striving. And it is this notion of home which infuses the play with its constant presence. It is the image which integrates the play's levels, tying the world of Mommo's story to the present existence of Mary and Dolly. In the story, Mommo and her husband are archetypal folk tale heroes, struggling for home against ferocious obstacles. The weather, like an evil spirit conspires against them, forcing them to take refuge on hostile territory. And Costello is specifically referred to as a "giant," making him the giant which the traveller must slay in order to reach home.

And this folk tale voyage for home is paralleled by Mary's search. "What am I looking for, Mommo?" she asks. "I had to come home. No one inveigled me. I wanted to come home." Later, when she takes up Mommo's story after the old woman has fallen temporarily asleep, she specifically links the search for home in the story with her own search. Adopting Mommo's voice she whispers "I wanta go home, I wanta go home." Then in her own voice she continues: "So do I, so do I. Home. (Anger) Where is it, Mommo?"

What is more, this sense of homelessness is also a metaphysical notion of man's lack of a place in the world. Mommo remembers her father's speculations as to how man and the earwig were the only two creatures for whom God could not find a use. God is a careless bumbler, who created man and then found nothing to do with him. Man has been expelled from Eden into a homeless world, and

Mary's attempts to construct a golden age of home and family are ruthlessly undercut by Mommo's refusal to recognise her: "There was happiness here, too, Mommo. Harmony?" "You can be going now, Miss."

The richness of this idea of home in the play is that we not only travel with those who are seeking home, we also wait with those who are at home, abandoned and bereft. In this way, the idea of home is created dramatically as something which does not yet exist but must be brought into existence in the play, for there are two incomplete forces which must be brought together: those who are voyaging towards home, and those who are at home, waiting anxiously. We are conscious of Mary, Dolly and Tom as the children waiting for their grandparents to return from the fair, with an inescapable sense of impending disaster hanging over them.

In the present, there is Dolly's son Michaeleen sick with tonsils, waiting for her to return home from her assignation to have sex in a ditch. In the story, Costello tells the children in the pub the "someone is comin' anaways if ye all aren't good." And in the present Mary makes herself a child at home: "What time is it? Half-nine. Someone will come yet." And these two opposite ends of worry and expectation, the struggle to get home, and the waiting at home of the abandoned child, are united in Mommo. She is the traveller of the story, trying to get home. But she also becomes herself a child again, a child who is brought sweets by Dolly, as she, in the story, brings sweets for Dolly, Mary and Tom: like a child she says "An' I never done nothin' wrong." and then, like a good girl, she is given sweets: "Do 1 like them ones?" In this image Mommo ties the two counterbalanced tensions of the play together.

But home in the play is not something which is to be easily achieved. Until the end of the play, when home is brought into existence, it cannot be reached safely. Mary's attempt at homecoming has been unhappy, and in the play she threatens to leave again and gathers her clothes together for packing. There are two more horrific images of disastrous homecomings. Dolly's husband Stephen works in England and returns home for Christmas, the great season of universal homecoming which is on the way. He is informed of Dolly's infidelities by his mother:

"Then waitin' for the hero, my rescuer, the sun shining out of his eighty-five-pounds-a-week arse, to come home at Christmas ... Old Sharp Eyes whisperin' into his ear about me. Oooo but he waited. Jesus, how I hate him! Jesus how I hate them! Men! Had his fun and games with me that night, and first thing in the morning. Even sat down to eat the hearty breakfast I made. Me thinkin', still no warmth, but maybe it's goin' to be okay. Oooo, but I should have known from experience, about-the-great-up-stand-in'-Steph-en-evra-body's-fav-our-ite. Because, next thing, he has me by the hair of the head, fistin' me down in the mouth, Old Sharp Eyes there, noddin' her head every time he struck an' struck an' kicked an' kicked and pulled me round the house by the hair of the head."

And to this terrible homecoming is added another: the story which Mommo refuses to finish tells of what happened when they finally arrived home from the laughing contest. Tom, the youngest child, has been burned to death in an accident with a paraffin heater, a fate hinted at only obliquely in Mommo's reference to "the cursed paraffin." Two days later, her husband dies, as Costello dies in the original story which Murphy was told, just as he had "put the kettle on the hook." But this ending to the story, this source of grief, is what Mommo is holding back and what Mary is determined will be spoken out.

The relationship of the story to the world of the present in the play is not one of simple reflection. For what may, in the story, be an accident which actually happened, is yet contained within a formal structure which allows it to be postponed rather than faced. Mommo is a skilled, formal storyteller (Mary reminds her that "People used to come miles to hear you tell stories") and her language and technique are a part of the drama. She uses a baroque, highly stylised language, full of archaic syntax and remnants of Gaelic, which, along with the more obvious device of speaking in the third person about herself, distances the story from reality and insulates her from the grief which must emerge if there is to be peace. She also uses the storyteller's techniques of elaboration and postponement to avoid the finishing of the story, to stave off indefinitely the terrible ending which she cannot face.

This is hugely effective as a theatrical device, for it means that the play reproduces dramatically what it is about thematically. The play is about the postponement of grief, and it works by postponing the end of the story. The narrative is constantly interrupted by sequences of "live" action, so that the audience is left with the tension of frustrated expectation, needing to know what happens next just as Mary and Mommo need the story to reach a conclusion. The breaking and distancing of both the narrative and the action act to prevent our identification with the characters, excluding any outrush of emotion but building it up and storing it until the final moments when the story and the action dovetail in an overwhelming catharsis.

The folk-tale world of the story is therefore a way of concealing and postponing the reality of what it tells. And that folk-tale world spills over into the world of reality with damaging effects. Dolly confuses story with reality and tries to solve her real problems — the fact that she is pregnant by a man other than her husband — by inventing another story about it. She proposes that Mary should pretend that the child is hers, and then, after a year "It'll be easy to make up another story." Mary objects that this new fiction would merely ensure that "the saga goes on," and her aim in the play is to end the saga, to get out of the world of stories so that reality may be faced anew.

But she herself has lived a fairytale. She remembers an elderly patient to whom she became close.

"But one day she said, in the middle of-whatever-conversation we were having, you're going to be alright, Mary. Simple remark. But it took me by surprise. Like, as if it was a promised blessing. And why I should have carried it and — believed in it for, oh, twenty years? until recently, I don't know."

This is the fairy story of the princess who is blessed at birth by the good witch with an enchantment which lasts for twenty years and then fades. But *Bailegangaire* is, literally, about disenchantment, the breaking of a spell by the uttering of certain words, the words that will end Mommo's story.

It is in this idea that the play makes use of the language of Catholic magic, the notion that the uttering of words in prayer and supplication can in itself bring about change for the better. The release which comes to Mommo and her husband in the story is that they speak each other's names, and the release which Mary is seeking is that Mommo should recognise her and call her by name as she does in the final moments. This idea of recognition is connected to the fundamental wellsprings of the theatre, and is used in Bailegangaire in a way which taps in to its full meaning. In the Greek theatre, recognition scenes have their origin in the playing out of the myth of Dionysus, who dies, is buried, and is then resurrected. The resurrected or reborn god is recognised by certain marks, and in this scene of recognition is the origin of all others in the theatre.

At the end of *Bailegangaire,* the recognition of Mary is accompanied by the resurrection of God. The God who earlier in the play was a careless bumbler, ignorant of man's function and place in the world, has become the possessor of at least some wisdom:

"It's a strange old place alright, in whatever wisdom He has to have made it this way."

It is this underground connection to a very old story which gives to the conclusion of *Bailegangaire* its sense of classical form. At the same time, the goal of folk tale is reached, and home is finally created in the last words of the play:

"But in whatever wisdom there is, in the year 1984, it was decided to give that — fambly ... of strangers another chance, and a brand new baby to gladden their home."

This sense of resurrection is achieved through the imagery of Dolly's pregnancy. The play is haunted by the ghosts of children, from the imaginary "fondlings" at the end of her bed to whom Mommo addresses the story at the start of the play, to the dead Tom at the end. Here again, the world of the story and the world of the present action are connected through the imagery. Dolly threatens to kill her baby, in a speech which has clear resonances of the Kerry Babie's saga which was a very recent memory when the play was given its premiere:

"The countryside produced a few sensations in the last couple of years, but my grand plan: I'll show them what can happen in the dark of night in a field. I'll come to grips with my life."

Later, Mommo, in the catalogue of misfortunes during the laughing contest, comes to "Nothin' was sacred and nothing a secret. The unbaptised and stillborn in shoeboxes planted, at the dead hour of night treading softly the Lisheen to make the regulation hole — not more, not less than two feet deep — too fearful of the field, haunted by infants, to speak or to pray. They were fearful of their ankles — Hih hih hih. An' tryin' not to hasten, steal away again, leaving their pagan parcels in isolation forever."

This imagery of a haunting by dead infants makes the acceptance of Dolly's baby at the end a symbolic resurrection of the dead.

It is, in the end, not Mommo who finishes the story but Mary, the power of rebirth lying not with the old world of the past, but with the present and the future which Mary is free to face. She asks the question "Who were the dead?" and answers "Daddy," "Tom." She herself needs to be recognised by Mommo, but she has also gained the power of recognition herself, along with a power of blessing. For just as the old woman once told her "You're going to be alright, Mary," so she says, just before the conclusion "You're going to be alright, Dolly." In the process of her search, she has acquired a new power and a new confidence. She has also acquired something that no Murphy character has ever had before — a home and a refuge. With the ending of *Bailegangaire* a voyage which began in Murphy's plays over a quarter of a century earlier is completed.

The resonance of the world of *Bailegangaire* is so powerful in Murphy's work that it remains strong in his first novel, *The Seduction of Morality*, published nine years later, in 1994. Though it functions very much as a piece of prose fiction, it also takes much of its shape from that of the play. There is a woman in her thirties returning home to Ireland from exile, though Vera is a whore in New York rather than a nurse in England, in character an amalgam of Dolly's coarseness with Mary's refinement. There is the pull of a childhood rural world dominated by a grandmother, here called Mom instead of Mommo. There is the haunting effect of a terrible fire at the old woman's cottage, though in the novel it is the old woman who is its victim, not a child. There is the same mood of reflection on mortality and inheritance from the past. And there is the same final, hopeful image of a new baby opening up the possibility of a future.

Other elements of Murphy's dramatic imagery, the alchemy of The *Gigli Concert,* the gombeenism of Liam in *Conversations on a Homecoming*, also recur, but the central search for a relationship between a woman and her grandmother fixes the novel's main concerns in the mould of *Bailegangaire*.

What distinguishes the novel and explains Murphy's attraction to the form so late in his career, though, is the capacity it affords him to bring the different worlds of his plays into co-existence. His drama is so powerfully drawn to at least a loose preservation of the classical unities that it never allows him to really bring the distinct worlds of countryside, town and city together on stage. All three are used in his stage work, but never in the same play. The looser, more expansive nature of fiction allows him for the first time to make use of the interpenetration of country (Mom's old thatched cottage), town (the devastatingly satiric portrait of Vera's petit bourgeois family) and metropolis (the glimpses of Vera's other life as a call girl in the urban wilderness of New York). The metaphysical sense in his later plays that there are different levels of reality is here brought back into a literal, social meaning, one that is strikingly true to the nature of Ireland in the 1990s.

What lies behind this shift is a broader cultural change in Ireland itself. By the 1990s, the dramatic struggle between tradition and modernity in Ireland, set in motion in the late 1950s, was all but over. The clash which had given shape to Murphy's plays had lost its fury and been replaced by a stranger, more elusive sense of a place defined by the intermingling of many worlds. "Ireland" itself, the notion that had underlain so much of Irish theatre in the twentieth century and given it its unifying assumptions had become a more distant concept as the society fragmented and as a new kind of commuter emigration, people shifting in and out of the country in response to unstable economic moods, took hold.

The Seduction of Morality is set in the mid-1970s, but its mood is closer to the 1990s. In the background of the story of Vera's return from New York and the struggles within the O'Toole family for control of the hotel she has been left in her mother's will, the argument about tradition and modernity rumbles on. The newspaper headlines reflect the rows about the availability of contraception that raged in the 1970s as cyphers of that larger struggle, and the sermon in the church that The Greek, Vera's sybaritic brother-in-law visits, is about contraception, divorce and abortion. But this political struggle is already pre-empted in the novel. The "traditional" world in which the novel opens, the childhood world of Vera's years with Mom, is far from traditional, if tradition is taken to mean the nuclear family, monogamy and sexual continence. The very fact that Vera is fostered out to her grandmother is a rebuke to the notion of the nuclear family as the norm. When we learn that Mom had a child out of wedlock, that Vera's mother was pregnant with Vera before she was married, that Vera is, as she announces at her mother's wake, "a call-girl, a hooker, a prostitute" in New York, then the battle for a traditional, contraceptive-free Ireland is made to seem not merely marginal but surreal. That the latter revelation comes in a chapter called "The Family" is particularly pointed.

The effect of the novel, indeed, is to make the Irish nuclear family seem, not any kind of norm, but a specific, and relatively short-lived phenomenon. Before the world of the O'Tooles, there was Mom's early widowhood and child conceived out of wedlock. After it there will be Vera in Mom's house with her own child conceived out of wedlock. In the middle, tilted at this angle so as to seem strange, odd, and essentially comic, is the nuclear family of the O'Tooles, with their frantic power struggles over property and standing in the town. And property, indeed, is all that holds them together. Murphy is ruthless in his depiction of a family whose only inheritance is what was owned — the hotel, a pub, a shop. In reality, the family is nothing more than a series of alliances, rivalries and conspiracies over the control of the family businesses. Only Vera has another inheritance, a secret childhood. The story of the novel is her journey to recover that inheritance.

Linking the novel just as strongly to the world of *Bailegangaire* and *A Thief of a Christmas*, are its biblical resonances. These are not as structured as the echoes of the nativity story in the plays, but they are nonethless insistent. Finbar Reilly's drunken fantasies about Vera imagine her as both Mary Magdalen and Christ, a fallen woman and a new-born messiah to whom he will bring gifts of gold, frankincense and myrrh, and the confusion of sinner with saviour is typical of Murphy's inversion of religion.

The Book of Job's "naked came I out of my mother's womb, and naked shall I return thither" is Vera's essential truth. Even The Greek, fleeing from a sermon in the church, imagines himself as Christ, a flock of birds as his flock. He feeds them with the holy bread that he was given in church and slipped into his pocket.

A world of images and archetypes surrounds the characters, not so much to protect them or give them meaning, but to mock them and to highlight the absurdity that threatens their every action. Religious impulses and needs drive them, but there is no religion that can give them succour.

In all of this the novel, while depicting a society, also anatomises its absence. The world of the O'Tooles and their town, of their family alliances and hatreds, is collapsing. The religion that gave that world meaning and coherence is itself meaningless. The peace that Vera makes with her past, with her memory of Mom, is not a reassertion of any tradition other than the tradition of being out on your own, at an angle to the world. The life that Vera finds and makes is a life after death.

X

The Second Time As Farce

Tom Murphy's father was a carpenter by trade, a quiet and resourceful man. When he pictures his father from early childhood, before he emigrated to Coventry, the image that comes most easily to mind is of his father in his workshop making coffins. He sometimes had to spend a Sunday making a coffin, sometimes for a child. Death was an ordinary visitor, a comonplace of work, a thing shaped and smoothed by his father's deft hands. He remembers the smell of the pine. He remembers playing with the shavings of pine on the floor, remembers himself as a boy warm in the company of his father, lost in the curlings and arabesques of shaved wood that were the remains of someone else's death.

That tenderness in mortality, that strange bittersweet memory in which a lost family tie is recaptured amid the trappings of death, comes close to the mood of *Too Late for Logic*, staged at the Abbey in a production by Patrick Mason in the 1989 Dublin Theatre Festival. The memory itself has no part in the play, but the interweaving of death and lost ties of kindred is at its core. And it is, in the end, a kind of resurrection of the father.

If it is true that *Bailegangaire*, as suggested in the last chapter, represents a culmination for Murphy, an achieved reconciliation which his work had never had before, then it is also true that that play marked a kind of ending, even a death. That feeling of an ending could only have been deepened by the death, shortly after the play's run ended, of the great actress for whom it had been written, Siobhan

McKenna. Her performance as Mommo was as much a culmination of a lifetime's art for her as the play was for Murphy, and the play's metaphoric homecoming was also for her, a literal one, taking her back full circle to the Galway in which she had begun. That for her, too, the play should be both a re-birth and a farewell, a best and last performance, gave it a strange aura of both excitement and finality, of abundant life and of life ending.

Where can a writer go after finality except beyond the bounds of life? Where can a play that comes after a death be set except in the afterlife? The strange, haunted quality of *Too Late for Logic* comes from its being a play of the afterlife. Both literally (the action happens after the death of Cordelia and, perhaps, of the protagonist Christopher) and metaphorically (the image of Orpheus in the Underworld plays about the action) it has its theatrical life after death.

Nothing in Murphy is ever completely new, of course, and it would be wrong to think of *Too Late for Logic* as a breach with the body of work that culminates in *Bailegangaire*. On the contrary, images of afterlife take us right back to Murphy's very first play, *On the Outside*, where Joe and Frank exist outside the dancehall in a metaphorical Purgatory and end the play by getting away to Hell. Thirty years on, *Too Late for Logic*, returns to that purgatorial world, though in a form that is less directly social, more self-consciously imaginative, and ruefully aware of the transition from youth to middle age.

Likewise, images of the afterlife touch a number of previous Murphy plays. Francisco's child-like vision of Limbo, all tropical light and laziness, is essential to *The Sanctuary Lamp*. The mocking afterlife of the dead John F. Kennedy haunts *The White House* and *Conversations on a Homecoming*. JPW King has to "die" in the darkness of his blackest night before he can re-emerge into the afterlife of a new morning.

There are other ways, too, in which *Too Late for Logic* remains of a piece with Murphy's previous work. The church converted to a nightclub ("The Priory") in scenes 3 and 4 is reminiscent of the church of *The Sanctuary Lamp*. (Murphy told Marianne McDonald, in relation to that play that before he left England in the late 1960s, he had seen a "For Sale" sign on a church, and "I thought good, they're disintegrating.") The sense of Christopher and Michael, as brothers, being too halves of one disconnected whole personality (an image re-inforced in this case by having them married to sisters) is a familiar theme from most of Murphy's plays. And the way in which a demented obsession (suicide, revenge on Wally Peters) is transferred from the person who conceives it (Michael) to the person who is most likely to carry it to fruition (Christopher) is strikingly reminiscent of *The Gigli Concert*. So, too, is the way in which Christopher jumbles up his own life with that of a famous man, becoming Schopenhauer in his breakdown as the Irishman becomes Benimillo. More obliquely, there are Faustian parallels in *Too Late for Logic*, as there are in *Gigli*.

Christopher and Michael, for instance, are a kind of Faust and Mephistopheles, though the parallels are even more deliberately desultory. Faust's heroic striving for knowledge is reduced in Christopher to his ambition for the chair at Trinity College that has become vacant because of the comic fate that has decreed that Dr Wuzzler should fall under a bus. Michael as Mephistopheles may lead him into the Hades of the Priory night club, and into his brush with the afterlife, but it is an essentially farcical damnation. Chokki the dog (confused in his breakdown with Schopenahauer's dog Atma) is a suburban version of the black dog that comes to pursue Faust. More importantly, the disembodied voices, on tape, telephone answering machine, television and microphone, the play's central device, recall the voices that call to Goethe's Faust at the end of his journey, just as the shadows that appear at the beginning and end of the play are also suggested by Goethe.

The effect, though, is more mock-heroic than in *Gigli*. The references to Goethe, the continual thread of discussion of Schopenhauer, the subject of Christopher's televised lecture which is to win him the chair, and the references through music and imagery to Gluck's opera *Orpheus and Eurydice*, combine to create a constant backdrop of heroic Germanic Romanticism against which Christopher's troubles with his family and his job are enacted. The effect is sceptical and wry. Wheras in, for instance, *The Sanctuary Lamp* the identification with Oresteian characters makes Harry and Francisco seem much larger than life, in spite of their down-at-heel condition, here the backdrop of heroic Romanticism places the characters, particularly Christopher, at a comic distance, making them more like figures in a puppet show. If the first time of Schopenhauer and Goethe was tragedy, the second time of Christopher and Wuzzy is often close to farce.

This, in itself, marks one of the ways in which *Too Late for Logic* does represent a break with Murphy's previous work. Never before has the tone of one of his plays been set so strongly by middle-class Dublin. Murphy's previous work has been devoted to Outsiders, both economic and spiritual. He has remarked in relation to *The Sanctuary Lamp*, for instance, that in making Harry a circus strongman, "I couldn't have dealt with a solicitor, or a teacher, or a housewife." While there are insiders in *On the Inside* and *Conversations on a Homecoming*, there is no character like Christopher, a respectable university lecturer, from a socially respectable background, a member of the settled urban middle class. JPW King comes close to Christopher in some respects — devotion to intellectual gobbledy-gook, respectable semi-genteel background — but he is, by the time we find him in *The Gigli Concert*, a virtually destitute exile, whose situation outside of the mainstream of domestic middle-class life is stressed. Christopher belongs to that mainstream, even in his strained relationship with his wife and children. In that alone, Murphy enters new territory in *Too Late for Logic*.

He does not, of course, enter it uncritically. The play gives us a superb caricature of the Dublin middle-class male in Tony and Geoffrey, all the strutting idiocy, all the violent insecurity summed up in Tony's lager-and-lime soaked war cry of "I've had two trials on the possibles for my country." In this strand of the play's backdrop, we are given a comic variation on Dada's savage exclusion from golf club society in *A Whistle*, brought up to date with the whiff of stale cigarillos and the desperate lurch of the groper in the early hours of Dublin's Leeson Street nightclubs.

The only form which Irish theatre has developed for dealing with middle-class urban life is farce, itself the classic bourgeois form. The variations on farce in recent Irish plays like Hugh Leonard's *The Patrick Pearse Motel*, and Brian Friel's *The Communication Cord*, suggest that even if it is not a mainstream form as it has been in France and Britain, it is certainly a usable one in the Irish context, and one which can be turned to political or even philosophical ends, as Leonard creates a political farce about Irish nationalism, and Friel a farce about the theory of language and communication. *Too Late for Logic*, however, goes further than any of these antecedents in that it not merely uses elements of farce side-by-side with the language of philosophical discourse, but blends the two so thoroughly that they become virtually indistinguishable.

Christopher is a typical protagonist of farce: a middle-aged, middle-class man in the midst of a mid-life crisis, launched quite suddenly into a stream of events that carries him to the edge of madness. Christopher, alone, at work, on the brink of respectable achievement — Wuzzy's chair in Trinity — is invaded by domestic woes and

engulfed in an illogical but relentless sequence of events
that leads to his humiliation. As in classic farce, physical
objects (in this case the gun that Christopher acquires
accidentally from Michael, and the cigarette he gets from
his son Jack, rather than the usual doors, beds and
trousers) play a central role in the plot, suggesting the way
in which the protagonists have become the victims of
rather than the controllers of inanimate objects, and thus
themselves parts in an inanimate machine that they are
powerless to switch off.

What gives the play its strange tone, however, is that
this element of farce is inextricable from the philosophical
context of the play. Schopenhauer may be ridiculed by
Christopher's demented reduction of him to the mindset of
a man having a nervous breakdown on camera, but he does
provide the framework of the play nonetheless. If
Schopenhauer is mocked by providing the subtext for a
farce, equally the farce is deepened in being animated by
Schopenhauer's *The World As Will and Idea*. For the
puppet-show nature of farce is in fact very close to
Schopenhauer's view of the world. *Too Late for Logic* is, at
one level, a theatrical demonstration of this similarity.

Put at its simplest, Schopehnauer's view of the world is
that it is, in essence, the Will. Starting from Kant's
separation of the world into phenomena (things that act
on our senses, that are perceived by us) and noumena (the
essences of the things, the thing-in-itself), Schopenhauer,
in the book that Christopher decides to lecture on, *The
World as Will and Idea*, calls this hidden essence of the
world Will. It is, he says, "blind striving, obscure
inarticulate impulse," identified in part with the
inexplicable will to live and reproduce. Individuals are
mere objectifications of this Will. They exist within it,
though Schopenhauer does not put it like this, as
characters in a farce exist within the plot, puppets of a
blind, striving, inarticulate desire, usually expressed as
lust.

What Murphy gives us, therefore, is not so much a philosophical farce as Schopenhauer-as-farce. In a sense, *Too Late for Logic* is a dramatisation of, and at the same time a satire on, *The World as Will and Idea*. This is not such a strange theatrical notion as it seems, for it has very considerable antecedents, both in European and in Irish theatre.

Much of twentieth century theatre in Europe was formed under Schopenahuer's influence. Wagner, who did so much to re-shape theatricality for our century, was a disciple of Schopenahauer. So was Adolphe Appia, the designer who is one of the formative influences on modern theatre practice. So, to a considerable extent, was Strindberg. In the Irish theatre, Yeats's *The Cat and the Moon* and the figures of the Blind Man and the Fool in *On Baile's Strand* are dramatisations of Schopenhauer's image of the relationship between the will and the intellect being like "the strong blind man who carries on his shoulders the lame man who can see." And Beckett's *Endgame*, with the blind master Hamm, and the sighted but lame Clov is rooted in the same image. For Yeats, Schopenhauer "can do no wrong", while Beckett continued to read him for most of his life. *Too Late for Logic* therefore exists within a very strong current of Irish and European theatre, and it is a struggle with the pessimism of that cultural strain just as much as Murphy's earlier work is a struggle with the tragedy of the Greeks and the absurdity of much of post-war theatre. Wuzzy's theory that Schopenhauer had spent two days in Cobh, County Cork in 1802, is not entirely beside the point. For Murphy is again testing a broad European current of ideas against the actualities of Irish life.

Whereas for Yeats or Beckett, for Strindberg or Wagner, Schopenhauer is a serious influence in every sense of the word, Murphy's attitude is infinitely more playful and disrespectful. They, after all, are still Romantics of a kind, even Beckett, whereas Murphy is determinedly post-Romantic in his disillusioned sensibility. His use of Schopenhauer in *Too Late for Logic* is therefore bitterly ironic. Having used, for instance, Jung to secularise a Christian myth in *Gigli*, Murphy goes further here and uses 1980s life to secularise Schopenhauer.

Christopher is a poor man's Schopenhauer living in a poor man's post-revolutionary backlash. The 1980s is a pale, pokey imitation of the triumph of counter-revolution in Europe after Waterloo. The restoration of the Bourbons and the dashing of Romantic hopes finds a squeaky echo in the triumph of reaction in the 1980s and the transformation of yippies and hippies into yuppies with Guccis.

This ironic context is set from the start in Christopher's taped lecture, which he is playing back to himself. "Egalite, liberte, fraternite, said the bishops and princes, our royal arse. Which they replanked up on thrones... Faith, hope, charity? Feed the birds tuppence a bag." Christopher's wry "Hard to visualise it, so unlike our own times... a time of demoralisation, debilitating reverie, despair. A time of sad songs" merely draws attention to the fact that all of this is about the 1980s as much as the 1810s.

The emphasis on religious reaction in this formulation is not accidental. The bishops on their thrones and charity for the birds conjure up for an Irish audience at the end of the 1980s, the re-establishment of Catholic orthodoxy in Ireland in that decade. The insertion of a "pro-life" (anti-abortion) clause in the Irish Constitution in 1983, and the equally divisive referendum in 1986 in which a proposal to delete the ban on divorce from the Constitution was defeated, gave to the decade an aura of Catholic triumphalism, the tide of liberalism apparently turned back. Internationally, this was the decade of Reagan and Thatcher, of the seemingly irrestible rise of neo-conservatism.

The two oblique references to recent events in the play
re-inforce this mocking parallel with Schopenhauer's own
times. In Scene Four, Michael, discovered in The Priory,
drunk and belligerent, resists Monica's attempts to get
him to eat. "Do you respect a hunger-striker?.. The bloody
rights of any man?" The refererence to the hunger strikes
in the H-Blocks of Long Kesh prison camp in Northern
Ireland in the early 1980s is, in the context, scathingly
anti-heroic. The decision of nationalist prisoners to starve
themselves to death brought the optimistic idealism of the
1960s to a peak of despair. Michael's "rights of any man,"
refering back to Christopher's "Concept of human rights?
— Man's freedom at last?" in Scene One, is a blackly comic
reduction of post-Enlightenment despair to drunken
night-club angst.

The second reference to a public event of the 1980s is in
Christopher's demented lecture, delivered in the midst of
a breakdown triggered by Michael's grief. Describing the
prevalence of suicide in Schopenhauer's time, Christopher
rants about "The insidious appeal of suicide to romantic
minds. The incident of mass suicide! Oh yes, those have-a-
happy-go-lucky-Californian-day-caperers did not create a
precedent in the avocado or banana fields of Orange
County was it." The reference is clearly to the Jonestown
massacre in Guyana, itself a grotesque image of 1960s
hippy idealism destroying itself in madness and despair.
Again, however, the ludicrous language and farcial
dramatic situation emphasise the shoddy, second-hand
nature of the tragedy. Even the despair is recycled. In a
sense, *Too Late for Logic* is a search for a language of grief
for a world that has lost the ability to grieve heroically, a
centre of feeling for a world that is too aware of its own
shoddiness to feel anything.

The dramatisation of *The World as Will and Idea* in the
play is, therefore, mostly sardonic. Schopehauer saw life
as a struggle between Will and Idea, the latter being,
crudely, intellect. The intellect could diminish the

inescapable suffering of life only by suppressing the desire to reproduce, to have children. This essentially is the condition in which we find Christopher at the beginning of the play, a man who has left his wife and children in order to pursue the life of the intellect. This attempt to avoid the suffering of life is exploded with great exuberance by the arrival of his children, the world as Will, the "blind striving" that is embodied in the obscure desire to have children, literally at his door. With wonderful comic exaggeration, his son Jack coolly announces the return of family, of Will to battle with his Idea, with the line "Cornelia died at lunchtime, Uncle Michael is going to commit suicide, Mum said would you take care of it."

Michael to a large extent embodies Will in its blindest, most obscurely impulsive form of sexual striving. At the edge of the grave, in the margins of his wife's death, he makes sexual advances to virtually every woman he comes into contact with. He mauls Monica, paws his niece Petra, disappears to the bedroom with Jack's girlfriend Moreva at his own wife's funeral breakfast. And all of this rapacity is marked more by grief than joy, more by the defiance of death than a lust for life. It is Schopenhauer's "will to live", the unthinking impulse which keeps us from death.

Even Schopenhauer's understanding of the world as phenomenon and noumenon, taken from Kant, is dramatised in the play. The noumenon, the thing in itself, Kant's Ding-an-Sich may be no more than the nonsense of Christopher's "Ding-a-dong? Ding-a-dong. I didn't think I'd be saying it, but did he hypostasise the ding-a-dong? He did." But the play's central theatrical device is one in which we experience many of the characters as both disembodied voices and as real people, as, in Kantian terms, phenomena and noumena. Christopher (his voice on tape and his "real" self); Patricia on the answering machine, and then later as herself; Maud as herself and as an extension of the voice of the singer on the record player; and Christopher again as a voice through a microphone and then speaking himself directly to the audience, all appear in both guises. They are both phenomena presenting themselves to our perceptions in the theatre, and the presences behind those phenomena, both the ding-a-dong and the finger on the bell.

Also taking its shape from Schopenhauer is the play's brilliant use of time. On the one hand, the action loosely preserves a classical unity of time, everything happening within the space of a few days. In this narrow sense, the idea of time is very specific and obvious. From the start, two deadlines are set for Christopher. There is the televised lecture, his big chance to make sense of his life by succeeding to Wuzzy's chair amidst the acclaim of his colleagues and the general public. Virtually from the start, we are aware that this moment is approaching. And there is Michael's apparent deadline for suicide, "Saturday, D-day, and Phith!" which sets the train of events in motion. With both of these deadlines, there is a straighforward trajectory of time, a point of crisis towards which events are converging.

But there is as well a whole other sense of time. The opening sequence in which the figures gather on stage and Christopher seems to have shot himself suggests that the entire action is set in the past, that what we are to see is the explanation of how Christopher got to this point. We are pitched into a literal state of suspended animation. Christopher seems to be dead, but is only at that moment coming alive as a character for us as an audience. This strange sense of a play flickering on the borders between life and death, a play conducted between the animate (Christopher and the other people on stage), the inanimate (the gun and the cigarette which are key players in the plot) and the semi-animate (the recorded human voices), is again a dramatisation of Schopenhauer. For Schopenhauer, time is an endless, meaningless flow, the Will pursuing its own blind multiplicity. People have no real past and no real future, only a boundless, timeless present. There are no causes or effects, only the Will taking other forms. Thomas Mann's Buddenbrook, reading *The World as Will and Idea*, is filled with this sense of himself freed from "the deceptive perceptions of space, time and history, the preoccupation with a glorious historical continuity of life in the person of his own descendants... Nothing began, nothing left off. There was only an endless present." This is the state in which we find Christopher at the start of the play, stuck in an eternal present, labouring under the Schopenhauerian illusion that he is freed from the past and the future, and particularly from his own descendants. Those descendants come crashing in, reminding him not merely of themselves but of the death of Cordelia and the threatened suicide of Michael. Reminding him, in other words, that things do begin and things do leave off.

Scene Six, in which Christopher, picking up on a mad obsession of Michael's, goes off to shoot the schoolyard bully Wally Peters, who was, in their childhood, "more dreadful than God," establishes this second sense of time most clearly. Here Christopher walks into a blackly comic nightmare from Schopenhauer. Christopher, slipping out of sanity, is trying to prove that he is a man with a real past, and therefore, perhaps, a real future. Wally is that past, and if its hurts and insults can be avenged, Christopher can emerge from it.

But Wally and his wife Maud are not in Christopher's ordinary time-frame at all. They are like ghosts, trapped in an eternal present, embodiments of Schopenhauer's terrifying timelessness. Maud's record goes round and round again, maddened old schoolfriends like Christopher come again and again to shoot Wally. They are sealed off in a kind of Hell, reminiscent of Beckett's characters who are doomed to repeat every day what has happened the day before. Chrsitopher can no more affect them than he can affect his own past. He cannot live in an endless Schopenhauerian present, but must live with his past, and, like it or not, with his future, his children.

The way in which Christopher hangs in time like this, hovering between life and death, makes *Too Late for Logic* a return to Murphy's beginnings, to the Purgatory of *On the Outside*. Whereas that play had its focus primarily in the outer world of social conditions, *Too Late for Logic* is essentially a meditation on death itself. The political world remains as a context and an anchor, but the shape of the play is determined much more by artistic imagery, by Schopenhauer and the myth of Orpheus and Eurydice. If there were an epigraph to the play, it would be Schopenhauer's "Without death men would scarcely philosophise." Against it, however, would have to be set Jack's barb that "the very best way to stop thinking is to become a philosopher." Cornelia's death, and Wuzzy's impending death, bring on Christopher's philosophising. But that philosophising is itself dead, a puny finger in the dyke that keeps death at bay.

Just as Schopenhauer found a way beyond the meaningless in music, so here the story of Orpheus and Eurydice offers another, more hopeful paradigm of suspended animation, expressed most strongly in music. The play roughly follows the contours of the myth. The death of a woman (Cordelia) impels a man into the underworld (the Priory), but he looks back (into the past and Wally Peters) and must re-surface from the domain of death alone. Yet Orpheus and Christopher do re-emerge from death. And — in an ending which defies Schopenhauer as much as it defies death — it is Jack, Christopher's son, who is the re-born Orpheus, with a banjo or guitar instead of a lyre, singing his own psychadelic lyrics instead of the songs that stilled the tortures of the damned in Tartarus. Schopenhauer's belief that the desire to reproduce must be conquered if the Will is to be resisted is, in the end, contradicted by the play. Christopher's desire in Scene One to avoid "those complicated thorns of kindred in my side" has become, by the end of Scene Seven, "those children, beloved thorns of kindred...Beloved thorns? Yes. Beloved." The will to reproduce has become, for Christopher, the will to live, his children, banes of his life, become his guarantors against death.

Schopenhauer saw death as a philosophical necessity: "We are at bottom something that ought not to be: therefore we cease to be." The first half of this sentence is largely endorsed in Murphy's work. Both JPW King in *The Gigli Concert* and Mommo's father in *Bailegangaire* recognise that man is just one of God's litle mistakes, a thing that ought not to be. But the second part isn't, and *Too Late for Logic* is an argument with it, a comic acceptance of the fact that we don't cease to be just because we ought to. Christopher is not, after all, dead, and it is a cigarette given to him by his son that shows us that he will die slowly, bit by bit, day by day, and not suddenly, from a bullet through the head. He is granted the blessing of returning to the moments before the play began, when the cigarette he was smoking at the beginning was unlit, when the descent into madness had not begun, when the possibility of a comfortable distance from his family remained, neither so distant as to be alone nor so close as to be painful.

In this, the end of the play is a kind of repeat of the end of *Bailegangaire*: "it was decided to give that fambly... of strangers another chance." Christopher's family is a family of strangers, and the movement of the play is towards giving them a second chance. In this movement, and in the play's ultimate rejection of Schopenhauer's pessimism about human reproduction, Murphy comes close to forgiving the Irish family. The broken families of his plays, the inadequate, monstrous, gapped scarred families of almost every play of his from *A Whistle in the Dark* onwards are given a kind of ambivalent blessing. Christopher, Patricia, Jack and Petra, scattered at the beginning of the play do come together by the end, if only at a funeral feast.

This coming together is all the more remarkable because of the play's bold refusal of contact or even conflict. Michael and Christopher have only the most desultory contact throughout the play. Christopher and Petra speak to each other only in the last scene, and that is a bittersweet meeting, a coming together at last, but one which marks the finality of their separation. Christopher's attempts to communicate with Jack, and particularly Petra, are tactless, awkward failures. If drama is about the interaction of characters, *Too Late for Logic* is almost entirely undramatic. But the presence of a family behind this veil of silence and misunderstanding remains unmistakable, and the play of this forgoten, half-dead love behind the misconnections gives to the piece its own drama, its own clash of forces.

It is well to recall what happens in the most famous use of Schopenhauer in Irish theatre before this. In Yeats's *On Baile's Strand*, Cuchulain unknowingly fights and kills his son, and the ending is one of unrelieved grief and futility. Tom Murphy started out as a professional playwright with a first full-length play, *A Whistle in the Dark*, in which a father is still killing his son, albeit indirectly, and in which the grief and futility are fully as total as Yeats's. The other fathers of his plays, John Connor in *Famine* and Harry in *The Sanctuary Lamp,* are also associated with death, the former killing his wife, the latter responsible for the death of his child. Against that background, the full refusal of pessimism in *Too Late for Logic*, in which a father, inadequate, semi-detached and disloyal as he is, is still granted some measure of blessing, can be seen. Death has its dominions, but fatherhood offers its own unruly and unruled territory outside them. It is hard not to see in the shaping of that blessing the skilled hands of a coffin-maker working while his son plays.

NOTES

Chapter 1

1. Quoted in *Proud and Upright Men*. By Noel O'Donoghue, Dublin Road, Tuam, 1987. p.8

2. ibid. p.8

3. ibid. p.l8

4. ibid. p.9

5. ibid. p.8

6. Thomas Murphy. *The Gigli Concert*.

7. See the 1977 John Snow Memorial Lecture by T.K. Whitaker. Published in Administration, Vol 26 no 3, Autumn 1978, Dublin. pp 305- 17

8. Paul Vincent Carroll, *The Mystical Irish in The Vanishing Irish*. Ed. John A. O'Brien. W. H. Allen, London 1954., pp 63-64. 9. Bryan MacMahon, *Getting on the High Road Again in The Vanishing Irish* op cit. p. 207

10. All references are to *On the Outside/On the Inside*. By Tom Murphy, Gallery Press, Dublin, 1976, and in *A Whistle in the Dark and Other Plays*, Methuen Drama, London, 1989.

11. On the Inside, op cit.

12. Eric Bentley. *In Search of Theater*, Alfred A. Knopf, New York, 1953, pp. 329-330.

Chapter 2

1 . Quoted in The Moral Monopoly: *The Catholic Church in Modern Irish Society*. By Tom Inglis. Gill and Macmillian, Dublin 1987. p. 143

2. ibid. p.l97

3. All references are to *A Whistle in the Dark*. By Tom Murphy. Gallery Press, Dublin, 1984, and Methuen Drama, London, 1989. The earlier published version is by Samuel French, New York, 1970

4. Declan Kiberd, *Inventing Irelands in Ireland*: Dependence and Independence, The Crane Bag, Dublin, 1984. p. 20

5. ibid.

6. Bunreacht na hEireann. Government Publications Office, Dublin Article 41, p. 136.

7. Ivor Browne, *The Madness of Genius*, in Irish University Review, Vol.17, No I, Spring 1987, Dublin. p 133.

8. All references to *A Crucial Week in the Life of a Grocer's Assistant*, By Tom Murphy, Gallery Press, Dublin, 1976; and in *A Whistle in the Dark and Other Plays*, Methuen Drama, London, 1989.

9. The Moral Monopoly, op cit. p. 221.

Chapter 3

1. Eric Bentley, *In Search of Theater*, op cit. p. 336.

2. All references are to *The Morning After Optimism*. By Thomas Murphy. The Mercier Press, Cork 1973, and in Plays 3, Methuen, 1994.

3. *The Gigli Concert*.

Chapter 4

1. Thomas Kinsella, *The Divided Mind*, in Irish Poets in English. Ed. Sean Lucy, Mercier Press, Cork, 1973. p. 208 ff

2. Georg Lukacs. *The Historical Novel*, Penguin, London, 1969. p. 104.

3. All references are to *Famine*. By Thomas Murphy. Gallery Press, Dublin, 1977; and in Plays 1, Methuen 1992.

Chapter 5

1. All references are to *The Orphans*. By Tom Murphy. Published in Journal of Irish Literature, Vol III no. 3, September 1974, Newark, Delaware .

2. Georg Lukacs. The Historical Novel op cit. p. 146.

Chapter 6

1. All references to the stage version are to *The Patriot Game*, published in Plays 1, Methuen, London, 1992

2. All references are to *The Blue Macushla*, published in Plays 1, Methuen, London, 1992.

3. All references are to *Conversations on a Homecoming*, The Gallery Press, Dublin, 1986; and in After Tragedy, Methuen, London, 1988.

4. Details of the reaction to *The White House* are from *Irish Television Drama*: A society and its stories. By Helena Sheehan, RTE, Dublin, 1987, pp 213-5.

Chapter 7

1. All references are to *The Sanctuary Lamp*, The Gallery Press, Dublin, 1984, and in Plays 3, Methuen, London, 1994.

The earlier published version is by Poolbeg Press, Dublin, 1976.

2. Eugene Ionesco. Dans les armes de la ville, in Cahiers de la Compagnie Madeleine Renaud-Jean-Louis Barrault, no 20, October 1957, Paris.

3. Albert Camus. *The Myth of Sisyphus,* Gallimard, Paris, 1942. p.l8.

4. Gilbert Murray. Preface to *Iphigenia in Tauris*. Allen and Unwin, London, 1910. p.x.

Chapter 8

1. Christopher Hill. *The World Turned Upside Down*, Penguin, London, 1975. p.l63-164.

2. ibid. p.294.

3. All references are to *The Gigli Concert*, Gallery Press, Dublin, 1984, and in *After Tragedy,* Methuen, London, 1988 and in Plays 3, Methuen, London, 1994.

4 Carl Gustav Jung. *Memories, Dreams, Reflections,* Fontana, London, 1983. p.262.

5. The Douay Bible, Exodus, 3: 14-15.

6. Peter Brook. *The Empty Space,* Penguin, London, 1972, p.156.

7. *Memories, Dreams, Reflections,* op cit. p.417.

8. *The Empty Space,* op cit. p.157.

Chapter 9

1. All references are to *Bailegangaire*, The Gallery Press, Dublin, 1986; and in *After Tragedy*, Methuen, London, 1988; and in Plays 2, Methuen, London, 1993.

Chapter 10

1. Marianne McDonald. *Ancient Sun, Modern Light*. Columbia University Press. New York, 1992, p. 199

2. ibid. p. 198

3. All references are to *Too Late for Logic*, Methuen, London, 1990.

4. *The World as Will and Idea*, London, 1883, Vol 1, p 195

5. ibid. Vol 2, p. 241

6. Quoted in *Joesph Hone*, W.B Yeats 1865-1939, London, 1942, p. 392

7. Thomas Mann. *Buddenbrooks*. Harmondsworth, 1957, p 506-8

8. *The World as Will and Idea*, op cit, Vol 3, p 307.

Acknowledgements

One of the great advantages of writing about Tom Murphy is that I have been able to draw on the large fund of respect and admiration for both the man himself and his work in putting this book together. Many people have helped, some knowingly, some unknowingly, and I am grateful to them all. The unknowing help has come from all of those who have presented Murphy's plays at the Abbey and Druid Theatres over the last decade, and whose work has had an immeasurable bearing on the shaping of my responses to those plays. It is still impossible for me to contemplate the texts of Murphy's work without seeing and hearing Tom Hickey or Siobhan McKenna, Godfrey Quigley or Marie Mullen, and this book is above all an attempt to contain and recapture some small element of the magic of those performances.

Tom Murphy himself has always made it clear that his work arises out of his whole personality, and that intellectual ideas of the sort which can be dealt with in a book like this are only one aspect of that personality. I entirely accept this distinction, and I hope it will stand as a caveat over everything I have written here. This book is a personal response on my part to his work as a whole, and it remains the view of someone looking from the outside in. I did not ask Tom Murphy to explain his plays, and I have no doubt that the view from the inside must be very different. But Tom Murphy has been extraordinarily generous in answering questions, in providing me with background and with unpublished scripts, and that support has been of incalculable value to me.

Most of what I now know about Tuam and about the background to Murphy's early work came from Noel and Mary O'Donoghue. In particular Noel O'Donoghue's fascinating book, Proud and Upright Men proved to be very valuable and I have made extensive use of it. Their generosity, hospitality and knowledge were a great help to me.

Thanks are also due to the Gallery Press, publishers of Tom Murphy's plays, for permission to quote from their editions. Mary and Bernard Loughlin of the Tyrone Guthrie Centre, Annaghmakerrig, provided the refuge in which much of the book was written. preserving what vestiges of sanity remain to myself and my family. Garry Hynes and Colm Toibin stimulated some of the ideas which found their way into the book. though not necessarily in forms which they would recognise or accept.

Dermot Bolger has been the most supportive and persistent of publishers, and I am gratful also to reviewers of the first edition and to Marianne McDonald in her book Ancient Sun, Modern Light, for comments on it, some of which have been silently stolen for this edition. Finally, my gratitude to Clare Connell is, simply, inexpressible but it will make up in durability what it lacks in eloquence.

Index